WHY *SO* SERIOUS?

**THE UNTOLD
STORY OF
NBA CHAMPION
NIKOLA JOKIC**

WHY SO SERIOUS?

MIKE SINGER

HARPER

An Imprint of HarperCollins*Publishers*

HarperCollins books may be purchased for educational, business, or sales promotional use. For information, please email the Special Markets Department at SPsales@harpercollins.com.

FIRST EDITION

Library of Congress Cataloging-in-Publication Data has been applied for.

ISBN 978-0-06-339680-7

24 25 26 27 28 LBC 5 4 3 2 1

TO ANNIE, NATALIE, MOM, AND DAD

CONTENTS

INTRODUCTION

The sun-drenched café overlooked the riverbank where kids swam and locals drank.

A rental boat coasted by with DREAM CATCHER on one banner and KK JOKER on the other. The former was Nikola Jokic's most prized horse. The latter was the club basketball team bearing his namesake.

Aside from the floating advertisement, Sombor, Serbia, didn't publicize its most famous resident. Instead, it tended to protect him.

On one side of the quiet café was an upscale restaurant that specialized in the local delicacy, fish stew. On the other was a public beach where locals swam and sunbathed. In Sombor, it was called the strand.

There, on a late July afternoon in a quaint corner of Jokic's hometown, we sat with Isidor Rudic, the first coach who believed in Nikola. Coincidentally, two of Jokic's earliest teammates were swimming in the river. Soon they joined us to recollect.

Isidor had pictures to share and stories to tell. So did his former teammates. Isidor's assistant, Milos, jogged his memory. My translator, Marko, brought the stories to life.

After an hour or so, a storm started pounding the umbrellas above us. Isidor's pictures and relics, including jerseys and meticulous notes from their earliest practice days, were in danger of getting soaked.

We packed up our belongings—Isidor's papers and my recorder. He told us to follow him. He knew a quiet bar where we could continue.

Not a hundred feet from the café's parking lot, as the rain pounded down and beachgoers took shelter, Isidor pulled over.

"There's Nikola's car," he said. It was parked on the gravel road beside the beach shelter.

"Do you want to go inside?"

"I'd rather not," I told him.

Nikola knew I was in Serbia, but I was still trying to be respectful of his space.

Would he be disgusted if I invaded his privacy? I wondered. *Would he appreciate how far I've traveled?* I didn't know the answer.

Isidor didn't take my suggestion.

He wandered inside, where he found Nikola being hounded for pictures and autographs, even among locals. He was with his best friend, Nemanja Pribic, when Isidor explained what he was doing.

"There's some American here," he told him. "He's writing a book about you."

Within minutes, Jokic bolted from the shelter, wearing nothing more than his striped bathing suit. Amid an unrelenting downpour, I hopped out of the passenger seat of our car.

"Mike!" Nikola shouted.

Our embrace was genuine. Jokic made sure to introduce his best friend too.

The exchange lasted no longer than a minute. It was, after all, the middle of a rainstorm.

O

Nemanja Pavkov was among the very first people on the planet to recognize something special about the pudgy, curiously coordinated younger brother of Strahinja and Nemanja Jokic.

Pavkov was neither an NBA scout, nor even a local coach in Sombor, where Nikola Jokic was raised. He was just a twenty-two-year-old hooper hungry to dominate the local court in the summertime and learned quickly that doing so required Nikola Jokic's help. It didn't matter that Jokic wasn't in shape or that he would routinely arrive donning his signature look: untied shoes. It didn't even matter that Jokic was only thirteen at the time, nine years younger than his teammate. Pavkov discovered what others dismissed due to his appearance: Jokic was both gifted and intensely competitive.

"He was like a big teddy bear," said Pavkov, some fifteen years after the duo shredded opponents daily, bewildering those who dismissed Jokic as cuddly.

In Serbia, around the neighborhood, full-court games were atypical. It was strictly three-on-three, as sometimes a dozen teams waited on the sidelines for their chance to play. Like any respectable court, the winner stayed on while the loser had no reason to stick around. Their day was as good as over.

What Pavkov first noticed about Jokic was his competitive spirit. Even as a kid, he despised losing, no matter what game he was playing. A loss playing pickup meant having to find some other distraction to kill an afternoon. That was all the motivation Jokic needed. Pavkov, a short, stocky player, kept drafting Jokic for his team even as ignorant opponents sneered at his choice.

Jokic followed his two older brothers, Nemanja and Strahinja, into the sport but had a court sense that his bruising siblings lacked.

Strahinja's playing style was as unassuming as a bulldozer.

"When he shot it, it was like a bullet," Pavkov said, conceding that the oldest Jokic brother was a literal wall on defense. "He can only score if he dunked."

Nikola, on the other hand, wasn't physically imposing. He wasn't fast or athletic, at least in the traditional sense. But his intuition dictated the games. He only needed willing cutters—three-on-three afforded Jokic a surplus of space—and his teams rarely lost. Jokic played the conductor, using the rugged court as his personal laboratory. According to Pavkov, the no-look passes that now carve up NBA defenses began between the faded white lines, on the unforgiving rims, atop the crimson mesh court of those pickup games—a court situated in the shadow of the Sombor housing complex where Jokic's parents raised their three boys.

Save for a few trees that provided minimal shade and primitive bleachers on both sides of the court, Jokic's earliest court marked a humble and drab beginning to an improbable, astonishing journey.

With irreverence, wit, and guile, Jokic carved a path more unlikely than anyone ever knew. His story, from an obscure prospect to one of the all-time greats, hadn't been told—until now.

Pavkov, like everyone interviewed in this book, could not have predicted the heights Jokic would reach. And it wasn't until five years later, after Jokic signed his first professional contract with Mega Basket in Belgrade, that Pavkov noticed a small but significant change in his friend's approach.

With his shoes tied, Jokic started to warm up. He even started to stretch.

"Everybody was shocked," Pavkov said. "It was like, 'What the fuck is this?' From that moment, I knew he will succeed."

Now, a few hundred yards in the distance but perfectly visible from center court, towers a sun-drenched mural of Jokic dribbling, plastered to the side of a school that he attended. In a childlike font with big bold letters, the mural proclaims: "Don't be afraid to fail big."

CHAPTER 1

SOMBOR

If those pickup games represented Jokic's informal introduction to basketball, his official indoctrination was significantly more turbulent.

Jokic formally registered to play basketball in 2002, with a picture as rudimentary as a passport photo. Behind his sunken blue eyes, pale face, full cheeks, and overgrown haircut there was something mischievous about his seven-year-old gaze. It was as if he was already daring future opponents to doubt him based on his appearance.

That sense of confidence, of conviction in his abilities, would ultimately define him. Well before he was allowed to experiment, transforming the court into his own personal canvas, he had to reconcile with his conviction. His first coach, Gradimir Markovic, wasn't interested in Jokic's improvisational skills.

The demanding Gradimir oversaw the club, KK Sombor, and Nikola's generation of mini-basket—a kid-friendly version of the sport. There were shorter quarters, shorter rims, looser whistles, and a mandate that all kids play. But during practices, Gradimir was strict and disciplined. Tasked with introducing kids to basketball, he was hard on them. There was no room for Jokic's creativity to blossom. Even worse, it was frowned upon.

Gradimir's insistence on training hard spotlighted Jokic's lack of conditioning. As a kid, Jokic's friends called him lazy. They said he was just as content watching a game as he was playing one. During practices, he couldn't have been less interested in running hard, especially since the reward—freedom with the basketball in his hands—was discouraged.

What was the point?

Under Gradimir, there was no engendering a love of basketball. To

Jokic it felt like work. And given his ubiquitous stubborn streak, Jokic wasn't interested in participating on someone else's terms. Until 2008, his creativity—and thus his eagerness to participate—was stymied.

The team's success didn't placate his discontent. One season, they won a youth Vojvodina championship. In another, they finished second. Their run included an unimpeachable year-and-a-half stretch where they never lost a game.

It was an exceedingly successful generation of Sombor basketball, with Jokic a fixture—but not yet a star—of the squad. Emotionally, he was still growing.

Around 2006 or 2007, during a team-building camp in Studenica, Jokic was miserable. He didn't like his coach's unapologetic approach, and he didn't like being away from home. Tears flowed, and after a few days, he phoned his parents to pick him up.

Jokic was at a pivotal, tender stage of his development, at an intersection between pursuing basketball through adversity or leaving it altogether. The resistance he met wasn't worth it.

O

Were it not for Isidor Rudic, Nikola Jokic likely would've given up basketball altogether.

At thirteen, Jokic was stubborn, disinterested in anything outside of the games themselves, and emotionally fragile. When Isidor got to him, Jokic had one foot out of the gym.

Behind Isidor's stern appearance, with discerning eyes, an imposing beard, and an athletic build, was a thoughtful, considerate person.

Isidor couldn't stand the way Jokic's team was being developed. He didn't like how regimented the environment was or how restrictive the playing style had become. By February 2009, he committed to assuming responsibilities for KK Sombor and would take over as soon as he returned from a ski trip.

But while Isidor was vacationing, Jokic waffled. He got kicked out of one practice and then another. By the third practice, Jokic, always a quick learner, predicted the pattern. He chose not to show up.

"When I came back, there was no Nikola," Isidor said. "We needed to beg him to start again."

According to Isidor, Jokic was gathering his own intel. Jokic had already endured multiple trying seasons, as his engagement and motivation waned. Having grown tired of the only real coach he'd ever known, Jokic wanted to know whether Isidor would be the head coach moving forward. He wanted to know if it was worth investing his time. Even as a teenager, he was discerning. He returned to the gym only after securing the assurances he was looking for.

"If you didn't come back and coach the team, I wouldn't be in basketball anymore," Jokic told Isidor.

It was tenuous at first, but there was a bond. Though that bond strengthened over the four years Isidor coached Nikola, it was a relationship that took constant nurturing. Never once did Isidor take Jokic's fragile commitment for granted.

"I had a fight even with him, to be honest," Jokic said. "Not fight but argument."

Having seen how close Nikola was to walking away, Isidor didn't need any further reminder how delicate the situation was.

Just because he was there one day didn't mean he'd be there the next.

That was because Jokic's opinion of practice was tempestuous at best.

"All four years I had a battle with him over practice," Isidor said.

The first point that Isidor addressed was the one that carried the most appeal with Jokic.

"I completely changed the way of training," he said.

Isidor believed in encouraging the fluid, free-flowing offense that catered to Jokic's strengths. He recognized his unique ball-handling skills for a player of his size and how quickly he processed the defense. Unlike Jokic's first coach, Isidor empowered his playmaking. He wanted him to explore, to push boundaries, to probe defenses.

"He loved to play [whatever the defense] offered and not to follow the called play," Isidor said.

It was the beginning of his improvisational streak. To go rogue, Jokic needed the ball in his hands.

As the in-bounder, it often was. Once Jokic passed to Igor, the team's talented point guard, the defense would inevitably descend on the ball handler. Because of the way he looked, opposing coaches weren't concerned about Jokic's playmaking ability just yet. (More often than not, quality games were deemed lucky rather than anything significant.)

But as soon as Igor faced pressure, Jokic was the natural outlet. That, in Isidor's estimation, was where his point-center skills began to coalesce.

"I was not able to see which one of them, Igor or Nikola, would be the better player," Isidor admitted.

Even today, there's still a healthy debate among the teammates over which player was more valuable at that time. A handful, perhaps in jest, sided with Igor.

Regardless, Jokic loved the change. Within Isidor's style of play, he was engaged. And during his Pioneer and Cadet seasons—the levels of youth basketball Isidor coached Jokic—he had a talented team to complement him.

But he still hated practice.

Heading into the 2009 season, Isidor took meticulous notes about the team he was inheriting. Those notes revealed a distinct pattern about Jokic's attendance habits. When a game approached on the schedule, Jokic appeared at practice. When there was a lull, he was more likely to be swimming in the river than anywhere near a gym. The games, and only the games, served as his motivation.

During one damning stretch, Jokic appeared in the three practices leading up to a game. With no games on the schedule, he skipped the following twelve practices.

"Especially when the season ended, he didn't show up for practices the whole summer, or if he did, it was only a little bit," Isidor said.

As had happened with Gradimir, the more intense the practices became, the less likely it was that Jokic attended. Jokic became attuned to Isidor's practice routines. If he had to fake an injury to get out of a particularly rigorous practice, he would. But that presented another pitfall because Isidor didn't want to push any player who was hurt, particularly one of Jokic's size.

"There was always a problem when the conditioning practices were held," Isidor said.

Isidor learned to scheme the schemer. When Jokic feigned an injury ahead of a difficult practice, Isidor quickly pivoted, turning the training session into five-on-five games. Inevitably, Jokic bit.

"Okay, it doesn't hurt anymore," Isidor recalled Nikola saying, resuming the constant tug-of-war between player and coach.

Isidor understood Jokic's body well. Ahead of the 2009 season, he ran diagnostic tests on his players' high jump, long jump, 20-meter dash, and sit-ups. Nikola was proficient in every discipline except the crunches.

"I was sure if I could get him to lose weight, he would be even better," Isidor said.

Isidor was sensitive to Jokic's size, whether injured or not, and didn't make unreasonable conditioning requests. He also recognized how boring those practices were for teenagers. If he was going to optimize Jokic and deploy him as the team's secondary playmaker, he needed him to lose weight. He introduced conditioning drills disguised as ball-handling drills to make the sessions more engaging. This new wrinkle worked. By the end, Jokic's coordination was baffling.

"He could dribble with five balls at the same time," Isidor said.

Nikola's confidence was brimming. He was enjoying basketball on his terms. He found success playing his preferred style of basketball and couldn't help but test his newfound power.

Whereas the rest of his teammates showed up for practices, even into the summer, Jokic neglected them. In his estimation, they were boring and unnecessary. Plus, if there were no games on the schedule, what was the point of practice?

Jokic's rebellious streak mandated constant monitoring.

"Because Sombor is a small city, you see everybody in the streets," Isidor said. "When I saw Nikola with his parents, I asked him why he wasn't coming to practice. He said, 'Why would I show up when I'm the best?'"

CHAPTER 2

FIRST LOVE

Café Hilton is a laid-back, unpretentious bar with a relaxing, open-air patio nestled comfortably on a quiet block in Sombor.

It's casual and cozy, like the rest of the quaint Serbian city. This wasn't the place to party. Situated at the end of the block where the Jokics lived, however, it was probably the most consequential watering hole of Nikola's career.

Without the profound soul-searching that took place here deep into many nights, Jokic's story would have ended prematurely.

The unofficial team of advisors was Isidor, Nikola's father, Branislav, and their horse trainer, Vlada, who happened to be Nikola's best friend's father. They all had some stake in his future. Together they were responsible for developing his love of basketball as an early teenager.

He just wasn't interested in committing.

There were a few concurrent factors. While his two brothers pursued their own basketball careers, Nemanja in the U.S. and Strahinja in the highest Serbian league, Nikola's parents poured all their energy and attention into raising their youngest. As a result, Nikola grew up a bit spoiled, according to Isidor. Watching his interest in basketball fluctuate, Branislav wondered whether their coddling was hampering him.

Branislav was a former basketball player himself. He saw the trajectory of his two older sons and felt Nikola had even more potential. The timing was fortuitous. Branislav was inching toward retirement and had time to invest in his youngest.

All the interested parties had to contend with his first love: horses. Nikola's father and grandfather had worked with horses, and Nikola used to attend races with his dad growing up. Even as a child, Nikola was *always* at the stables.

Vlada, their horse trainer, took him to the racetrack often enough that some of the owners began to believe Nikola was actually Vlada's son. He was obsessed. Jokic was often at his happiest around the stables, watching races and caring for the animals. His favorite was harness racing, where horses pulled a two-wheeled cart—a sulky—around the track.

"The late Jovan Ladjar, a giant in harness racing, was the first to put him on a sulky and hand him the reins," Branislav said.

Naturally, Nikola's morning routine revolved around the horses. There were two shifts: one early in the morning and one in the afternoon. Before heading to school, he'd go to the stables near their home to clean the stalls and tend to the horses.

"I was once summoned by his teacher, who asked me why Nikola 'smelled,'" Branislav said. "I explained everything to her."

During that time, the stables were dingy and "kinda smelly," according to Nikola.

"Even if you take a shower or whatever, it kinda sticks to your skin, sticks to your hair," he said of the scent his teacher was concerned about. "Some people like it, some people don't."

Back then, his first love was a horse named Fantastic Lobel. Nikola's dad recognized his love and printed a picture of the horse, along with its name, on a shirt for his youngest son. Nikola called it his jersey.

"He constantly told me that he wanted to be a horseman," Branislav said.

Nemanja, his best friend and Vlada's son, said Nikola's obsession defied explanation.

"You need to be born with that," Nemanja said.

Nikola's exuberance over horses allowed him to "disconnect," as he said, and pour energy into his most beloved hobby. He was his happiest when he was around the horses. He loved the preparation and the training, the shoeing and the strategies. He savored talking to trainers and gossiping about the fastest horses outside of Sombor. Mostly he loved being with them, in nature, where he found it peaceful.

"The races are just like one minute," he said.

He became obsessed with the entire operation.

Though several people around Nikola shared his devotion to horses, they were adamant it not come at the expense of basketball. They saw too much potential.

"For Nikola, horses were his love, but basketball was something that he needed to do," Isidor said.

After numerous long nights, surrounded by dozens of discarded beer mugs, the Café Hilton crew reached a conclusion.

"I told him that because he was truly talented in that sport [the biggest, strongest, and best on the court], he should focus on basketball, earn money, and have as many horses as he wanted," his dad said.

Nikola had his own ideas.

Practicing hoops—a game where he already excelled—wasn't nearly as fun as drinking with his friends. Serbian culture didn't encourage casual teenage drinking, but it didn't frown on it either. Jokic, who loved dancing and built a deep catalog of Serbian songs in his head, was interested in socializing, just like the rest of his teammates.

Basketball practices were in the morning, so Jokic & Company had ample time to hang out and party at night. Isidor was savvy. He was on to their habits. Beginning in 2010, when Jokic was fifteen, Isidor roamed Sombor with a breathalyzer (which he still has) and often popped into the local bars unannounced. In Sombor, everyone knew everyone. If one of his players was carousing, there was no hiding from their coach.

"At the time in Serbia, when you're like fifteen, sixteen, seventeen, you start drinking, and he didn't allow us to drink," Nikola said. "I think we respect him so much, and didn't want to ruin that respect."

The consequences were simple.

If caught once, they'd miss one week of practice. A second time yielded a month of no practice. If anyone was caught a third time, they'd be kicked off the team, future NBA champion or not.

"All of them stopped after the second time," said Isidor, including Nikola.

At Café Hilton, every aspect of Nikola's development was dissected, including the hurdles.

"He was teased a bit because of his 'larger' build, but he overcame it as he grew and felt more dominant on the court," Branislav said.

After every practice they talked and analyzed his state of mind. While other parents drove Nikola home, Isidor and Branislav schemed to meet later that night. If Branislav picked Nikola up from practice himself, he'd drop him at home and then take the short walk down the block to the café for further discussion. If Nikola skipped practice altogether, as he often did, it prompted another meeting.

"Brana saw something in Nikola that he didn't see in Nemanja and Strahinja," Isidor said.

Branislav did his best to nurture that spark, even if it grated on his son. Nikola didn't yet recognize it, but his talent needed unpacking.

"He had a tough nature, and I was a bit of a demanding dad because I always pushed him to train and play with full force, which often annoyed him," Branislav said.

They all tried to convince Nikola to commit.

"The biggest problem at the time was that Nikola wasn't interested in practice at all," Isidor said. "We were spending days and nights to formulate a plan to get him to the gym."

How can we push him without pushing him too hard? How can we make him comfortable so that practices aren't such a chore? How can we contend with the horses?

When Nikola was sixteen, he walked away from basketball for four months.

"My dad went to talk to [Isidor and Vlada], and I was with Vlada, the horse trainer," Nikola said. "In that time, that was my biggest [hobby]. I wanted to do just that. He starts, 'Okay, when you gonna start going back to practice?' . . . Now I think it's funny."

The group devised several coordinated schemes to motivate him.

When Nikola left his condominium, Isidor just happened to be there with his car and asked him about coming back to practice.

"We tried to make it look like it was spontaneous, but it wasn't," Isidor said.

Next, they took the equestrian route.

When Nikola was at the horse stable with Vlada, Isidor would get a call to spontaneously show up. This wasn't bank-heist sophistication, though their schemes did indicate how hard they tried to get Nikola to reengage.

Their next ploy was the craftiest and struck at Nikola's heart. Vlada's sons played basketball, and he knew of Nikola's fleeting interest toward practice. Vlada was at the intersection of Nikola's two hobbies.

"Brana went to my father and said, 'Come on, you need to help him get back to basketball and to make a condition, if he wants to do the horse thing, he needs to go back to basketball,'" Nemanja, Vlada's son, said.

The horse thing.

Nemanja had gone to horse races as a kid, but his interest fizzled over time. He never questioned Nikola's love and just accepted that the sport—chariot racing—resonated with his best friend.

"There's more love for horse chariot racing as a sport than love for horses overall," Nemanja said.

Nikola's unofficial team leveraged that love. The Café Hilton group had established a foothold.

The late nights at the café tended to bleed beyond midnight, as the topic always revolved around Nikola's mercurial motivation. There was no quick fix or easy solution. Nikola was stubborn.

"It was a process which lasted four years," Isidor said.

How could they convince Nikola to prioritize basketball? Better yet, why did they care so much?

Branislav's motivation was clear, but Isidor didn't have time to invest like this in every kid. What differentiated Nikola?

"I noticed that he was becoming a leader even if he wasn't the best player on the team," he said. "But I didn't see this big career coming."

Jokic maintained he wasn't ready to abandon the sport altogether even though he needed a break.

"I was not [that close to leaving entirely] because I still enjoyed playing outside, still enjoyed playing basketball," he said. "I wouldn't completely give it up because I really loved the sport, and I enjoyed the sport. I [thought I] will eventually come back at some point, but in that moment, I didn't care about basketball."

Jokic also wasn't convinced his unofficial team—Branislav, Isidor, and Vlada—was totally fixated on motivating him.

"They say that, but I think it was just an excuse for drinking and having fun," Nikola said.

○

Isidor's teams practiced twice a day in the summer. In a curious twist of fate, the morning session was almost always at the hippodrome—the now-infamous track where Nikola owned and trained horses.

There Nikola followed one mandate. The horses were the priority; the team's conditioning drills were not.

While his teammates ran the exposed dirt track on the outside of the ring, Nikola trained his horses on the inside.

The scene was preposterous. His teammates were incredulous.

During one morning session, Nemanja and his teammates pleaded with Nikola to train with them.

His fitness unlocked new levels to their potential. They needed him to run.

Nikola, stubborn and sarcastic, reminded his friends they held little jurisdiction over his actions. Jokic momentarily dropped his feet off the chariot he'd been driving and mimicked jogging with his teammates.

That was the best they were going to get. He did as he pleased.

The scene was a microcosm of his relationship with his teammates. They worked hard; he worked with horses. They ran in the summertime; he didn't. They would've been justified in their frustration that Nikola continued to see playing time despite a shoddy practice record except that they all liked him. He was funny and unselfish. Of course, they all wanted to win and understood that Jokic facilitated that. That was the uneasy balance Isidor had to strike.

"If Nikola was thankful for something to me," Isidor said, "it's that I found a way to handle that."

Isidor had other frustrations when it came to workouts at the hippodrome. The track was so long that he couldn't police his guys' effort like he wanted. When he yelled, his voice would trail off, message unsent. Occasionally he'd ride a bike around the track to enforce the summer workouts. One summer, parents were encouraged to come to the track to watch their kids train. Nikola's mom, Beba, was in attendance.

She was the anchor of the family, according to Nebojsa Vagic, Nikola's godfather. She was humble, smart, and down-to-earth, and her voice was often in the back of Nikola's mind.

"She's there to always show them where everything began," Nebojsa said. "They know. They cannot forget. They weren't born in a Rolls-Royce."

Beba sensed Isidor's frustration mounting at how little his team, and specifically her son, cared about the conditioning. She sought to reassure him.

What she said that day reverberated in Isidor's head for more than a decade.

"She said, 'Coach, why are you so mad? One day Nikola will go to the NBA and will buy this hippodrome.'"

CHAPTER 3

GROWING PAINS

Locally, Jokic's legend was growing, but outside of Sombor, there was still healthy skepticism.

During the 2009–10 season, Nikola, now fourteen going on fifteen, and another teammate, Petar Potkonjak, were invited to Belgrade for a national team camp on the strength of Isidor's recommendation. Both had succeeded at a regional camp and secured an invite to the more prestigious event. All the elite clubs and coaches would be there, mining the ranks for future talent.

The camp began at 7:30 in the morning, which required a 3:00 a.m. wake-up call in Sombor. It was early, but the exposure and opportunity were worth it. The group piled into a car and headed south to Belgrade. Because of the stakes, outside coaches and parents weren't invited to the camp. There were prospects from Partizan and Red Star, the two most prominent clubs in Serbia, and others from smaller yet still noteworthy clubs like FMP and Hemofarm. Coaches from those clubs guided the prospects through one session in the morning and another in the afternoon.

By 5:30 p.m., Isidor was waiting in a car outside the gym, eager to hear how the day had gone. His guys had gotten the exposure they deserved.

When they reached the car, he was met with silence.

His first thought was that his two best players, in front of a national team audience, had gotten into it.

Had an argument upended their exposure?

Finally, they broke.

"Coach, we got up very early to be here, and we don't know why we came," they told him. "We won't come to this kind of training session in Belgrade anymore. It's better to train in Sombor."

Petar revealed he'd played two minutes in a scrimmage. Nikola had gotten off the bench for just a minute and a half. The trip, bursting with potential, was a bust.

It wouldn't be the last time Nikola was ignored.

Because of all the sessions at Café Hilton, Isidor was acutely aware of Nikola's emotional state. When Jokic later attended—and completed—a ten-day basketball camp at Zlatibor as a teenager, there was reason to celebrate.

The last camp he'd been to, in Studenica, he'd been miserable and needed his parents to pick him up despite the hours of driving such a trip would entail. This time, with plenty of communication back home, at least he'd survived the camp.

At least one representative from Partizan, one of the two most storied clubs in Belgrade, was invited to evaluate Jokic at the Zlatibor camp. It could've been another seminal moment in Jokic's career. The best club team in Serbia had come to see if he was worthy of a professional contract in the coming years.

Perched on a balcony overlooking the court, Partizan coach Goran Tadic peered over the railing and shared his unfiltered thoughts.

"You called me for this guy? I'm not even going to the court. We have many guys like this in Belgrade," Isidor recalled Tadic saying.

Only a few years later, after Jokic established himself at Mega, the Belgrade-based club he'd eventually join at eighteen, Partizan representatives would stew over their mistake. They once had a chance at Jokic. And whiffed.

O

In 2010, Nikola's entire team followed Isidor's lead and transferred clubs to KK So Kos.

Nemanja, Nikola's best friend, was practicing with their former club in the offseason but when Gradimir Markovic, the former-coach-turned-president, wouldn't allow him to formally join, Isidor decided to uproot the entire team.

"I think he understands us, and that whole group of people look at him like a big brother, like someone who is not old, not young, but we heard stories about him," Jokic said. "I think we had a huge respect for him as a group, and he really took care of us."

The group had formed a special bond. Nikola didn't have the gaudiest stat lines, and he rarely led the team in scoring. But his teammates loved to play with him. If they were open, he'd find them in space. Even during practices, his teammates loved to play with him because of his unselfishness and his competitiveness. It was relatively easy to tolerate his tardiness and truancy with practice. His easygoing nature and insistence on turning everything into a joke made it even easier.

No matter the sport—volleyball, soccer, Ping-Pong, or basketball—Nikola excelled. In every competitive setting, he wanted to win. The coordination he developed in each discipline seemed to pay dividends in all the others.

"He was born talented," said Lonki, a teammate and friend since the second grade.

His talent, coupled with his mischievous streak, occasionally got him into trouble.

In practices—that is, when Jokic attended—Isidor insisted on honing fundamentals. During one three-on-none drill, the goal was to pass the ball with two hands on fifteen consecutive occasions. Nikola couldn't help himself.

At the tenth pass, Jokic whipped a one-handed dish to a teammate. Isidor stopped practice and made them start over. The next round, Nikola did it again. Fed up, Nemanja remembered Isidor issuing an ultimatum.

"Whoever passes the ball with one hand is going to the locker room," their coach said.

Whoosh.

The very next time Nikola touched the ball, he flung his signature one-handed pass. True to Isidor's word, that was the end of Jokic's practice.

Throughout their four years together, the longest amount of time he spent with any single coach prior to reaching the NBA, Isidor kicked Jokic out for his refusal to run, for dabbling with alcohol, and for testing the limits of Isidor's authority. The passes that once got him booted from practice were the same ones that would later twist defenses into knots.

Jokic's mounting legend may cloud Lonki's memory, but his recollection of another game in 2011 was plausible nonetheless.

In his version of events, KK So Kos was slaughtering their opponent by forty points in the third quarter of a game in Futog. With the game already out of hand, Lonki remembered Nikola heading to the locker room midway through the quarter, changing clothes, and leaving the gym altogether. He and his father were headed to a horse race.

His skills were no longer needed in the gym.

Isidor recalled a less theatrical but equally comical version of events. They were scheduled for two consecutive games against Futog, to make the most of gym times and accommodate budgets. KK So Kos was the better team and, as such, traveled with a smaller roster. The first game, So Kos boat-raced their opponents, 114–61. With little to no reason to play, Jokic approached Isidor.

"I'm sorry, coach, but we are much better than these guys," Jokic told him. "I'm going to the horse race."

Horse races always took place on Sunday afternoons, while kids' basketball games were scheduled for Sunday mornings.

"I even had to rush him to the racetrack during halftime to make sure he didn't miss anything," Branislav said.

Though there's a box score to back up Isidor's version of events, both iterations underscored an essential current in the Jokic formula. Without motivation, in other words, a competitive environment, Jokic wasn't any more valuable than a benchwarmer. If a game wasn't worth his time, he'd let everyone know. If he felt he played more than necessary in a blowout, there was a good chance he'd pick up a few cheap fouls and expedite his visit to the bench.

Jokic was always, unapologetically himself.

O

Nikola never looked like the rest of his teammates. He was taller than them, yes, but he was heavier too.

Poor eating habits didn't help his size, nor did his aversion to practice. His frame contributed to the way he was perceived.

Nikola's size played a factor in what opponents and talent evaluators thought of him. There was no avoiding the obvious: he didn't look the part of a budding pro prospect. It affected how people judged him, and how he looked at himself.

Like any teenager, Nikola was self-conscious about his body, according to Isidor. His self-awareness began during the 2010–11 season, when his teammates had started to develop muscles and he was still chubby.

During that season, Jokic waited until he was the last one in the locker room. It was only after all of his teammates headed to the gym that he changed into his basketball gear.

Jokic was fifteen at the time. It's not hard to imagine puberty, raging hormones, and body image creeping into his self-consciousness. Physically, he was a late bloomer.

Ahead of a home game that season, according to Isidor, one assistant coach crossed a line. As Jokic was getting dressed before a game, the coach began mocking his body and teasing him for his size.

"Boobs and bakery," he told him. "Boobs and bakery."

Jokic left the locker room and headed to the bench with tears welling in his eyes. When Isidor asked what happened, his blood curdled. He banned the coach from entering the locker room again and forbid him from interacting with Jokic.

"He's a jerk," Branislav said. "Because of that teasing, I took Nikola away from him. . . . Because of his thickness, he could tease him."

The coach lived in the same building as the Jokics and would often see the family.

"I told him I would beat him if he continued with such nonsense," Branislav said. "He would go to the media years later and boast that he was Nikola's first coach. I told him, 'Don't mention my family in public.'"

The assistant, according to Isidor, took it a step further. He was a Partizan supporter, and after making fun of Jokic, was the one responsible for inviting the club to the camp at Zlatibor, where he'd been dismissed.

The coach tried to take credit for discovering Nikola, then tried to leverage his association with him with other players. In reality, he had hardly anything to do with Nikola's development. He only served to impede it.

○

What the coach did was despicable, but Nikola's frame did limit him on the court.

"All of that helped Nikola to try to do some other things with his type of body on offense and defense," Isidor said.

It made him process the game differently. To pick up on an offense's habits. To take calculated risks based off an opponent's tendencies. To hunt for attainable advantages.

With Jokic at center, the team implemented a zone to try and mask his defensive limitations. Isidor knew he wasn't agile. The scheme allowed him to defend, snatch rebounds and outlet in transition. In the zone, he, theoretically, had protection. But the application reinforced another essential quality of Nikola's: his intelligence. As soon as Isidor explained the basics, Jokic was already asking pertinent questions.

Who rotates in this scenario? Whose responsibility is that swing pass?

While the rest of the team tried to grasp the basics of a zone defense, Jokic was already processing its nuances. Of course, as soon as Jokic snatched a rebound, everything was on the table. He might lead a fast break or heave a full-court pass. Or he might get caught between possessions.

"After he threw the ball, he would start running to the other half of the court," Isidor said. "There were some times that we had already scored, and the other guys were running back on defense, while Nikola was still trying to run on offense."

Nikola had legitimate limitations, but others were self-imposed. His stubborn streak, evident in his practice record and his insistence on throwing one-handed passes, translated to games too. If anyone cared to share their suggestions from the stands, there was a high likelihood he'd do the opposite to illustrate how little he cared what others thought.

If he was told to hustle, for example, he was apt to plant his feet on the offensive end and wait for the court to flip.

During one home game, Branislav levied some criticism at Nikola while he was at the free-throw line.

Shoot with a higher arc, he told him.

Jokic wasn't interested in what suggestions his father had for him.

"He threw both free throws almost to the top of the hall," Branislav said. "Since then, I've calmed down a bit."

In a constant act of defiance, Jokic preferred to play on his own terms. So, he did.

CHAPTER 4

TASTE OF SUCCESS

Nikola's generation of basketball players (1995) was excellent, and because the levels of Serbian basketball were broken down into two-year windows, every other season he was grouped with kids born in 1994. Despite being older, that group wasn't as talented. Playing alongside the '94 group was seen as a demotion.

During most of the 2010–11 season, Nikola played on the club's developmental team.

"The reason why we transferred him to that group was to try and wake him up," Isidor said.

Heading into the season's final regional tournament, their head coach abandoned them, thinking that they wouldn't be able to compete. Isidor, with Nikola engaged, took over the team and unexpectedly seized the title.

The next season, with Nikola on the first team, was even more fulfilling. KK So Kos buzzed through the regular season. They smacked Vojvodina Novi Sad (Nikola's next club) by 50 points at home and 20 points on the road. They hadn't lost a game all season as they approached the round-robin style Final Four of the Vojvodina regional championship.

There, again, was Vojvodina Novi Sad. In their third try, they finally bested KK So Kos. But because of the nature of the round-robin tournament, Nikola's team survived. They won the 2012 Vojvodina regional title for Cadets.

"In that time, [Isidor] was the best we ever had," said Nikola, who still considers Isidor a friend to this day. "He taught us some stuff and we played good. We were like a really good bond of guys together. . . . He understands us. It was I think the huge respect we had for him."

The picture celebrating their championship run is eerie. Wide grins crept across a handful of the teenagers while a slight smile spread on Nikola's face. In the back row, five of Nikola's teammates clasped their hands behind their backs. Nikola, perhaps stubbornly, draped his left hand over his right in front of him.

While every single kid wore a medal for the shot, the light danced radiantly off of only one of them: Nikola's.

It was a turning point in his career. Four year earlier, he'd all but quit. The practices and the requisite effort weren't worth it. After that game, Nikola grasped something about his potential. He understood that if he took the game seriously, there was a career waiting for him in basketball. Maybe the NBA was still far-fetched and unreachable, and maybe he'd settle in Europe. But there was already enough evidence. He knew there was something worth chasing.

O

The Cadet championship was in April 2012, and Isidor still wanted to test his team heading into the summer.

KK So Kos didn't have a senior-level team. He applied with the core of that Cadet team, along with a few older players, to compete in a summer league qualification series for promotion to the senior-level league.

The team traveled to Novi Sad and faced off against Slavija Novi Sad, whose team featured Dusan Domovic Bulut. The 6'3" guard was, at one time, the No. 1–ranked three-on-three player in the world according to FIBA and would later star in Ice Cube's nascent Big 3 league.

Nikola was just seventeen at the time, ten years Bulut's junior. The game was competitive but KK So Kos fell by two points. Afterward, Nikola was furious. He felt the refs robbed them. Bulut tried to console Jokic, conveying his newfound respect for him.

"Don't be mad, shit happens," Bulut told the rising star. It didn't help. Nikola was still incensed.

Strahinja, Nikola's hulking older brother, was in the stands for the game. So was Ljuba Anicic, the head coach for Vojvodina Novi Sad. Together they plotted Nikola's next stop, reaching an agreement for him to continue his career at Novi Sad.

"My eldest son, Strahinja, who lived in Novi Sad after quitting basketball due to an injury, watched that tournament," Branislav said. "He told me that Nikola must go 'further,' and that's how he joined KK Vojvodina, and later Mega from Belgrade, and beyond."

While Strahinja insisted, Nikola resisted.

"Nikola was crying," Isidor said.

It had nothing to do with the stinging defeat. He wasn't ready to move on from Isidor, from his teammates, from Sombor.

Branislav was against the move too. The Café Hilton group had made significant gains with Jokic in terms of his practice commitment. What's more, the team was starting to gel. He was also concerned about Nikola, his youngest, leaving home and leading a professional lifestyle without his oversight.

"Nikola adored his two older brothers, who, because of basketball, had left home, one to Subotica [Strahinja] and the other to Vrsac [Nemanja]," Branislav said. "Nikola's departure to Novi Sad, and later to KK Vojvodina, was not easy for my wife and me because, in previous years, we ran every weekend for our sons' matches. We didn't want the third one to leave home."

For Branislav, there were too many unknowns.

"After one month or two in Novi Sad, he will come back to Sombor, and we will have lost him forever," Branislav told Isidor.

Strahinja was bullish and unrelenting. He had Nikola's career in mind. He wasn't going to allow his youngest brother to falter.

CHAPTER 5

NOVI SAD

Nikola never had much choice in the matter of leaving Sombor.

Strahinja, who already lived in Novi Sad, vowed to his family that he'd look after his youngest brother. He argued it was time for Nikola to become more mature and take some ownership over his career. He even rented Nikola an apartment and helped keep him fed from the bakery he owned. Almost all of Nikola's breakfasts came from Strahinja's place.

"They were actually really good," Nikola said.

At the time, Nikola admitted he was a bit shy and, as the third child, somewhat spoiled. To have Strahinja look after him, employing his brand of oversight, meant Nikola had familial support, but that wasn't the only factor.

"At that time, Nikola was afraid of Strahinja," Isidor said.

As a kid, both Strahinja and Nemanja tried to toughen their youngest brother. Nikola relished being around them no matter the cost; they, in turn, took the liberty of terrorizing him.

Once, the three brothers were out fishing.

"They were doing something they weren't supposed to do in my mind, when I was like fourteen or fifteen," Nikola said. "I said, 'I'm gonna tell Mom and Dad.' Then my brother stood on my arms and like threw knives right around my head."

Through tears and clenched eyes, Nikola vowed not to tell their parents about his brother's indiscretions.

"Nowadays, that would be a problem," Nikola said.

Back then, he conceded, it was strictly "brotherly love."

The Jokic household could barely contain the three rambunctious boys. They used to play indoor basketball together, with a hoop mounted on the door. The teams were fairly lopsided: Strahinja and Nemanja versus a young Nikola.

"You can imagine what happened there," Branislav said. "They beat him with no mercy."

But Nikola cherished the time he had with his older brothers, even as they pounded him.

The games they'd play on that hoop were legendary.

"If I touched them, it's a foul," Nikola said. "And then, if they like, basically kill me, it's nothing. And if I start crying, they didn't want to play with me."

Despite their double-digit age gap, Nikola savored being near his brothers. When they traveled around Serbia for basketball games, he was more than game to accompany them for a few days.

"I loved to spend time with them," Nikola said.

If Strahinja was going to facilitate a transfer for his youngest brother, Nikola had no choice but to begrudgingly accept.

"Most of the guys from that team, if they were offered to go to Novi Sad Vojvodina, they would've accepted it happily, but Nikola wasn't like that," Isidor said. "He was not happy with that move."

Strahinja had played on bigger clubs and understood the negative associations of strong, slow, and plodding.

According to Ljuba, the head coach at Vojvodina Novi Sad, Strahinja was deliberate about where Nikola would continue his career. To Strahinja, it was important that Novi Sad develop Nikola's strengths rather than pigeonhole him as a back-to-the-basket center. Strahinja knew as well as anyone what Nikola was capable of.

It was also important that Novi Sad had a junior-level team, one where development was prioritized over results.

Ljuba was adamant that Jokic not split time between both levels. If the organization decided it was right for him to play on the senior circuit, which was discussed, Ljuba didn't want him to return to the junior squad. He didn't think any player should be receiving mixed messages. That idea, he said, stemmed from Aleksandar Nikolic, a legendary figure and one of the founding fathers in Serbia's rich basketball history.

Ljuba's point was the senior team played one game a week. The results mattered. Growing prospects wasn't the priority. Besides, the coach of the senior team offered no guarantees that Jokic would play.

Instead, Ljuba elected to develop him as a leader of the junior squad. On the senior team, that level of empowerment, for a seventeen-year-old, wouldn't have happened.

The organization couldn't offer any money, so it was fortuitous that Strahinja oversaw Nikola's accommodations.

The organization was so broke that Ljuba sometimes paid for gym time out of his own pocket. Other times they benefited because Ljuba's mother worked at an elementary school, and he negotiated free gym usage with the school principal.

But Nikola needed Novi Sad, like Novi Sad needed him. Had he remained in Sombor as a junior prospect, one year before his eighteenth birthday, his professional prospects would have plummeted. There was a reasonable chance he would've remained undiscovered.

At the time, Novi Sad didn't have the same reputation as the more established clubs like Red Star, Partizan, and Hemofarm, but they were respected. So was the league. At Hemofarm, Nikola Milutinov, now a staple on the Serbian national team, starred. At Mega, the next stop on Jokic's basketball odyssey, future NBA guard Vasa Micic was blossoming into a feisty floor general. The gyms around the league were buzzing. Word had spread about the talent of that generation.

"He chose us," Ljuba said.

Igor Kovacevic, then in management for Novi Sad, believed Nikola may have been just a month away from quitting basketball altogether. Upon arrival in the summer of 2012, he noticed no professional habits.

"He loved horses, hamburgers, and Coca-Cola," Igor said.

One of his teammates, Marko Brankovic, said Jokic was a frequent visitor to a local pizza chain close to his apartment. The two hung out often there, watching EuroLeague games, guzzling Cokes, and playing *Pro Evolution Soccer* on PlayStation.

Despite a typical junk-food filled teenage diet, Jokic shocked coaches with his natural abilities. The team's conditioning coach, Aleksandar

Jovancevic, had a wrestling background and liked to train players in his gym without their shoes on. The padded, uneven surface was meant for combat sports, not necessarily training basketball players.

The first time Nikola walked in the gym, he had his high-top basketball shoes on with his trademark untied laces. He spotted a ball, walked over to it, and started juggling.

At first, he flicked the ball with one foot and then the other. He passed it up toward his arms, then his shoulders, and then his head. Aleksandar was watching—and counting—in amazement. On a foam mat, with untied shoes, an unknown, tall, chubby kid juggled it seventy consecutive times on a whim.

"In that environment, with those shoes, everything was unreal and I was fascinated with what I saw," said Aleksandar, who'd trained thousands of athletes in his career.

It wasn't natural for a guy as big as Jokic, with muscles as indiscernible as he had, to be as coordinated and smooth as he was. Aleksandar spent most of his time with the senior team and had few expectations when he volunteered, without pay, to train the junior squad too. What he saw in Jokic was stunning.

It had nothing to do with aesthetics. Perhaps other coaches wouldn't have given him a second look had they fixated on his leisurely, relaxed disposition. Aleksandar noticed his motor skills were off the charts, his coordination with the ball astounding. Beneath the surface, his talent was undeniable.

"He was different," Aleksandar said. "He wasn't like the other guys."

Aleksandar told the rest of the team to keep warming up, while he ran to the café to inform Novi Sad's management of what he'd seen.

"People, we have something worth a million," the trainer said.

Predrag, the team manager, was on holiday that summer when he got an excited call from Ljuba.

"Come to practice and see what I have found," he told him.

There was no glossing over the way good things happened when possessions funneled through Jokic, or the way loose rebounds seemed to gravitate toward his hands.

"He was fascinating everybody," said Aleksandar.

"Everybody saw," Predrag said.

CHAPTER 6

LJUBA

Ljuba didn't want Nikola playing both levels of competition for Novi Sad, but he did register that team for the Srpska Liga, a third-tier senior league in Serbia. That way, Nikola would get experience against older players without the pressure of having to win. It also allowed for two games per week, one on the junior circuit and the other against seasoned veterans.

"I saw him developing in that league and playing every week," Ljuba said. "Each week it got easier for him against bigger and older guys. It was nice to watch how one little boy is dominating older guys."

It didn't matter the opponent. Nikola carved up the thirty-year-olds like he did the junior circuit.

What most impressed Ljuba about Nikola was his composure, especially in the Srpska Liga. Their team would travel to small, rowdy gyms and Nikola wouldn't get rattled. In crunch time, in hostile environments, he consistently delivered. To Ljuba, that spoke volumes about his mental makeup, competitiveness, and gamesmanship.

In Nikola, Ljuba saw a big, coordinated body, with good dimensions and an uncanny feel for the game.

"He had slow legs because he was overweight," Ljuba said. "But I saw that he had very long arms, and very fast hands. Also, he saw everything on the court. Maybe he wasn't able to do everything on the court but he saw everything on the court."

Aleksandar shared a theory with his athletes that there were limits, physically, to what they could do with their arms and legs, but that mentally, their creativity couldn't be bound. In addition to his coordination, what distinguished Nikola was his mind. His processing speed masked his physical limitations. When he wasn't able to jump as high for rebounds, he learned to tip the ball to himself instead, or read the trajectory of a miss faster than his opponents. He learned to compensate.

He was also determined. When Aleksandar introduced a particularly grueling exercise in practice, Nikola didn't quit until he'd finished it. He and his teammates would do partner sit-ups, with their legs wrapped around their partner so gravity became an obstacle. They needed to finish fifteen to twenty of them, without falling. And since Nikola was paired with a fellow big man, falling, from a meter up, hurt. In one practice, Nikola kept struggling. And falling. Aleksandar proposed a different exercise. Nikola refused. Finally, he finished the drill.

"I was fascinated by him because he wasn't ready to give up any time," Aleksandar said. "He, all the time, continued to work. He refused to surrender."

Igor noticed his zealous approach to defense. On one play, he'd strip the ball from an opponent's top playmaker. On the next, he'd body-check someone else. As a seventeen-year-old, he said he was playing like a thirty-year-old EuroLeague player. Still, though his hands and timing were elite, his vertical limitations were obvious.

Offensively, Igor couldn't compare him to anyone. His style was too unique. His influence in the attack was too entrenched. Igor mentioned Hakeem Olajuwon, whose post moves were deft yet teachable.

"With Nikola, it's not like that," he said.

He arrived at Novi Sad with a perfect shooting form, and Igor gushed. Even his misses were pretty.

Collectively, Novi Sad's brain trust understood that he was unique and could be deployed in innumerable ways.

"I'm gonna tell the same story even if Michael Malone is here," Igor said. "I really believe that if he went to any other coach, he wouldn't play. He was lucky to go with Ljuba. . . . If there's no Ljuba, Nikola's not playing today."

Ljuba fancied himself old-school. He'd grown up watching the former Yugoslavians of the 1970s and '80s. In Jokic, he saw someone he'd seen before.

"When Nikola came, I saw he can play like Kresimir Cosic was at that time," Ljuba said.

Cosic was Croatian-born, and at 6'11", broadened the boundaries of what a big man could do on the court. Cosic became famous for playing all five positions, for facilitating out of the high post, for serving as the fulcrum of an offense.

Predrag had grown up with the same Yugoslavian golden generation. Vlade Divac, Toni Kukoc, Drazen Petrovic, and Dino Radja all had an outsized influence on his basketball philosophy. After the six months Nikola spent in Novi Sad, Predrag remembered Ljuba predicting to newspapers what was on the horizon.

"He will be a lot better than Divac because he's a lot more talented than he was at that age," Ljuba said.

○

Miroslav Pasajlic was Novi Sad's official point guard, but his play became inextricably linked to Nikola.

Together they were tasked with initiating the offense. As defenses descended on Miroslav, they adjusted. They devised a scheme where Miroslav would in-bound the ball, since opposing centers never pressed all the way up on Jokic. This turned him into the de facto point guard.

"He's the same player as he is now," Miroslav said. "He did everything on the court."

Nikola hadn't practiced with the team before he made his debut in a scrimmage against Partizan, then the best team in the country. He'd only just met his teammates in the locker room prior to tip-off.

When he arrived, Miroslav remembered him as shy and introverted.

"He looked like he wasn't happy to be there," he said.

Then he went out and dominated, with something like 25 points and 10 rebounds, according to Miroslav.

His first two games, Jokic registered an index (a compilation of counting stats) of 50 against Partizan and 49 against Hemofarm, respectively. After the second game, the team made fun of him for his declining production.

"It was very hard to not notice him," said Marko, another teammate. "He was [toying] with the basketball."

Igor was struck by the deliberate yet varied ways in which he moved. It was obvious to him how calculated each decision was. He couldn't believe that someone so talented had been such an unknown commodity in Serbia.

"He was like a miracle," he said.

At the beginning of his time in Novi Sad, Marko said Nikola was quiet and content living in his own world. He didn't like going out chasing girls. The only girl he cared about was Natalija Macesic, though they weren't then in a relationship. He'd met Natalija when he was fourteen or fifteen. She grew up only a few minutes from Jokic's home. According to Marko, she was all he talked about. Back then, he was too nervous to ask her out.

Toward the end of 2012, Nikola's life was relatively simple.

Everything he did revolved around sports: watching them, simulating them, or playing them.

If Nikola was disappointed that he wasn't at a more renowned club, it took only a month or two to get over it. Miroslav described celebrating a teammate's eighteenth birthday, which turned into an excuse to hang out and drink.

"All of us got drunk in that party," said Marko. "Joka was dead drunk."

The party went until 5 a.m., even though they had a Srpska Liga game, on the road, against the best team in the league that night.

Novi Sad won.

"After that, he started smiling more," Miroslav said.

Nikola was living in an apartment close to Miroslav's school, and whenever Miroslav felt like playing hooky, he'd wander over to the apartment and ring the intercom. At 7 a.m., Miroslav would trudge into the room where Nikola was already playing computer games and chugging Coca-Cola.

"Don't worry about me," he told him. "Let me play."

O

In games, Nikola was unrestricted.

"We gave him freedom," Predrag said.

They didn't want him to develop as a traditional center. They encouraged him to pursue a hybrid role.

There wasn't much that he's doing now that he hadn't at least tried in Novi Sad. He excelled at leading breaks. He stepped confidently out from the 3-point line. He threw blind passes to spaces he expected his teammates to inhabit. When they were out of position, and the ball soared out of bounds, Nikola shrugged his shoulders.

It was their fault they were standing in the wrong place, not mine.

He drained floaters, scored through double teams, took defenders off the dribble, tipped in offensive rebounds with one hand, and more. Nikola was in his lab, assessing his powers.

In a game against Red Star, the supposedly ground-bound prospect dunked. Only a few possessions later, he gobbled up a steal, took off in transition, dribbled once behind his back, and whipped another behind-the-back pass to a running teammate, who fed it back to Nikola for the layup. The sequence was emblematic of his tantalizing potential. A reminder that he wasn't to be kept in a box.

Like he does today, Nikola played games within the game. He'd loaf around the court, seemingly content to let gravity dictate his next movement, before lunging into action. On in-bounds actions he'd play possum, lulling his defender to sleep before shoving him aside, his post position already established. When engaged, he'd run hard, but if he'd ignited a fast break chance for his team, there was a decent chance he'd just stay on the defensive end rather than jog past halfcourt. Reverse cherry-picking.

His body language improved as he got more comfortable with his teammates, but there were still telltale signs of Nikola's temperament. If he had a mismatch, and a teammate launched an errant shot instead, he was apt to roll his head in disgust.

That was not the right basketball play.

Even as the de facto big man, Nikola never liked being the screener in pick-and-rolls. It devalued his abilities, diminishing him from a dynamic facilitator to a decoy. Once when he pleaded with a guard for the ball and the guard refused, instead calling for him to set a pick, Nikola set a screen so soft he neglected to make contact with his teammate's defender.

Nikola elevated his passive aggression to an art form.

When he moved, he ambled and swayed like a buoy floating in the ocean. Most of his top speeds resembled the last mile of a marathon. His complaints to referees were enthusiastic and comical. On bad calls, he'd flare both wrists at a 90-degree angle, leaning back in disbelief. In blowouts, his body language fell comfortably between boredom and indifference. In many ways, he was a jester, tilting and bending the game to his own pace.

O

Ljuba and Predrag were more than happy to put the ball in Nikola's hands and let him probe the defense, but it came at a cost. Miroslav's father wasn't happy watching his son, the point guard, get overshadowed.

He didn't like that Nikola seemed to enjoy endless freedom on the court, his wayward passes never punished while his creativity always stoked.

Most parents, according to Predrag, voiced their displeasures at the referees and their frustrations at the coaches. Branislav and Strahinja, though they attended every game, didn't do that. Having invested so much in his future, they reserved their criticisms only for Nikola.

Miroslav was the captain of the team. When his dad conveyed frustration that his son wasn't being featured enough, Ljuba kicked Miroslav out of a game.

"He was my best point guard and my only point guard," Ljuba said.

Ljuba said he didn't show up to practice for a week before his father apologized, and he was allowed to return.

In contrast, Ljuba lauded Nikola for how polite and grounded he was during his six-month stay.

The only confrontation he ever got into with Nikola was engineered. Ljuba forced Nikola and Miroslav to play one-on-one, beginning at half-court. The drill was rigged.

"Obviously, Miroslav was faster and he was cutting Nikola and making layups, and the reason I decided to do that was because I wanted Nikola to play defense, to try to play against point guard, to make his legs faster," Ljuba said.

Nikola hated that his defense was getting exposed. He also didn't like losing to anybody.

"Nikola was really mad," Ljuba said.

He wore his emotions on his sleeve, loafing in disdain and bobbing his head in protest.

When Nikola played defense, he was more apt to roam the paint than stay attached to the opposing big. He didn't need to move as much and could play a style of zone within the defense itself. If an action didn't involve him, he'd stand upright near the hoop while waiting for a shot to carom. Defensively, he wasn't going to overexert himself.

But that had more to do with his attitude than it did his conditioning.

Years later, as Nikola's legend grew, Predrag took exception to the idea that Nikola was always just some overweight kid with a basketball. He was bigger than his teammates, but he wasn't close to fat, as portrayed in some younger pictures. Predrag thought the overweight stories were a marketing ploy later cooked up in Belgrade.

It was true, however, that both his coaches and Strahinja wanted him to monitor and control his weight. If nothing else, they felt it was essential to his development.

O

Whether because of his talent or his personality, or both, Nikola's teammates loved him.

If there was innocent teasing, Nikola was usually behind it. On bus rides, Jokic always sat in the second row, just ahead of Predrag and just behind the youngest guy on the team.

"The whole trip, Nikola was twisting his hair, flicking his ears, trying to tickle him," Predrag said.

When the team played soccer, all Jokic wanted to do was dribble the ball through his teammates' legs and embarrass them. In pickup basketball games, Nikola tried to deke his defenders with some new dribbling trick he unfurled.

"Break his ankles" was even more devastating in Serbian. It referenced the flaky, doughy pastries that Nikola devoured as a kid.

Send him to buy a burek.

The insult hit even closer to Jokic, whose weight was a constant topic.

When the team trained at Aleksandar's wrestling gym, Jokic weighed himself at the start of practice. Occasionally, others would sneak behind him and discreetly press their foot on the scale. Inevitably, Nikola would step off disgruntled and dismayed at his bloated size. After practices, without any other assistance, he couldn't believe how much weight he'd lost.

The few times it worked, Aleksandar reveled in Nikola's confusion, since it was so often their budding star who was behind such pranks.

When he wasn't sending someone to buy a burek, Nikola was spinning the ball on his fingers, his nose, or even the equipment inside the gym.

"He was making a circus over here," Aleksandar said.

CHAPTER 7

MISKO

Sixty miles away from Novi Sad, European superagent Misko Raznatovic was perusing the junior league box scores in the newspaper.

Two weeks in a row, Raznatovic saw numbers that astounded him and piqued his interest. Raznatovic, the founder of Mega Basket in Belgrade, almost always sent his scouting team to assess a prospect before deciding to pursue him or not. His team would offer an opinion, Misko would observe, and they'd proceed as necessary.

But Jokic was different.

"I decided let's go for him," Misko told the *Denver Post*. "I never do [it like] this."

Ljuba said that both Partizan and Red Star, the two most heralded Belgrade clubs, registered some interest in Nikola but added that Red Star's curiosity had been more pronounced.

"There were talks with Red Star, for sure," Predrag said.

Novi Sad's management was more eager to see their star continue at Mega than the other two more established clubs because they knew what it would mean for Jokic's development. At Red Star or Partizan, there would be immediate pressure to win. At Mega, thanks in large part to Misko's directive, they could afford to let him blossom.

"When we decided, we had a couple offers before we take Misko," Strahinja told the *Denver Post*.

Strahinja was essential to the process. By taking responsibility for Nikola's future, he inherited all the baggage that came with it.

"There were people with bags and bow ties who tried to manipulate, but my oldest son had his own vision, and that's how it ended up," Branislav said. "It didn't hinder him at all."

More than a decade removed from that pivotal moment, Misko was still emboldened by Jokic's choice.

"We came first," he said.

But even if they hadn't, Misko was confident they'd still have been his choice because of their developmental reputation.

Prospects, Misko believed, understood it was easier to grow at Mega.

At that point, Nikola wasn't in the pipeline for Serbia's youth national team. And recognizing that Nikola needed more exposure than he was getting at Novi Sad, Strahinja once again spearheaded the transfer.

If a player was turning eighteen, as Nikola would in February 2013, and didn't intend to stay with his current club, also as Nikola planned, the cost of a buyout was ten thousand euros.

What seems now like the deal of a lifetime was all it cost to acquire a player under Nikola's circumstances.

"But [back then], he wasn't worth more than that," Misko said.

CHAPTER 8

DEJAN

Once Nikola arrived in Belgrade, he wasn't allowed to practice.

Mega's head coach, Dejan Milojevic, and its training staff deemed him so far removed from a professional fitness level that they were concerned about him getting hurt. As an eighteen-year-old, they were worried that he wasn't physically equipped to handle bigger, stronger professional players. Or even the rigors of two-a-day practices.

"Push-ups are not some drill that's super valuable to basketball, but the point is, if he cannot do a few push-ups . . ." said Dejan, implying all that needed to be said.

For a month, Nikola worked on his strength and fitness with the team's training staff.

"He needed patience and love," Misko said.

Dejan was the perfect coach to provide it. He was a decorated player, winning three consecutive MVPs in the Adriatic League. A 6'7" power forward, Dejan wasn't the biggest, but what he lacked in size he made up for in craft, physicality, and determination. He played with tenacity and heart and blended a bruising style of strength with deception.

As a coach, even though he'd never been one before Mega, he had a gift for relating to players. He understood how to unlock their potential, often catering his philosophies to his players' strengths. He was fond of saying coaches, like GPS systems, were only as good as the coordinates given to them.

In other words, Dejan could steer Nikola, but without believing in his potential and envisioning what he could become, that guidance was fruitless.

From the start, Dejan recognized something unique about Mega's new prospect. He wasn't dissuaded by his body type. In fact, it was the opposite.

If a player arrived on Dejan's doorstep more physically mature than his peers, he couldn't help but ask himself a poignant question: *Was this player more talented than his competition or was he just stronger?*

Immediately, Dejan was encouraged by the fact that Nikola had dominated his prior stops despite his apparent indifference to fitness. His measurables—his height and wingspan—were undeniable. His hands were fast, he processed the game quickly, and his coordination would be impressive for any player, let alone a big man.

But Dejan, like Nikola's prior coaches, soon learned about his tepid relationship with practice. Motivating him, he conceded, was a challenge. Getting up for games wasn't the issue. It was the mundane drills that were a chore.

"Yes, of course," Dejan said, adding that he was no different than any young player. "But he always liked to compete."

From then on, every drill Dejan designed had a competitive element. He wouldn't just tell his players to make fifty shots. Instead, he'd pit them against one another. There needed to be enthusiasm and energy in the gym. This was a competitive environment he was trying to foster.

Dejan mandated one-on-one games. It wasn't one-on-one in a traditional sense, since each drill had to mimic a gamelike situation as closely as possible. One-on-one could commence, for instance, out of a pick-and-roll drill, so as to practice attacking a defender or picking up an offensive player with momentum. Dejan emphasized closeouts, all within the confines of the competition itself.

He also found improvement was limited if they only stuck to positional groups. Nikola played one-on-one against everyone, guards included. If the flow of a game could present cross-matches, then that's what they were going to drill.

There were also two-on-two and three-on-three games. With a teammate or two, Nikola's impact was magnified. The spacing, the ball movement, the anticipation allowed him to showcase his vision and wile.

Ratko Varda, the team's starting center and resident veteran, was nearing the end of his career. He suffered an Achilles injury the season before and wasn't even sure he could keep playing, let alone play effectively. Before he called it a career, Dejan and Misko convinced him to come to Mega to mentor their young core. They wanted him to set an example for the rest of the team.

"I was looking at them like my kids," he said.

His early impression on the tall one?

"Who is that fat guy?" he wondered aloud.

Ratko saw an eighteen-year-old immature kid, not a budding professional.

"Nikola didn't really care about basketball," Varda said.

Varda and Jokic were frequent one-on-one opponents. On offense, the bigger, stronger, more experienced big man plowed through Jokic. Defense was a different story. Dejan taught Nikola a playground move where he'd whip the ball behind his back, then pass it through his defender's legs. When Nikola executed it against Ratko, yielding an uncontested layup on the other side of Mount Varda, the veteran was dumbfounded.

"What the fuck?" Varda proclaimed.

At the next practice, Nikola unfurled another move that left Ratko in shambles.

The veteran couldn't stop the intrepid eighteen-year-old.

"I will punch him," said Ratko, turning to Dejan in astonishment. "I cannot do anything."

Perplexed by his ingenuity, Ratko finally found a way to slow him down. He caught Nikola, ostensibly by accident, with an elbow and served the upstart a gash that required five or six stitches in his mouth. According to Ratko, Nikola was happy to spend the next three or four days back home in Sombor.

Even then, when Nikola was toying with Ratko, embarrassing him with all his dekes, the veteran wasn't a total believer in his potential.

He thought he'd be a good European player, with the *potential* to have an impact in the NBA. At best, maybe another Vlade Divac.

No one, Ratko said, believed his current level of dominance was possible.

The impact he had on Mega was immediate, according to the team's power forward at the time, Nemanja Radovic. Nikola initially arrived on the club's junior team during the 2012–13 season but was promoted soon after. Everyone wanted to play with him because of how unselfish he was. Even then, Radovic said, he was mentally a few steps ahead of his teammates.

"Nikola was so special," he said.

Beyond his skill, there was a charisma that was as infectious as his unselfishness.

"Having fun," Radovic said. "He was having fun from the first moment."

Nemanja Pavkov, Nikola's childhood friend from Sombor, was among the beneficiaries of Jokic's newfound wealth. One of the veterans on Mega told Nikola to get drunk off his first paycheck.

Nikola listened.

"Hey brothers, I have five hundred euros," Nemanja recalled Nikola saying. "We need to drink all of that tonight."

According to Pavkov, about a hundred people drank on Nikola's tab.

"He bought everything for everybody."

O

At Novi Sad, Nikola had been a hybrid forward-center. Dejan decided he'd be best suited as a center and developed him as such.

Positionally, Nikola's most unique attribute was his ballhandling. If he could snatch defensive rebounds, it allowed their offense to instantly engage. Dejan wanted him in transition, where he could spot mismatches and thread needles. He wanted him to push the ball, lead the break, and compromise the defense.

If you have the open floor, push it.

Nikola's other elite skill was how quickly he made decisions. It didn't matter if that led to risky or errant passes. Dejan encouraged him to go.

"Make the right mistake," he told him.

They occasionally ran a pick-and-roll drill where coaches would flash their fingers on the sidelines to dictate a certain sequence. A 1/3/5—odd number—meant one action while 2/4 meant another. After Nikola mastered the simpler drill, coaches resorted to putting two hands up. Now he had to process *and* calculate what was being asked of him.

In between practices, Nikola and Radovic would hit the arcade together. He gravitated toward one game where he'd have to touch a screen as soon as a light flashed.

"It was crazy how fast his hands were," Radovic said.

Nikola's speed, on the court and off, compelled the coaching staff to stay creative.

Dejan introduced various pump fakes and deceptive shots that added to his arsenal, but that was hardly his biggest influence. What mattered most was Nikola's approach to the game as a whole, his decision-making within the gym, and how he stitched his gifts together.

It helped that Dejan saw advantages where other coaches might have fixated on flaws.

Nikola wasn't too slow. He played at a different pace. He wasn't unathletic. His coordination was astounding. From the right vantage point, anything *could become an advantage.*

Whatever attributes a player had, Dejan catered his coaching style to work with them. His gift was in adapting to his players' strengths, not imposing his philosophies with an iron fist.

Dejan often wondered what would have happened had he not encouraged Nikola to hunt transition opportunities or if he prohibited him from exploring the depths of his passing. What if he limited his playground to the paint, like a traditional center, or even worse, trained him as the stretch four like many in the NBA projected him to be?

Nikola stuck on the perimeter might as well be confining a Ferrari to a school zone.

Dejan couldn't help but joke about his influence.

"I unleashed him," he said, tongue glued to the side of his cheek.

CHAPTER 9

STRAHINJA

While Misko has celebrated his role in Nikola's discovery, even he knew that the backbone of Nikola's success was Strahinja, his massive older brother.

Anyone who had interacted with the family knew it too.

"Strahi had a vision that no one really probably saw," said then–Nuggets GM Tim Connelly, who recalled Strahinja serving as the family spokesman.

He essentially handcuffed himself to his younger brother, ensuring he didn't falter.

"He definitely sacrificed his life to help me," Nikola said.

Strahinja negotiated his transfers. He vetted offers. He provided food and living accommodations in Novi Sad. In Belgrade, he was there to ensure he never strayed off track.

"Strahinja devoted his life to Nikola and his basketball development, especially after Nikola's move to Belgrade," their father, Branislav, said.

When Nikola was at the gym, he was with his teammates, who adored him. Between that time, though, he was still a vulnerable eighteen-year-old.

"If he didn't have Strahinja, he would've been really alone, and I'm not sure having in mind how he was fragile in that time, would he survive?" Misko said. "And maybe he would've said, 'No, I don't want to stay, I want to go back.'"

That was a threat Nikola seemed to dangle at every stop on his path. Goran Cakic, who was a teammate of Nikola's at Mega and became the GM while he was there, felt it too. If Nikola got bored or frustrated, there was always the risk he'd walk away. It was the only time Goran ever felt that way about a player.

"When he liked to play, he destroyed everybody," Goran said. "When he don't like to play, he didn't play."

Even then, Nikola's relationship with basketball was complex and sensitive. Despite his talent, he never needed basketball. It was still a job. A fun one, and one he was good at, but a job nonetheless.

Strahinja played high-level basketball in their home country as well. He knew the pitfalls young players could fall prey to. Nikola wasn't exactly a wild adolescent, clubbing every night or chasing girls, but he was still susceptible.

Their other brother, Nemanja, had been a teammate of Darko Milicic's in Serbia. After Milicic was drafted No. 2 overall to the Detroit Pistons in the 2003 draft—sandwiched between LeBron James and Carmelo Anthony—he invited Nemanja to take up residence with him in his suburban mansion. Nemanja, then a scholarship player at Detroit Mercy, saw the trappings of life as an NBA player. He realized how quickly things could deteriorate when basketball wasn't the priority.

"Even Darko said that my brothers can teach me all the bad things," Nikola said.

The blueprint for what *not* to do had been lived. Nikola was on a different path.

Strahinja eschewed his life for Nikola's, sacrificing his personal ambitions for his brother's pursuit. He moved to Belgrade and served, again, as Nikola's support system. Of course, Nikola loved having his older brother by his side.

"I kinda miss those kinda days," Nikola said.

Strahinja knew all too well Nikola's shaky commitment to practice and dubious dietary habits.

Without his influence, there was no telling whether Nikola would've succeeded.

"It was fifty-fifty chance he was not [going] to become well-paid basketball player," Misko said.

○

The practices, especially the conditioning drills, were grueling.

Nebojsa Vagic, Nikola's godfather, saw how essential Strahinja was in those moments.

"Strahinja, he was locomotive of his career," Vagic told the *Denver Post*. "Nikola was young, a bit sensitive because he didn't know the world, he didn't know the street. . . . But Strahinja, on the other hand, he did. He was just barging through life in some difficult moments and Nikola was just following him."

Goran, the team's general manager, found Nikola unique in that levying typical punishments or criticisms didn't work with him. The persistent threat of him leaving may have given Nikola some bizarre leverage, but the amalgam of Dejan's vision and Strahinja's constant oversight seemed to register.

"Strahinja was like a John Deere tractor," Vagic said. "He was unstoppable with support toward Nikola. He always believed that Nikola needed that support."

To accommodate their players, Mega offered a life coach to help ease their transition into the professional realm. She would organize small breakout groups designed to address whatever off-court issues or questions a player had. The idea was to establish professional habits.

According to his teammate Nemanja Radovic, the woman tried hard to understand Nikola's admittedly complex motivations. She could never get to him. She did work with everyone but couldn't crack Nikola.

She eventually decided it was a fruitless endeavor and she was better off not doing anything.

"She said to him, 'You just keep playing. You just do what you do,'" said Radovic.

Nikola found the entire exercise useless.

"Whatever she would try to do, he would destroy her," Radovic said.

Added Nenad Miljenovic, the team's point guard and Nikola's close friend: "He was always answering the opposite of what she wanted to hear."

"That's Isidora," Nikola said. "I actually really like her . . . I was just young and liked to be difficult."

Besides, whatever headway she attempted to make with Nikola, Strahinja had already been there. Nikola's support system, with his brother and dad attending games, was sound.

"Mentally, [Nikola] was so tough," Nebojsa said. "You can't change him."

Nikola didn't have the same aggressive gene as his brothers, or Nebojsa for that matter, but he understood the implications. All three influences were older than him and had lived through the Balkan Wars of the early 1990s. That hardened them and reinforced their collective resolve.

"Nikola knows when it comes to survive, you have to show some teeth . . . even if you don't know if you're going to take that bite or not," Nebojsa said.

CHAPTER 10

MEGA BASKET

In the summer of 2013, Nenad Miljenovic, a heady point guard, heard whispers about a young, talented big man making an impression in the months before he joined Mega.

"Couple of people talked to me about it, 'Hey, he's really talented,'" Nenad said.

He watched as Nikola, then just a rotation player, helped Serbia's FIBA Under-19 team earn a silver medal after falling to the U.S. in the title game in Prague.

"Yeah, I can see flashes, but he was not dominant," Nenad thought at the time.

The MVP of that tournament was none other than Aaron Gordon, Nikola's current teammate. The head coach of the U.S. team was current Chicago Bulls coach Billy Donovan, shepherding a team full of future NBA players. Donovan remembered Serbia's connective tissue on the court. Regarding Nikola specifically, it was his hands. His touch around the rim, at eighteen, was sublime. But nothing suggested Nikola would ever surpass the handful of lottery picks he faced in the final—not with their talent and not with his body.

"It's pretty amazing what he evolved into because I think if you would've looked at that team and would've said, 'Okay, [Jahlil] Okafor or Nikola.' Everybody would've said Jahlil," Donovan said.

As Nikola developed, his priorities crystallized. Donovan couldn't claim to see then what's become inarguable since: winning, not stats or individual acclaim, is what drove him.

"I think the one thing that was probably hard for me to see at that age, I think the one thing he doesn't get enough credit for, in my opinion, is you see him run and play, and the way he plays and how easy it sometimes comes, but I think he's really competitive," Donovan said. "And I think winning is of the highest priority for him. Everybody talks about the triple-doubles, and no one's seen a center like this, I don't think people talk enough about that he's all about winning."

Donovan had been around enough basketball players to know the innumerable motivations that could drive a player. Jokic, he later deduced, was wired differently.

○

Nenad began training with Mega in August 2013. The early impression Nikola left on him was jarring.

One of their earliest games came against Kosta Perovic, a former second-round pick of the Golden State Warriors. When he was drafted, he'd been playing for Partizan, but after a short stint in the NBA he was at the back end of his career playing for BC Enisey, a Russian team. The fellow big man was born exactly ten years to the day before Nikola. His basketball trajectory was littered with victories while playing for decorated EuroLeague clubs.

"My god, what he did to him," Nenad said.

Nikola's domination was so unique that Nenad thought it was a fluke. He had never seen someone play like Nikola, pirouetting in the paint like a ballet dancer. Nikola's style was the same as it is today: spot a weakness and exploit it, whether it was a gap in a passing lane, a slow rotation, a mismatch, or something else. Nenad couldn't ignore how much fun the big man was having. At eighteen, he was more reckless than he is today, more willing to experiment. But that made his bizarre style even more entertaining.

"You can imagine how it looked," Nenad said. "When it was working, it was unbelievable."

Nenad still had his doubts. *Would it translate in a real competitive setting? Were his gimmick moves sustainable?*

Nenad had never seen a seven-footer playing one-on-one from the perimeter, carving crazy passes through the defense and pump-faking defenders out of their shoes. He was clearly talented but with a style so outlandish it warranted healthy skepticism.

"It was still too funny to be real," he said.

Ratko saw how determined their other teammates were to make an impression in practices, to stand out to the coaches, and it underscored his appreciation for Nikola's approach.

"I loved him differently than other players because of his mentality," he said.

Ratko derived immense joy from that season in Belgrade. The pressure to win wasn't what it had been earlier in his career, and his role, as a glorified babysitter, was new to him. He took enormous pride in the fact that they'd beaten Red Star once and made it all the way to the Serbian Cup final. Their quirky blend of talent and toughness surpassed all his expectations.

But there were other questions beyond whether Nikola's unique game was sustainable. Serbian coaching was strict and regimented. There wasn't any space to Jackson Pollock the basketball court with passes.

"Who is gonna let you play like that?" Nenad wondered.

Goran, the general manager, believed it wouldn't have happened at Partizan or Red Star. The pressure to win at Mega wasn't nearly as robust as it was at either of Belgrade's more storied clubs. Goran felt he was fortunate to have landed where he did.

"We can handle this here," Goran said.

The patience that Misko preached, that Nikola needed, was available to him. There were no directives from Misko to Dejan either, for how to develop him in the gym. Misko told his head coach that he was talented and to take care of him. Nothing more. Misko trusted Dejan's instincts.

Even if a coach saw Nikola's creativity, most other organizations were too structured to let an eighteen-year-old play the way Nikola did. How could a coach justify playing him through the litany of turnovers his passes could yield? Some of his turnovers were *loud*. But the directive came from the top. Without Misko's blessing, his players' organic growth might never have happened. (In the already-saturated space of Belgrade basketball, it was a shrewd business move by Misko to differentiate his club's directives.)

Nenad has considered the alternative. *What if he had developed in a restrictive environment at a more renowned European club? What if he hadn't reached the NBA as early as he did? What if he neglected his body?*

The pivot points were innumerable, but Jokic's route was crystallizing.

"After two years in Mega, after a game in Sremska Mitrovica, my son, Strahinja, and Misko Raznatovic told me that Nikola was on the path to the NBA," Branislav said. "I asked them, 'Are you two on drugs?' But it happened."

O

When Radovic played with Nikola throughout the 2013–14 season, he remembered the long, unforgiving bus rides and the suicide sprints. He couldn't shake the suicides.

When Dejan felt his team hadn't competed like he expected them to, there were punishments. During his career, he'd been a fighter. As a new coach, he sought to hold his team to the same standard. After the first underwhelming performance, it was 50 suicides. The next was 55, and then 60, and so on. The drills could last up to two hours.

Radovic said he'd stopped feeling pain about halfway through the drill. Then his body shifted into autopilot.

If a teammate didn't finish in under thirty seconds, the whole team would repeat. The exercise was grueling, with the potential for humiliation.

"Nikola in that moment, he was so chubby," Radovic said. "I mean, he was chubby when he got to the NBA, but back then he was really chubby."

Nikola struggled to keep up. When he wasn't able to finish in time, there were tears. He'd cry from how difficult the sprints were, how depleted his body felt.

"His soul was out of his body," said Ratko, sympathetic to his fellow big man's plight.

Ratko asked Dejan whether the unconscionable number of sprints were really necessary. Dejan was unequivocal. *They need it. He needs it.*

The tears came not from his inability to complete the sprints, but because his inability was costing his teammates.

"He looked at basketball like a game on a phone, like he's going to the next level," Radovic said. "He doesn't have any pressure. He's so good at it. But he liked his teammates. And he didn't want anybody to suffer because of him."

During punishments, according to Radovic, Dejan laughed. He wasn't remorseless. He was trying to strengthen their mental resolve. According to Ratko, a player's salary could hover around five hundred euros per month, which was too small a wage to dock from his players' pay. Instead, Dejan made them run.

"I think Dejan understood how special he was," Radovic said.

Finally, they were allowed to go home. His teammates had gotten behind him in the drill and pushed him, more mentally than physically. Like the painful ab workouts back in Novi Sad, Nikola had refused to quit.

CHAPTER 11

RIDDLER

Misko fawned over his fingers.

During an offensive possession, while Nikola was fighting for positioning under the basket, his teammate missed everything. Air ball.

Nikola read the trajectory, redirected the ball, and glanced it off the backboard for a basket.

Nobody can really do this, Misko said to himself before accepting reality.

"It's from God," Misko said.

Meanwhile, Ratko marveled at his ability to corral five offensive rebounds on a single possession.

"He has unbelievable feeling in his fingers," he said.

Goran was similarly amazed at his touch.

When Nikola shot the ball, it rattled around the rim two or three times before gently falling through the net. The same shot from someone else could ricochet off the rim in untold directions. The shots looked the same coming off the players' hands, but they never responded the same. Cakic couldn't believe what he was seeing. There was a running joke at Mega that made more sense the more they studied him.

"For him, the rim is bigger, and it's a little bit slanted," he said.

The game came easily and effortlessly to Nikola, as if something were tilting the scales in his favor. He couldn't help but enjoy it and tinker with his gift. Outside of conditioning drills, everything he did came with a smile.

Nikola employed the same trick he used on Ratko in their one-on-one battles against another teammate, Novica Velickovic.

Put the ball between his legs. Confuse him.

The through-the-legs ploy was, at best, flashy and, at worst, disrespectful. When a defender was playing him too close, Dejan wanted Nikola to keep the opponent honest.

When he unleashed it against his latest victim, Novica chased the brazen eighteen-year-old around the gym, furious at being made the fool.

There wasn't a moment where Nikola wasn't searching for a way to entertain himself at someone else's expense. Missing shoes? Nikola was often the culprit.

Ratko was the last guy on the team worth instigating, though his temper made the prospect alluring.

Once during a game at Cibona, Ratko, the team's elder statesman, was disgusted with their effort and ripped a sink off the bathroom wall. As the lone veteran on the squad, Ratko felt it was his job to set an example, to strike fear in his teammates' eyes.

"The sink is in his hands, and he didn't know what to do with it," said Nenad, who couldn't stifle a laugh during the incident.

Radovic recalled an incident where someone locked Ratko in the locker room. Furious, the big man smashed through the door when no one brought him a key. The door remained in its place; there was just a Ratko-sized hole in the middle.

Who was responsible, a decade later, remained a point of debate.

"We didn't want to snitch on Nikola," Radovic said.

But Nenad maintained that he himself played a significant role in the prank. And even if Nikola hadn't been formally responsible, he knew of the plot against the grizzled veteran. When Dejan inquired, no one said a word. In some ways, it was the kids against the adults.

At the time, "nobody really knew [who did it]," Nenad said.

Once, during a trip to Bulgaria, Nenad flipped the script on his friend. The team needed to prepare their passports ahead of the border.

"Somehow his passport gets to me," Nenad said.

Curious at what a young Nikola looked like, Nenad peered inside and was greeted with a photo of a disinterested, chubby face staring blankly at the camera. In 2014, Twitter was in its nascent stages, and Mega's players, while known, hadn't yet passed the tipping point of being famous. Struck by Jokic's adolescent features, Nenad Tweeted his passport photo. At first it was funny, but after ten minutes of ample engagement, Nenad regretted the decision. Jokic's home address was on the photo.

Naturally, Nikola took it in stride. Today the cropped photo is still in regular circulation across the internet.

During one game in the 2013–14 season, Nikola met his foil. Mega was playing against a third-division team, which featured a crafty, ground-bound forward with a bag of tricks similar to Nikola's. His name was Djordje Djordjo.

Among the lower leagues in Serbia, he was famous.

"He looked like a construction worker," Radovic said.

But the savvy veteran, eager to compete against a team from the Adriatic League, gave Nikola fits. He mocked him throughout the beating, leaving Nikola dejected and frustrated. For a player who'd largely coasted, this humbling experience wasn't the worst thing that could've happened to him. It was yet another instance where Nikola revealed how much he cared.

When facing Red Star, a Mega rival, one of their players, Rasko Katic, consistently picked on Nikola during games. He couldn't understand it. One night, Nikola went to Ratko, the team's enforcer.

Why was he targeting me?

He was comforted by the fact that Ratko had his back.

"Okay, I don't care," Nikola said. "I have Ratko behind me, I got Novica behind me. I got Dejan behind me. He can't do anything."

That season, Mega met Red Star in the 2014 Serbian Cup final, an upstart against an established power. Down 81–80 with four seconds left and the ball, Dejan drew up a play for their point guard, Vasa Micic. When Red Star clamped Micic, preventing him from getting the ball, Nenad's inbounds pass landed in Jokic's hands.

Jokic's decision was almost premeditated—odd because it was the antithesis of how he dismantles NBA defenses nowadays.

As Jokic tried, unsuccessfully, to find Micic, Nenad cut backdoor with *no one* in the paint.

"I was wide-open," Nenad said.

Jokic didn't see him. With Micic out of the play and the window to Nenad closed, Jokic took three dribbles and gathered into a contested jumper. The look didn't even draw iron.

He dropped his hands to his knees, draped with dejection in Mega's infamous pink shorts. Katic, Jokic's nemesis, rejoiced and sang along with Red Star's boisterous fans.

○

Still a teenager, Jokic was learning what it meant to be a professional.

Radovic, who was single, tried hard to convince Nikola to go out and live like a typical eighteen-year-old. He wanted him to enjoy being a professional in Belgrade, to take advantage of everything in front of them.

Nikola wouldn't budge. Even though he was living alone at the time, everything he cared about was at his fingertips. His time was spent playing PlayStation and FaceTiming Natalija, who'd become his girlfriend despite moving to the States.

"He had his girlfriend, he loved her from the beginning," Radovic said. The distance was painful.

"He came one day to practice and he said, 'I don't want to play anymore because I'm super depressed with Natalija going to the States,'" said Dejan.

With his girlfriend in the U.S., Dejan theorized it motivated him to work even harder to reach the NBA.

He was loyal and in love.

On one hand, Mega should have celebrated how little concern there was that Nikola would get himself in trouble off the court. On the other, his habits weren't exactly professional.

Jokic lived near Ulica Gladnih, a street in Belgrade famous for its fast food. Radovic said he'd order two or three burgers at a time. For dessert, it was two or three crêpes. That appetite, paired with a healthy diet of video games, could kill an afternoon.

Other times, Ratko said a group of the younger guys went to a video game arcade to play *CounterStrike* for hours on end.

Nenad wasn't interested in video games like some of his teammates, but he did play *NBA 2K* with enough of his friends to become competent. Unlike Nikola, he hadn't mastered the game. Once after practice, Nenad took on Jokic at his apartment.

Nikola trapped Nenad full-court on every possession, forcing a long, dangerous pass to the frontcourt to de-escalate the pressure. It yielded a turnover at least 50 percent of the time.

"He was using the game basically against me," Nenad said.

In his low-stakes games with friends, Nenad had never faced the kind of defensive intensity Nikola foisted on him. As the game slipped away, Nenad grew angrier and angrier. Nikola laughed at the success of the strategy and thoroughly enjoyed his friend's exasperation.

"I was so mad," Nenad said.

The teammates he was close with learned his rhythms. They understood that basketball, as good as he was, wasn't what defined him.

"There's a part of him that you can reach in a certain way, but you've gotta be a certain type of person," Nenad said.

Nenad found that they both shared a dry, biting sense of humor. They loved to mess with one another, their sarcasm turning into a language in and of itself.

"He's not a guy who's gonna be ready to give his time to anybody," Nenad said. "You have to earn it."

CHAPTER 12

DISCOVERY

It was February 2013, and the snow crept all the way up to Rafal Juc's knees.

"It was in the middle of wintertime in freakin' Lithuania," Juc said.

Juc, who was still years away from becoming the Nuggets' lead European scout, was in the nascent, gritty stages of his career. What may have been reckless didn't even register.

He nudged his foot in the door of the basketball world when he landed an internship with the Polish basketball federation. He did everything for the organization, from coaching and administrative work to public relations and marketing.

His position afforded him access to international prospects and the opportunity to travel to various basketball events across Europe. With access to prospects came access to the scouting world. Juc soon discovered he could be a valuable source of information for international scouts curious about Poland's players. There was a professional network waiting to be stitched.

Before that exposure, Juc wasn't entirely sure where his passion for basketball would take him. His height made any professional playing ambitions a nonstarter. But he kept plodding until it became all too obvious: scouting was his calling.

"That's my dream job," he told himself.

When he discovered the possibility of scouting as a profession, Juc didn't leave his desk for three days. He was so obsessed, even his mom became concerned. He consumed everything the internet had to offer about the scouting world. He researched the pathways of NBA scouts in an effort to bolster his chances of becoming one. He sent reports to established scouts, eager for feedback on his player assessments.

For two years, Juc traveled Europe building connections and evaluating players. He had financial help from his family to fund his dream, but he took side jobs to make it work. Whatever it took, he was willing.

Which was how he found himself . . . *in the middle of wintertime in freakin' Lithuania.*

There was a Nike under-18 tournament for all the top teams in Europe. To save money, Juc took an overnight bus. Once he arrived, he headed straight to the gym to scout for twelve consecutive hours.

As lonely and competitive as international scouting can be, there's still an element of camaraderie to those who do it. Juc caught wind of a dinner later that night. It was as valuable a tip as any he'd ever receive.

"I was not even invited to the dinner, but I overheard that all the most important scouts and agents and team representatives were getting dinner together," Juc said. "So I just decided to kind of force my way."

Those scouts and agents had budgets, and therefore had taxis and rental cars at their disposal. Juc didn't.

He trudged his way through the snow to the restaurant. It was a bold move, but what adventure isn't?

"I'm gonna run through a wall just to make my dream happen," he said.

Juc showed up late, legs cold from his jaunt.

"I see there's an empty chair, so I just make myself comfortable," he said. "And somebody taps me on the shoulder and tells me, 'Hey, this is my chair. What are you doing here?'"

It was Rich Sheubrooks. He was one of the first U.S.-born scouts to move overseas and had been responsible for several big prospects landing in the NBA, including future Hall of Famer Pau Gasol. He also worked for Nike and helped populate the Nike Hoop Summit.

Juc had one friend at the table who vouched for him. His name was Yarone Arbel, then a scout for the Pelicans. Among all the scouts Juc had reached out to, only Arbel had responded. He told Sheubrooks to give the precocious kid a shot.

"Rich being Rich, he basically said, 'I'm gonna give you a chance,'" Juc said. "You have sixty seconds to tell me which international players I should invite for the Hoop Summit game."

Juc's jaw dropped.

"Hey, buddy, like fifteen seconds have passed," Juc heard through his astonishment. "You better start shooting those names."

Juc rattled off his list. He crushed his impromptu audition. Sheubrooks was impressed but didn't tip his hand. Juc couldn't gauge his reaction. Finally, after a few tense beats, one of the pioneers in international scouting told Juc to pull a chair up. He was in.

He gave Juc his business card and told him to come to his hotel the next day. It was then two months ahead of the Nike Hoop Summit in Portland, Oregon.

Juc's determination was palpable. Sheubrooks sensed it and offered to pay his way to Oregon, where he arranged for him to be on the support staff and take care of accommodations.

Juc's snowblown path to the NBA was becoming clearer.

"I feel like that was a defining moment of my life," he said.

O

At the Hoop Summit, the scouts and executives Juc had researched were sitting next to him.

"That week in Portland allowed me to connect with a lot of NBA people, including Tim Connelly and Arturas Karnisovas," he said.

Connelly was then the assistant GM of the Pelicans, and Yarone, who vouched for Juc in Lithuania, ensured they'd spend time together. Juc's path still wasn't cemented. Most scouts had worked in the U.S., and he figured the best route to the NBA was through a graduate assistant role. With Connelly's extensive network along the East Coast, Juc landed a job at St. John's.

Things moved quickly after that. In the summer of 2013, Connelly became the GM of the Nuggets. He asked Juc, pointedly, "Do you want to go to college or do you want to be pro?"

Karnisovas, then the assistant GM who was in charge of the Nuggets' international scouting department, conducted the interview process. It was August 2013, and Juc was at the FIBA under-20s tournament. Once again he spent the day scouting before staying up all night preparing materials to submit to Karnisovas.

At twenty-one, Juc was offered the job.

"I never even read the contract," he said.

He was the youngest international scout in the NBA. Juc didn't fit the typical profile of a scout, which generally meant a former player or coach with years of international experience. But he was connected and his opinion was already respected.

Before Juc landed with the Nuggets, he had already compiled lists of international players, complete with reports and intel on each. He loved the traveling component of the job and had made a point to connect with coaches across Europe. In the scouting world, those relationships were invaluable.

"I just did it for myself," he said, with a sneaking suspicion that perhaps his work would later be rewarded.

One of his first tasks with the Nuggets was to provide a list of the top international prospects. Though not near the top, Nikola Jokic was on his list. Juc viewed him as a long-term project, a secondary prospect.

Juc had first seen Jokic when he arrived at Mega for the 2012–13 season and he was only playing for their junior squad. Occasionally he practiced with the main squad, but he didn't really demand attention just yet.

Mega harbored so much prospective talent that Juc was a frequent visitor. Like any good young scout, he needed to water those connections.

In Juc's mind, it wasn't until Serbia's FIBA U-19 run in the summer of 2013 that Jokic became worthy of more serious study.

"I always tell people that, especially in international scouting, the biggest benefit we have is the ability to evaluate guys over a period of time," Juc said. "With Joker, every single time I would see him he would become better and better."

Juc kept noticing Jokic's propensity to improve. He saw little moments that hadn't been there the last time he evaluated him. Juc heeded a lesson he learned from Sheubrooks: it wasn't how a guy looked on a given day but how he looked from evaluation to evaluation. To the best scouts, context was crucial.

"Maybe if you go to Mega once and you just see this chubby, gangly guy, kind of loose, on the outside it seems like he doesn't care, but if you know the whole story . . ." Rafal said.

There was a story there. His job was to discover it.

Part of his process involved picking Dejan's brain. Rafal asked about certain players, and sooner or later, the conversation always steered back to Jokic.

Juc remembered the way Dejan talked about him. The way he beamed at his growth, and deemed him his next project. Comparisons were difficult for someone as unique as Nikola, but Dejan did his best. He called him a Boris Diaw type. Neither was a chiseled prospect, but both had an innate feel for the game.

"In scouting, we are so biased looking for whatever's attractive," Rafal said.

He also noticed how hard Dejan rode him. The cultural differences between coaches in the U.S. and coaches in Serbia are stark. Dejan was aggressive with his coaching. He was in Nikola's face, making physical contact and taunting him. Certain barriers got crossed in order to produce more mental toughness. His oldest brother used similar tactics.

"[Strahinja] would get on his ass. . . . It was almost borderline embarrassing," Juc said.

Delivered the wrong way, Juc used to say, "the message can be a bullet." However, Dejan and Strahinja had strong enough relationships with Nikola that they could push him in uncomfortable ways.

It was tough love from those who were most invested in Nikola's success. Rafal saw it and made note of it. Context was everything.

○

Rafal Juc was only twenty-one at the time. He was still forging his scouting philosophies, which made vouching for a prospect like Nikola difficult.

Furthermore, when he traveled to Denver for the type of front-office debates that shape so many draft decisions, there was a language barrier he needed to overcome. Sitting beside him, debating the pro potential of various prospects, were Connelly, one of the youngest and most innovative GMs in the NBA; Karnisovas, a European legend; and former NBA player Jared Jeffries, among others.

"That was kind of overwhelming for me," Juc said. "That's why, I maybe regret not pushing more for Joker. I was hedging my bets on him."

But Connelly and Karnisovas empowered their young scout. They had hired him and valued his insight. They wanted his opinion known.

"Obviously, there was a huge concern over his body and athleticism," Juc said, while offering an interesting perspective to the debate. He tried to qualify his judgment with a lesson.

Oftentimes, we make something important because we can measure it, he thought, *but we don't always measure it because it's important. Jokic wasn't even a part of the organization before he compelled the front office to consider auditing their process.*

Juc surmised that maybe the tests gauging a player's athleticism were outdated. Or at a minimum, incomplete. How could a team quantify Nikola's hand-eye coordination or the speed at which he downloaded a defense? Could a test really capture the way Nikola's touch was unmatched, or his footwork unique? Like Dejan said, there was an advantage in being different, and one that a speed test could never calculate.

The tangibles were obvious. Even though he didn't have a chiseled frame, he had legitimate height, an enormous wingspan, and big hands. The concerns about his body were fair, but Juc remembered another adage he'd been taught: the easiest thing to develop in the NBA is a player's body.

The NBA had access to the latest research, the best coaches, and the newest equipment. If a player had everything but an NBA-ready body, maybe there was an opportunity to bet on upside. Perhaps in the right environment, a player could thrive.

Rafal believed scouts could be divided into two camps: opportunistic and conservative. Connelly, who liked to describe himself as "obnoxiously optimistic," encouraged his staff to seek opportunities for the former. They tried to identify potential breakout players who might mandate drafting them a year early.

Connelly insisted on empowering his staff. That meant championing the opinions of his scouts in the field. And no one had a better sense for Jokic than Juc.

Before Connelly ever became the continent-hopping executive who transformed the Nuggets' organization, he was a lowly scout in the Wizards' front office. He cut his teeth in the film room, where many executives and future coaches start their journey. Perhaps that's why he maintained so much respect for those who did the work.

When Connelly took over for his close friend Masai Ujiri following Ujiri's exit to Toronto, the Nuggets were on a run of ten consecutive play-off appearances (though only once past the first round). They fired former coach George Karl, replacing him with first-time head coach Brian Shaw. Their infrastructure was in flux, with a path forward that was equally as dubious.

Connelly wanted to maintain that level of success while simultaneously stamping his own vision on the organization. Danilo Gallinari's ACL tear undermined that mission, as did Andre Iguodala's decision to leave Denver in free agency in the summer of 2013. Through the first six weeks of the following season, the Nuggets went 14–9 behind a core of Ty Lawson, Randy Foye, Kenneth Faried, Wilson Chandler, and J. J. Hickson. But injuries to rotation pieces JaVale McGee and Nate Robinson beset their depth. The season was already unraveling when veteran guard Andre Miller verbally jousted with Shaw over playing time, leading to a suspension.

Connelly's first year was veering off the tracks.

Amid a February losing streak, Connelly watched in his basement as his team got run out of the gym by Minnesota. Due to injuries and Miller's suspension, Denver's only point guard was Foye.

"I told [my wife] Negah, 'All right, I tried, gave it our best effort,'" said Connelly, resigned to how his inaugural season was unfolding.

The Nuggets were going nowhere fast. The roster wasn't old by NBA standards, but they were far from a young team with a burgeoning future.

The following summer, Connelly leveled with team owner Josh Kroenke about the direction of the franchise.

One toe in, one toe out wasn't what he'd envisioned. He told him this wasn't thematically how he viewed roster construction. Were they contending or were they rebuilding? Straddling both lanes often yielded little in the NBA. Not to mention, Connelly had his own vision for team building. He sought high-character players, who were smart and cared about winning. Equally as important, Connelly coveted players who didn't take themselves too seriously. After all, as Connelly often reminded himself, this was a game.

Not that basketball wasn't a business, and not that Connelly didn't take winning seriously, but if you couldn't laugh at yourself, Denver probably wasn't the right fit. The season was long and grinding. In establishing a culture, Connelly wanted guys who wanted to be there.

"Josh was like, 'Screw it. Go with your gut on things,'" Connelly said.

It was a watershed moment that altered how the Nuggets' brass conducted their business. With Kroenke's blessing, they weren't beholden to the franchise-record 57 wins of the 2012–13 season or the good-not-great Carmelo Anthony era.

They had no idea whether constructing a team in that vein would yield a championship, but Connelly didn't have to waste any energy considering what the Nuggets *had* been. His sole focus was building for the future.

And if there was a chance to take a second-round swing on a self-deprecating center with an awkwardly effective style, how much downside was there really?

CHAPTER 13

HOOP SUMMIT

The scary part about the Nike Hoop Summit was that everyone was there.

The weeklong event was based in Portland, where executives from all thirty teams convened to watch dozens of the top NBA prospects compete in practices and scrimmages. It culminated in the game itself—a show-down between the top U.S. talent against the best international prospects. It was a fixture on the scouting and pre-draft schedule, a place to confirm suspicions or sharpen opinions on potential draft picks.

In 1998, Dirk Nowitzki parlayed a 33-point performance in Portland into the ninth pick of the draft to Dallas. Two years later, Tony Parker made a strong impression that led to a first-round selection a year later from San Antonio. Marin Sedlacek, a Serbian scout (working for the 76ers in 2014), helped recruit both future Hall of Famers to the Hoop Summit. Marin was both the assistant coach for the international team for twenty years and the director of the Nike European camps.

Marin knew of Nikola as soon as he arrived at Mega. He was intrigued by his rare combination: a point guard's mind trapped inside a center's body. He saw his intuition on the court and his unwavering confidence against bigger, stronger players. Unlike most scouts, Marin wasn't deterred by Nikola's lack of physicality or even his limited athleticism. To Marin, a longtime international scout, neither defined a prospect. He was most fixated on Nikola's innate court sense and his rare skill set.

"I saw something which the other people who saw him first or second time on the practice court didn't see," he said. "They were teasing me, 'You think he can play against Okafor?'"

Jahlil Okafor headlined the U.S. team, while Karl-Anthony Towns was the biggest name on the international squad. Both sides were teeming with NBA potential, with numerous prospects firmly on Denver's radar.

Logistically, it was easier to have seen the elite U.S. prospects, so the Nuggets made a dedicated effort to scout the international practices. And Jokic, due to the extensive work Juc had already done scouting Mega, was firmly in their crosshairs.

Had that work not been done prior to Portland, perhaps his performance would've been a blip. Had they not seen him collectively, maybe the same excitement wouldn't have percolated. The week helped galvanize their opinions.

Juc, who wasn't there in person, woke up to a text on the team's group thread.

"Joker just pumped somebody out of the gym."

The benefit was in seeing prospects of similar ages and talent levels compete against one another. When Jokic faced glorified construction workers in Serbia, it only taught scouts so much. Seeing him against other highly ranked players validated what he was doing in Belgrade. It also helped confirm that there was legitimate talent waiting to be discovered in the Adriatic League.

The Nuggets were unique in their commitment to Europe. Juc was deeply entrenched with his relationships in the Balkans, and Karnisovas, a legend while playing for Barcelona in the EuroLeague, was highly respected as an international scout. Connelly spent extensive time scouting Europe and was heavily invested abroad. They were as well positioned as any franchise to unearth someone like Jokic.

The barriers—of scouting Europe, not to mention Karnisovas's understanding of European players—tilted in their favor.

"In that time, you're depending on reports, suggestions, authority of guys who are working international scouting," Marin said.

Technology wasn't the same. Highlight reels on Instagram couldn't ping around the globe in seconds. Information, from trusted sources, carried weight.

For a franchise to take Jokic, one needed to dismiss whatever soft European stereotypes still permeated NBA front offices. Dirk's ascendance in Dallas had eased some skepticism. Plus, the allure of finding the *next* Dirk was tantalizing to every single front office in the league.

In Juc, Denver had intel. In Connelly, it had an unconventional leader with one foot abroad. And in Karnisovas, it had someone to bridge the gap and assuage whatever doubts still existed.

Arturas and Marin were old friends, dating back to Karnisovas's time playing for Barcelona. During one scouting trip, Arturas had dinner at Marin's house before watching Nikola play at Mega. Marin sensed Jokic was on his radar. He thought that if Denver had a chance, they'd pick him.

"I knew that he liked him," Marin said.

At the Hoop Summit, which took place two months before the draft in April 2014, Towns and Okafor were the buzziest names, but the rosters were stacked. Myles Turner, Justise Winslow, Kelly Oubre, Tyus Jones, and Stanley Johnson were all on the U.S. team. Jamal Murray, Clint Capela, Trey Lyles, and Emmanuel Mudiay helped comprise the international squad.

Marin received Nikola when he arrived for his first trip to the U.S. He explained the process and outlined the expectations for the curious center from Belgrade. Marin asked if he was interested in going to college and was swiftly rebuffed.

Furthermore, as part of the Hoop Summit experience, players who didn't intend to go to college could go to the Nike employee store, where apparel was heavily discounted. College attendees risked an NCAA violation. According to Marin, Nikola collected lists of apparel for guys who couldn't shop for themselves.

On the court, Jokic didn't *look* the part like Capela, Okafor, Towns, or Turner did. He was long and skinny (the conditioning under Dejan had paid off), with muscles that couldn't be described as defined. He didn't jump like Capela and didn't have the heft of the other elite big men. With them, it was easy to see a future NBA frame. With Jokic, it was easy to see him getting steamrolled in the paint.

"I think it was a mixed bag," said Karnisovas of Denver's assessments. "The skill level was there but it was just awkward to watch, right? Awkward projection."

Jokic did have unique skills; they were just less tangible compared to his counterparts. He was light on his feet and his touch around the rim was ridiculous. His 3-point stroke was smooth and reliable. He wasn't scared to hoist either.

Before the Hoop Summit, Misko told Nikola that he had to present a certain profile to NBA scouts.

"They have to think you're a shooter," he said.

Within the practices and scrimmages, Jokic shined. He played pick-and-roll off Murray and Mudiay, ironically two future teammates in Denver. He finished cleverly around the rim, with reversals, ball fakes, and deceptive finishes he learned in Belgrade.

"Nikola was doing all the funky stuff he did in the NBA, shooting under guys' arms," Nuggets GM Tim Connelly said. "People were being critical of Capela and not realizing the out-of-shape guy was really unique."

Nikola's footwork was already polished. He dropped touch passes through unsuspecting defenders, finished under and through Towns, and flashed a basketball IQ that was rare for an NBA player, let alone a teenage prospect. In the breakout groups—centers on one basket, guards on the other—he deftly navigated the spate of defenders that dotted the international team's depth chart.

What he lacked in athleticism, he made up for with a deep reservoir of tricks.

"When I was in Houston, we had [Luis] Scola," Karnisovas said. "The post moves that Scola would have would be these multiple pivot moves, and the defenders wouldn't even know where he's at after like three reversals. So, Joker was using the same post-up plays and just made a lot of guys in Hoop Summit look silly."

Trey Lyles, who was on his way to Kentucky and would later join Jokic in Denver, remembered the practices vividly.

"Nobody knew who he was," Lyles told the *Denver Post*. "I think it was the second day of practice. He just totally went off and was killing everybody."

Capela, a long and bouncy center from Switzerland, had significant buzz going into the event. He had all the athletic tools to make NBA front offices drool. In terms of aesthetics, he was at the complete opposite end of the spectrum from Jokic.

"He's never been [athletic]," Capela said. "[But] from playing in Europe, he was kind of doing everything already."

Capela remembered Jokic splashing a few 3-pointers and noticed his skill along the interior. The Nuggets quietly noted how often he scored against Capela and how frequently his pump fakes baited opponents off the ground.

Capela played well that week, but because the curious oddity from Belgrade got the better of him, the event may have hurt his draft stock. While it didn't move the needle much for Jokic, likely because of how he looked, most executives took the matchup as a referendum on Capela. (Two months later, the Rockets selected him at No. 25 overall.)

Two days after Jokic reached Portland, two other large Serbians arrived. Speaking in their native language, they announced themselves to Marin as Strahinja and Nemanja Jokic, Nikola's two older brothers. They knew who Marin was and the influence he wielded within the organization.

At the end of one practice, Strahinja asked for a word with Nikola.

"If [Marin] tells you to be in a basketball stance on your head instead of your legs, you need to do that," Strahinja told Nikola. "You need to do anything he tells you."

Marin started laughing. Strahinja snapped back, telling the sage scout not to laugh. He was dead serious. They put their trust in the scout's hands.

All throughout the practices, Jokic stood out. Not just how he looked, but his impact. What Juc had believed about his potential going into Hoop Summit had been validated by more experienced NBA executives. The Nuggets tempered their excitement. There were still reservations about his body, question marks of whether it would translate to the best league in the world. Jokic himself wasn't even convinced he was an NBA player, telling a reporter that perhaps the EuroLeague was in his future.

As their four-man party left the gym one day, they batted opinions back and forth like a piñata.

Some of their staff was intrigued with Jokic. Others were fixated on how he looked.

"Dude with man-boobs?" one staffer said.

At that time, no one in their group was pushing to use a first-round pick on him.

Besides, he was no longer their secret.

"Other teams were there too," Karnisovas said.

In the game itself, Lyles and Towns earned the start while Jokic came off the bench. In the backcourt, Murray and Mudiay dominated the ball. It was a showcase after all, and every prospect was trying to flash his potential to pro scouts. Murray hit two quick 3-pointers and Mudiay continued to hunt—and force—his offense.

After a week where Jokic had played the fulcrum of the international team's practices, he was largely an afterthought. Sets tended to avoid him, perhaps due to others' selfishness.

When he did do something positive, the ESPN broadcast butchered his name.

"Yuck-itch."

He was trying. When the international squad launched a 3-pointer, Jokic, who'd been standing on the perimeter, crashed the glass. It was an atypical show of effort and one indicative of the stakes. It didn't help that Okafor, then the No. 1 prospect according to ESPN's rankings, barreled through Jokic on offense, seemingly targeting the lanky center. Defensively, Jokic looked vulnerable.

On one dead-ball sequence Okafor appeared to knock into Jokic, which he didn't appreciate. Jokic took exception and smirked.

At least he was competitive. At least he was unafraid.

The U.S. team handled the international squad, and Jokic, playing less than sixteen minutes, didn't make a noticeable impact. The momentum he built over the week fizzled a bit. He finished with just 5 points, 7 rebounds, and zero assists.

If he'd dominated the game like he did throughout the week, there was no chance he'd last until the second round. The feedback Misko got from his NBA sources wasn't encouraging.

"So-so," he said. "It was not so great."

For Denver, the game was a blessing in disguise.

CHAPTER 14

NO. 41

Ten days before the draft, Misko announced he was pulling Jokic's name from the draft pool.

The international early withdrawal deadline was approaching, and Misko used it to his advantage.

He tweeted: "Nikola Jokic, 95, [will] withdraw his name from the draft. He will play next year for Mega Vizura!"

Only, Misko didn't officially pull Jokic's name. Interest in his client had been tepid, at best. Without any guarantees, he wanted to know how NBA teams actually felt about Jokic.

When America woke up to his tweet, he got his answer.

"One of the biggest complainers was Denver, so I smelled that he had a good chance to be there," Misko said.

Misko had reason to trust Denver, stemming from a prior relationship.

"An unsung hero in all of this is Joffrey Lauvergne," Connelly said of another one of Misko's clients who played in Belgrade.

The Nuggets acquired him on draft night in 2013 and vowed to bring him to Denver. Connelly didn't draft guys to stash them overseas. He drafted them to play in the NBA. The rapport, between agent and club, mattered.

When the Nuggets inquired about Jokic, Misko had reason to believe they were sincere.

Following Hoop Summit, Rafal headed back to Serbia, to vet every single angle one more time. Juc was essentially a journalist who published nothing for public consumption. Most times, his—or any scout's diligence—didn't go anywhere. But that was the draft process. Learn, vet, and store. In the NBA, information was the most valued currency.

Rafal had a goal to see a player three times before the draft, to see the incremental improvements a player made as he monitored them. Those visits also yielded valuable information. The closer it got to the draft, though, the more Juc learned to couch what he heard.

Information tended to get sanitized as draft day neared. No one wanted to hinder a player's draft status as they were on the verge of achieving their dreams. Even coaches weren't reliable. They tended to let their emotions sway their opinions. A player's strengths were emphasized, their flaws overlooked. Juc was attuned to the biases.

Dejan had a different dilemma. When NBA personnel inquired about Jokic, they weren't even sure he was a worthy NBA prospect.

He's not athletic, he's too slow and can't jump high enough, he heard. *His defense will be a liability. If he wasn't a traditional five, and wasn't quick enough to be a stretch-four, what exactly was he?*

NBA personnel projected Jokic as a stretch-four, though Dejan insisted he could play the five. Players being caught between positions can occasionally be a death knell in the draft process.

"I honestly had a problem convincing people from NBA that Nikola is an NBA player, especially at the five," he told the *Denver Post*. "I was talking always that he's a center. Yeah, he plays uncommon center, but his main position is five. . . . And people from [the] NBA struggled seeing that. They looked at him more as a No. 4, but I had my reasons. . . . He can defend better No. 5, and he's probably one of the best pick-and-roll players in the world."

When arguing his point, Dejan fixated on Nikola's defense—the sticking point for scouts. Dejan reinforced his gigantic frame, elite hands, intelligence, and anticipation. He also knew how strong he was, even if it took some squinting. He believed athleticism wasn't just about leaping ability. It was the combination of all his attributes. Dejan insisted Nikola could defend at an NBA level, scoffing at those who rendered him undraftable because he didn't look the part.

"Today, he's one of the strongest players in the league, together with the skill that he has, that's why probably he's unguardable," he said.

That 2013–14 season, Rafal saw the ball skills, his coordination, and his strength. Rarely, if ever, did Jokic get pushed off his spots. He also noticed a significant change in the narrative and tenor around Jokic: He was more mature. He was more developed and dedicated as a player.

Juc thought he was coming together as both a player and a person.

○

Entering the 2007 draft, Connelly, then in Washington, was bullish on an oversize European center. Marc Gasol was slower than the typical prospect but his pace was effective. His IQ and tempo masked his athletic deficiencies. Connelly talked to people close to Gasol who insisted there was more than met the eye.

Don't fixate on his body. Fixate on his game.

Gasol had legitimate height and a brother who was already an NBA All-Star. Furthermore, he could pass, shoot, and handle. Besides, if he didn't pan out, it was a late second-round pick. A miss wouldn't have been detrimental to the franchise. The Wizards gave Gasol serious consideration, but it wasn't Connelly's decision to make.

With the 47th pick, Washington selected Dominic McGuire. Gasol was off the board at the very next pick.

Rafal remembered one of Connelly's dictums: *History is the best indication of the future.*

Before the 2014 draft, the Nuggets pored over film of eighteen- and nineteen-year-old Gasol. They also studied Marcin Gortat and Nikola Pekovic, both as teenagers, to establish apples-to-apples comparisons for Jokic.

Connelly had seen the mistake before, comparing prospects to established NBA players. The practice almost invited errors. There was also still a market inefficiency relative to how guys looked.

They tried to discover what physical limitations Gasol had rendered immaterial.

"In terms of skill level, how high the skill level, passing, shooting, dribbling, high basketball IQ, but the physical profile is the one that makes you pause," Karnisovas said of Nikola. "At the same time, obviously, when Marc was coming out, that was almost the same questions."

Connelly thought he was looking at a ghost.

"Eerie similarities to Gasol in terms of feel for the game, passing ability," he said. "Both guys weren't svelte."

The Nuggets had seen enough. They were confident that Nikola's atypical style, paired with a body they felt would improve in an NBA environment, was worth the gamble.

The Nuggets promised they'd take Nikola Jokic with the No. 41 pick, according to multiple sources. For their plan to come to fruition, they just needed him to still be there.

As reassuring as that was, that Nikola was guaranteed not to fall beyond No. 41, how strong a commitment was it really when the Nuggets had multiple picks earlier in the draft?

The Nuggets owned the No. 11 pick in the 2014 draft and flipped Creighton's Doug McDermott to Chicago for Nos. 16 and 19 in the first round. Scouting was Connelly's specialty. The more swings they took, the better chance they had at landing foundational pieces.

At No. 16, Chicago selected Bosnian center Jusuf Nurkic, a bruising big man from the Balkans. He was physically imposing but couldn't bend a court like Jokic. Three picks later, the Bulls chose Michigan State's Gary Harris, a crafty, two-way shooting guard, to bolster their backcourt. Harris had a football background and the Nuggets loved his combination of toughness and athleticism. Both were on their way to Denver.

Nurkic was talented yet traditional. He played with his back to the basket. In Jokic, Denver could take a swing on a complete outlier for the position, someone equally comfortable operating from the paint or the perimeter.

"By then we really felt strongly," Karnisovas said. "It's just like, is it gonna happen? It's anticipation. Pick by pick it's going, and then information flow . . . 'Oh those guys are not picking [him], those guys aren't picking, those guys might.'"

Juc's diligence gave the Nuggets as much information as any team about him, and their Gasol study allayed concerns about his utility. But the draft was still a crapshoot, with twenty-two other franchises slated to pick ahead of Denver at No. 41.

"Do you try to move up to get him?" Karnisovas said, floating the idea that every executive has asked themselves when awaiting a target on draft night.

The Nuggets knew they weren't the only suitors.

"[Teams] were chasing we just didn't know where," Karnisovas said.

At No. 41, as a Taco Bell commercial ran and Jokic himself slept through the drama, the Nuggets pulled off the biggest draft-night steal in NBA history.

It was an unremarkable, humble start to an improbable story.

A few years later, Connelly learned that Utah had been interested in Jokic as well. But by then Jokic was already on the ascent, and it was fair to wonder, in retrospect, how strong the interest actually was on draft night.

Before the night was over, two other Serbians, Vasa Micic and Nemanja Dangubic, were selected from Mega. Both players were taken by the 76ers, who'd spent extended time scouting the Belgrade-based club.

They, along with the rest of the league, had missed the treasure hiding in plain sight.

CHAPTER 15

SANTA BARBARA

After landing Jokic, the attention turned toward making him a viable professional.

In late July and early August 2014, Misko arranged for Nikola to train at P3 (Peak Performance Project), in Santa Barbara, California, the famed biomechanics lab that specializes in analyzing body movements and optimizing athletic performance.

Though it was Misko and Nikola who took the initiative, the Nuggets simultaneously conveyed an essential message to their latest draft pick.

If you're going to be a professional in the NBA, we have to address your physical profile, they said. *You might not run faster or jump higher, but your nutrition needs to be a priority.*

On Nikola's end, there needed to be a commitment to his body.

When Arturas visited Nikola in Santa Barbara, he met Strahinja and Nemanja for the first time. He also met Jokic's girlfriend, Natalija. That's when it dawned on him. Nikola's support system was entrenched; they'd either find success in the NBA, or fail in the NBA, as a unit. His family was a collective package.

A photo from the visit showed both Nikola and Strahinja wearing graphic Nike tees and loud, color-coordinated Nike shorts. Somewhat ironically, Nikola's shirt read: "Up the Tempo."

The brothers' casual flip-flops belied the purpose of the trip.

"At that time, I'm looking at his diet too," Karnisovas said. "After the meal, he takes like a huge tub of freaking ice cream. I'm like, 'Is he gonna offer me some?' And he starts eating out of it, by himself, with this huge bottle of Coke."

The Nuggets assistant GM squirmed.

If Nikola was going to make it in the NBA, his diet needed a thorough audit.

While his family was there for roughly six weeks, the Nuggets did their best to make them feel comfortable in the States. This was Denver's first chance to formally connect with the Jokics, outside of the work that Rafal had done.

Connelly and Arturas agreed that the best person to build a bridge between his family and the organization was a goofy, self-deprecating, energetic figure.

"We sent our special assignment person, Jim Clibanoff," Rafal said. "He's the easiest person to connect with."

Clibanoff, the Nuggets' director of scouting, was ebullient and silly. He didn't have a mean bone in his body. Or a serious one.

"Arturas says to me, they might not get your sense of humor," Clibanoff said. "Tread lightly."

Arturas was sensitive to how a foreign family might receive Clibanoff. The franchise didn't need to alienate him only a month after drafting him. But Denver's brain trust underestimated how disarming and endearing Clibanoff could be.

Clibanoff drove to their rental home a few miles outside Santa Barbara. There was nothing ostentatious about the place.

Without having a plan for dinner, the group settled on cooking their own food. It was an ideal, intimate setting for relationship building.

The group headed to the grocery store, where any concerns Arturas had about Clibanoff meshing with the family evaporated.

Before long, Clibanoff, who stands 5'6" on a good day, hopped into a grocery cart being pushed by Nikola and Nemanja. In the now-infamous picture, beside a mac-and-cheese stanchion, Nikola wore his preferred Nike graphic tee: "Break'n Ankles, Shatterin' Dreams," and Nemanja sported a Nuggets hat.

The special assignment was going swimmingly.

Heading into the night, Clibanoff figured he might spend a few hours with Nikola's family before venturing elsewhere, not wanting to occupy too much of their time. The goal wasn't to be intrusive. It was to establish trust. The introduction turned into a four- or five-hour affair, where Clibanoff immersed himself into their group and slowly began to understand the Serbian family's close-knit dynamic. Throughout the whole night, basketball was barely discussed.

Clibanoff understood the investment his brothers made in him and witnessed the young love budding between Natalija and Nikola.

"They were just so captivating as a family unit," he said.

CHAPTER 16

P3

Nikola arrived at P3 as unassuming as any NBA prospect ever had.

At that point, in the summer of 2014, there might have already been one thousand NBA players to filter through P3's gym, according to its founder, Marcus Elliott. Athletes utilized P3 for all types of reasons, from performance enhancement to basic raw assessments. Jokic went there to refine a body that served as his biggest impediment to NBA success.

Elliott was used to working with Olympic athletes, who rarely had much slack in their system. Overall improvements tended to be marginal. The NFL athletes were next, honed and optimized far better than basketball players. NBA players generally arrived at P3 all over the fitness spectrum.

NBA players' schedules featured games year-round. There was an eight-month season, a couple of weeks off to recover, followed by pickup games to prepare for the next season. All guys did was play. They weren't accustomed to looking under the hood.

"We never find NBA players that are optimized from a development standpoint," Elliott said.

From that perspective, Jokic was far from his peak efficiency.

The team's biomechanist remembered just how far away. Jokic sat, slumped in a chair, as they explained data from his first assessment to him. As the team pored over their target goals—based on their initial evaluation—one of Jokic's brothers grew restless. He got up from the corner of the room and walked over to his kid brother.

"This [information] is all good," he said.

"But what about this?" he asked, lifting up Nikola's shirt and exposing a midsection that needed work.

Elliott appreciated the directness. The gesture, while funny, wasn't personal. Besides, no one was more self-deprecating than Nikola himself.

Jokic wasn't a heralded prospect, and his second-round credentials made his NBA future a maybe, at best. Still, at P3, court times were an essential part of the formula. Basketball players tended to want to play basketball.

Of the hundreds of NBA players who came through P3, most worked on the court at least five or six times a week. P3's general manager asked Nikola for his preferred court times.

Nikola responded: "No basketball. Basketball good."

"This," Jokic said, grabbing his potbelly, "not so good."

Elliott and his staff were bewildered. Not just at the candor but the humor. And what Nikola's joke revealed about him. They'd never had a prospect, or a professional for that matter, opt *out* of playing basketball in lieu of working on their body.

For the entire six-week stay, Jokic didn't touch a basketball. What struck Elliott, more so than Nikola's comment, was the internal confidence that such a comment conveyed.

"In his mind, he's good," Elliott said.

That made the purpose of the trip relatively straightforward. His body was the objective.

When Jokic was at P3, he worked out hard, with consistency and purpose. He'd be in five or six times a week, including an occasional two-a-day.

"He had as big of an improvement as we've ever seen from somebody in a moderately short stint," said Elliott, who believed those sessions could've amounted to the first real workouts in his life.

What was pivotal, Elliott said, was that Jokic was still at a relatively young training age. His body responded exceptionally well to the physical work. He was adaptive and resilient. He'd just never undergone that type of focused work before.

When Jokic arrived, he made history.

"He had the lowest vertical jump of any NBA athlete that we've assessed," Elliott said.

But upon departure, his jump numbers were up two and a half to three inches—a rare and significant leap. His speed, force, mechanics, and knee extensions all improved too.

"Everything was up," Elliott said.

NBA players used to arrive at P3 eager to improve their vertical jump, but Elliott noticed a small but significant shift. More and more players wanted to address their lateral movements—which may not have earned them an invite to the Dunk Contest but could have extended their NBA careers.

"I love that Jokic makes the case that vertical jump is at least overrated, if not irrelevant," Elliott said.

As encouraging as his improvements were, that was only part of the revelation. The larger conclusion was even more compelling.

O

At the start of the 2023 NBA season, Elliott said nearly two-thirds of the league had visited P3. They'd recorded and analyzed well over one thousand players, which yielded corresponding and statistically predictive data.

Using a machine-learning model called principal component analysis, P3 collected thousands of data points on athletes' movement quality, then sorted that data into relevant clusters. They weren't just evaluating how fast an athlete ran or how high they jumped; both could be determined by the naked eye. They assessed things like movement symmetry and balance—secondary performance metrics that P3 deemed far more statistically significant than traditional measurements.

For example, Luka Doncic has trained with P3 since he was sixteen. One of his superpowers is decelerating, an advantage he wields by doing it faster than almost anyone. Dejan, Nikola's coach at Mega, seemed to grasp this concept early when he concluded that Jokic's slower tempo was actually to his advantage.

There was a sort of hidden language below the surface, discernible only when viewed underneath their microscope.

The most significant cluster of NBA players P3 has found are deemed kinematic movers. These athletes don't tend to jump very high, don't run fast, are a little above average laterally, but in general are below average in most categories. What they are, however, is symmetrical, low injury risks, and balanced. They move equally well to their left and right. They rotate well off both legs. They jump well off either leg and jump well off both.

"We think of them as the Swiss Army knives of NBA players," Elliott said.

The prime example is New Orleans's C. J. McCollum, who seems to be good at everything on a basketball court yet doesn't excel in any one thing. Others who fall into that coveted data set include New York's Mikal Bridges, Atlanta's Trae Young, and Phoenix's Bradley Beal. Kinematic movers tend to be guards or wings who remain effective even if they lose one skill because of their innumerable other ones.

If Zion Williamson lost his brute force, or Ja Morant lost his quickness, how impactful would they be as basketball players? Kinematic movers had the coveted ability to adapt.

Most importantly, the kinematic movers have by far the highest winshares and longest careers among P3's clusters. Had Jokic fit neatly into this category, he would've been the tallest kinematic mover P3 had ever recorded.

But he didn't. Not exactly, anyway.

Jokic straddled the data points between kinematic mover and "traditional big"—a cluster that didn't portend a long NBA career. Jokic fit, uncomfortably and hilariously, between P3's most successful cluster and one prone to failure. Jokic is enough of a smooth mover, shooting equally well off either foot, for example, that he displayed kinematic traits. His awkward lumbering, however, not only flashed characteristics of a "traditional big" but also seemed to create a new category entirely. Unsurprisingly, Jokic was incomparable.

CHAPTER 17

STASH YEAR

The Santa Barbara trip signaled a shift in Nikola's professionalism.

If the Nuggets were going to commit to him, he needed to commit to himself. At P3, he did that.

The Nuggets decided that Nikola, at nineteen, would head back to Mega for another year in Belgrade, with the understanding that they didn't like leaving their draftees in Europe for long. They wanted him to mature, while sensing how close he was to realizing his dream. Ultimately, the Nuggets' brass felt draft-and-stash prospects should get the chance to succeed or fail in Denver, under their system, in their gym, with their coaches. If he succeeded, it would be a referendum on their developmental program. The same principle held true if he didn't make it.

"Our mentality was, if player fails, he fails with us," Karnisovas said.

Misko immediately noticed a difference in Nikola heading into the 2014–15 season. His confidence, after getting drafted, was brimming. It was obvious to Misko the physical gains Nikola had made and he predicted a leap in performance.

"He came with a little bit different body, he looked stronger, just bigger overall," said Nenad Miljenovic, Nikola's close friend and Mega's point guard.

During the 2013–14 season, Nenad and Nikola had both come off the bench. Nenad was backing up Vasa Micic, who'd been drafted by the 76ers but had transferred to Bayern Munich heading into the next season. Ratko Varda's one-year stint with Mega was over, clearing a pathway for Nikola to start.

On the court together, both Nenad and Nikola shared a proclivity for passing. Even if Nenad was officially the point guard, Mega essentially employed two primary distributors. It was a devastating combination of unselfishness. Nenad estimated that 80 percent of their actions involved pick-and-rolls, at the top of the key, between the two of them.

Either Nenad fed Jokic for a bucket, or the ball was in the hands of an even better distributor. That season, Nenad, not Nikola, led the Adriatic League in assists.

"It's easy with the guys who know how to play," Nenad said.

As heady players coming off the bench the year before, they quickly learned how to optimize one another. As starters, their intuition for the other's game was already cemented. But their style, and their success, weren't universally lauded.

There was some disdain at the way Mega was approaching competition. Under Dejan, with Misko's blessing, the players with potential played. Nenad sensed a disrespect toward their team since, the thought was, anyone could put up numbers playing that freely in an environment devoid of pressure. *The point was to win, not to develop players.* It was the antithesis of how the best clubs in Serbia approached the game.

Mega's players were just messing around, so the thinking went. A gimmick. Certainly, Nikola's experimental style reinforced that belief. Opponents, unaware of Nikola's newfound commitment, continued to guard him how they always had—one-on-one.

"Because he was so young, and the way he played, and the way he looked, I don't think too many teams really respected him as much," Nenad said.

There was an asterisk next to Jokic's success, a skepticism that his impact was really that profound. The deception became an advantage.

O

Entering that season, Mega moved its home games to Sremska Mitrovica, where they had a friendly scrimmage against Partizan scheduled.

Prior to the game, and because this was their first season in the new arena, Nenad and Nikola ventured to a local school, tasked with promoting the team. At the elementary school, they took dozens of pictures and videos with the kids. Nikola, in his element, played endlessly with them.

His joy around kids, and his willingness to accommodate them, was ever-present. Around them he could be goofy and silly, always eager to undermine his status as a professional basketball player with a joke.

The occasion included autographs, and Nikola was happy to oblige. He signed and signed until everyone was taken care of. Mega played the exhibition against Partizan, and won, yet the next day, Nikola appeared with a cast on his right hand.

Nenad looked at his friend and burst out laughing.

There's no possible way you injured yourself between the game and now, he said.

"I injured my tendons when I was writing the autographs," he told him.

Misko was incensed. He had never heard of anything like it. No one had.

"What the fuck?" he said, his eyes rolling at the memory.

CHAPTER 18

DIPLOMACY

The Nuggets were intentional about trying to identify draft targets, including Nikola, before their breakout seasons.

For example, numerous lottery picks came out of the 2014 Hoop Summit, but every single one of them got selected a year later, in the 2015 draft. Karl-Anthony Towns and Jahlil Okafor were both top-three selections. At No. 7, the Nuggets drafted Emmanuel Mudiay, right before Stanley Johnson, Justise Winslow, Myles Turner, and Trey Lyles were picked.

Drafting Jokic a year early prompted a type of parlor game within the Nuggets' front office.

If Jokic had withdrawn from the 2014 draft and returned to Belgrade to author a stunning season at Mega, how high would he have gone a season later? they would ask themselves.

One of the top prospects that season was a 7'3" Latvian, with hybrid big-man skills and perimeter range. One Nuggets front office member distinctly remembered Connelly wondering aloud: Are we sure Jokic isn't better than Kristaps Porzingis?

Nuggets staff members developed a routine. When they came to work, the eight-hour time difference between Denver and Belgrade allowed them to gather around a conference room and stream Jokic's games at Mega.

It was early October 2014, and in his first game, Jokic dominated with 27 points and 15 rebounds. Nenad, his running mate, registered 26 points and 10 assists. Jokic played loose and with joy, taking calculated risks when appropriate.

Connelly, who tended to be overly optimistic about his players, had an inkling about Jokic after watching that season debut. He started to believe Jokic had the potential to be special.

That conviction bled into conversations about the 2015 draft. When Connelly claimed he'd draft Jokic over higher-rated prospects, including Porzingis, he'd hear it from his colleagues who were still skeptical.

"You're out of your mind," they told him.

But Connelly couldn't shake his intuition: Jokic popped off the screen.

A few weeks later, after watching another game of his on a random weekday, Connelly was even more bullish. Jokic was dynamic *and* special. Connelly's internal ceiling for him was rising. In comparing him to Porzingis, the stretch-four out of Latvia, Connelly felt Jokic was already a better rebounder, passer, and post player.

"I was pretty convinced, and that's with immense respect to Porzingis," Connelly said.

The flashes Denver's front office saw from Jokic the previous season were becoming more consistent. It was obvious he was on the verge of breaking out if he hadn't yet already.

Having established relationships with all the relevant influences in Jokic's sphere, Rafal was the man on the ground in Belgrade. He was Denver's eyes and ears, conveying messages from Nuggets staffers to Mega coaches whenever necessary.

He estimated he saw Jokic around ten times that season. While there, he met with Nebojsa, Nikola's godfather, Misko, Mega's coaching staff and management, and Nikola's brothers, if they were in town. The purpose was to ensure they were all on the same page with his growth, a subtle reminder that Denver intended to bring him over the next season.

There was an art to Rafal's visits. He never wanted to intrude on Nikola's space but wanted to ensure their latest draft pick felt supported by the Nuggets organization. As the team representative, Rafal also didn't want Nikola to think he had arrived yet. Everything Jokic wanted was still in front of him.

That season, Juc coordinated visits for most of Denver's front office. Those visits almost always included dinner, where Denver's front office watered crucial relationships and underscored the trust that had already been established.

Upon arrival, Connelly remembered getting picked up from the hotel in Nikola's Toyota Yaris—a compact car that had no business housing a seven-foot frame. From there he first met Strahinja at an upscale restaurant called Dorian Gray in Belgrade. It was in a part of town nicknamed "Silicon Valley," where surgically enhanced women tended to convene with older men.

When Strahinja walked in, and Connelly went to introduce himself, he was taken aback by his mangled finger.

What happened, Connelly asked.

"Training accident," Strahinja replied.

What became immediately obvious to Connelly was how tight-knit Jokic's family was. Within this setup, the Nuggets felt their goal—of letting him develop one more season in Belgrade and of maintaining trust abroad—was feasible.

Denver's diplomatic strategy was by design. It wasn't as if they were adding more than one or two foreign players per season. It was important to Connelly to make sure they didn't feel isolated playing abroad.

Nikola's early success that season begat another issue.

Arturas watched from afar as Nikola tallied impressive efforts on a near-nightly basis. The team's conversations and group chats were lively and animated throughout his games. He was so good that there was no more flying under the radar.

His play was garnering real interest from European squads, which created the possibility that he might not even make it to the NBA. After all, playing at the highest levels in Europe was once Jokic's stated goal.

During a game against Cedevita, in early December, Jokic was abysmal.

"He was just off," Rafal said.

His body language and energy weren't there. One source recalled him being pouty and lethargic. Rafal surmised it could have been the increased attention, that perhaps he was finally feeling pressure. Rafal liked to compare him to an artist, and that as a creative, he needed to be in a proper headspace. Jokic was 1-of-8 from the field, with 6 points, 6 rebounds, and 1 assist in a blowout loss at home.

It was arguably the worst game of his career in front of some significant company.

"I just spotted in the VIP area that there was [the] Barcelona GM," Rafal said.

Something clicked in Rafal's head.

What if he was there for Nikola?

Rafal called Arturas, who'd starred at Barcelona during the mid-1990s.

"Anxiety kicks in because I know how aggressive those teams are," Karnisovas said.

The concern was always that Jokic could sign with a major European power, to a long-term deal, with a significant buyout, all of which would complicate his path to Denver. Karnisovas was instrumental in assuring that didn't happen.

The truth was that Barcelona did intend to sign him that day. The transfer was negotiated and near finalized with Misko and Mega. But Nikola was so unimpactful and sluggish, it gave their management pause. Misko suggested waiting a few more games before finalizing, but Barcelona was spooked. Karnisovas, momentarily relieved, was stunned that one below-average game swayed their decision.

He intervened, reassuring Jokic and Misko that the Nuggets were still heavily invested in their second-round pick. The plan was for Jokic to finish that season in Belgrade before debuting in Denver.

(There was even some discussion of bringing him over earlier than that.)

The impression Jokic left on Barcelona's management didn't dissuade the Nuggets. They scouted him accurately. If anything, the episode showed how fraught the situation was.

But the sting for Jokic lingered.

The following game, at Partizan, Jokic was off too. In 24 minutes, he failed to log an assist in defeat. Two games later, Nikola managed just 6-of-17 from the floor. Another game, and another loss, he shot just 3-for-11. Mega went into a tailspin, at one point losing six of seven games throughout December and January. It wasn't until Jokic came off the bench (only for one game) that both he and Mega temporarily reset.

Nenad, Mega's point guard, sensed his resentment over the Barcelona rejection. He even recalled Jokic gaining weight, a tell that his momentum—from the draft to Santa Barbara through the start of the season—was broken.

"He was so fat," Nenad said, sensing a bout of depression at his lowest point of the season.

"That body was like a fifty-year-old," he said.

He tried to coax him out of it, but even though he'd been drafted, Jokic didn't feel his future was secure.

Late in this slump, following a loss to Olimpija, there was a significant moment that illustrated Jokic's resolve. Yes, Barcelona passed, and yes, he'd gained weight in the aftermath of that decision, but, at his core, he was still deeply determined and stubborn.

Nenad and Nikola were horrible defensively in the loss. Individual defense, pick-and-roll coverage, communication, it was all porous and unacceptable.

A day or two after the game, there was a team meeting, which Misko attended. The meeting consisted of defensive lowlights from Nenad and Nikola paraded in front of the whole team. Misko, serving as both an agent and the club owner, was so mad he stripped Nenad of his captaincy. Nenad could only listen. There was no rebuttal, just acceptance. It was already tense, and players had a healthy fear of Misko before he turned his attention to Nikola.

They paused on one of Jokic's defensive mistakes, and Misko asked Nikola pointedly: "Do you like Dejan?"

For two-plus years, Dejan had groomed Nikola. He believed in him and emboldened him. The question was meant to be patronizing.

Obstinate and nimble, Nikola didn't tell Misko what he wanted to hear.

"I only like my mom and dad," Jokic replied in front of the whole team.

Misko wasn't accustomed to being shown up, not publicly and not by a member of his club and certainly not by one of his clients. But Nikola was not going to be strong-armed.

Misko told everyone to clear the locker room.

Teammates wondered whether Misko was going to cut him from the team altogether. The team's group chat crackled with nervous curiosity. When Jokic eventually responded, he cut through the tension with a hot knife.

"Man, nothing happened," Jokic told them. Misko reinforced that that level of defense was unacceptable before the rest of the conversation became mundane.

As Jokic's agent, Misko was never going to alienate one of his NBA clients. As Misko's client, Jokic wasn't going to be intimidated. The episode was significant, but Jokic was still mired in a slump.

With a foggy future, Misko waffled on whether Denver was the ideal place for his client to land. After all, the jump—from small European club to the NBA—was atypical. There were still questions about his size, intensity, and approach to the game. Could all of those doubts be allayed at the highest level of basketball in the world?

Since his body would likely make or break his career, Karnisovas asked Misko an astute question: Which environment would be most beneficial for his frame? The point resonated with Misko. Karnisovas promised patience in Denver.

Jokic had another concurrent dilemma: he missed Natalija, badly.

The Nuggets understood how influential she was to him. She was in Oklahoma on a volleyball scholarship, then worlds away from Nikola. But his loyalty to her, even as a teenager in Belgrade, was unflinching.

"You could easily see that he was just miserable," Rafal said.

On one of the rare occasions the team went out together during the 2013–14 season, Nikola had a few drinks before getting emotional about her.

Nemanja, Nikola's best friend, understood what his first and only girlfriend meant to him.

One night, he and Nikola were at a Kafana drinking when a song titled "Damn America" started playing. At that time, only Nikola knew Natalija was headed to the U.S. Sad about her departure and emotional over its implications, Nikola was so dispirited he took his phone and smashed it against the wall of the Kafana.

He was lovesick. He was also determined to join her there.

○

In late February, Mega lost to Red Star again in the final of the Serbian Cup championship, but Jokic's momentum was building.

He'd strung together enough quality games, despite his temporary malaise, that he was in contention for the Adriatic League MVP. Heading into the final week of competition, Nikola trailed Nenad by a meaningful, though not insurmountable, margin.

When Nenad suffered a calf injury in the penultimate game of their season, he wasn't able to practice for a few days. Dejan decided he'd come off the bench for their last game, which almost never happened. Nikola had his opening. As a reserve in limited minutes, Nenad played fairly well. Jokic, however, dominated. He ripped off 28 points and 15 rebounds to seize the league MVP title.

"He killed it," Nenad said, begrudgingly tipping his cap to his deserving teammate. Back in the locker room, Dejan cackled at Nenad's frustration.

Following the conclusion of the Adriatic League, Mega's schedule flowed into KLS, the larger Serbian league.

By late March and early April, Nikola had shrugged off the Barcelona disappointment and was torching opponents. Each game he flirted with double-doubles. Back as the starter against FMP, he reeled off 24 points and 19 rebounds.

For three months, Nikola was on a heater. He was energized, happy, and engaged. Perhaps motivated by Denver's encouragement, he sensed how close the NBA was.

"He was killing people," said Nenad, in awe of his unique dominance.

"It's not possible [that he's this good]."

Thirty-three points against Partizan. Another 34 against FMP.

There, in the heart of the KLS schedule, was Vojvodina Novi Sad, Nikola's old team.

Prior to the start of the game, Nikola was warming up when Ljuba, his head coach from Novi Sad, approached him.

"Why did you come here when you know you're going to lose?" Nikola teased before venturing back to his bench with a big, silly smile on his face.

The game was physical and tense and, according to Nenad, borderline dirty. Jokic hammered his old squad, pacing Mega with 28 points and 15 rebounds (but only 1 assist). The outlier, though, came from the free-throw line, which Nikola visited 20 times. As a team, Mega went to the free-throw line 49 times compared to just 13 for Novi Sad.

Novi Sad's side felt they'd been robbed.

After the game, Nikola came to Vojvodina's locker room to speak with every one of his former teammates and coaches. According to Igor, then in management at Novi Sad, Nikola acknowledged the lopsided whistle and congratulated them for the tough competition (Mega survived, 88–87, in overtime).

"Now in my fiftieth year in life, I think Nikola Jokic's story is the most interesting in the history of sports," Igor said. "Not Novak Djokovic, not some Formula One driver. For every sport, you need talent and to work hard and be lucky. . . . It was unbelievable that nobody in Serbia knew that kind of player existed."

Jokic arrived at Novi Sad an undisciplined, out-of-shape seventeen-year-old prospect. Less than three years later he was destroying the best talent basketball-rich Serbia had to offer.

CHAPTER 19

SUMMER LEAGUE

The first thing Nikola's godfather, Nebojsa, needed to address was his running.

His canter was, objectively, goofy. When he was tired, or disinterested, Nikola would sway from side to side, ambling up and down the court.

It didn't look professional because *it wasn't professional.* And Summer League, his debut with the organization that drafted him, was approaching.

"He needed to start running without inclining to one another side, being like a clown, now he's a Joker," said Nebojsa, who himself was a basketball coach. "At that time, it wasn't serious."

Nebojsa was tasked with preparing him for Summer League in Las Vegas. For the preceding three weeks, Nebojsa, Strahinja, Nemanja, and Nikola worked out together, every day, twice a day. They wanted to polish his ball skills, address his strength, build his stamina, and try to add something to his game prior to Summer League. It was the first time Nikola had worked with Nebojsa in earnest.

Eager to see the work pay off, his brothers trailed him to Vegas. They took up residence at the Hooters Hotel but made themselves more than comfortable at the Bellagio, the Nuggets' team hotel. They intruded on Nikola's room, making his space *their* space. But it wasn't an imposition whatsoever. Whatever they did, they did together.

The room looked like any inhabited by three brothers—a colorful setting to consummate the franchise's partnership with Team Jokic. As Connelly and Karnisovas came to sign Nikola's first contract—a three-year, $4.1 million deal—there was one slight impediment. The brothers had strategically placed a fake brown rubber swirl—prank poop—that Denver's executives had to move to sign the contract. The gag landed.

"It was awesome," Connelly said.

Playing alongside Emmanuel Mudiay and Gary Harris, Jokic was far from the headliner of Denver's Summer League roster. Mudiay, who'd teamed with Jokic at Hoop Summit the prior year, was the heralded No. 7 pick from the 2015 draft. Harris, following a quiet rookie season in Denver, needed more seasoning and was back in Las Vegas for a second consecutive summer. Both played more—and were more productive—than Jokic.

In five games, he averaged 8.0 points and 6.2 rebounds across 21 minutes per game.

But there were a few contributing factors outside of Jokic's control. As Michael Malone's staff settled into their new roles in Denver, Micah Nori, an assistant with Malone from their time in Sacramento, served as the team's Summer League head coach.

"We had just got there, so I really didn't even know who Nikola was," Nori said.

He was more concerned with integrating Nurkic into the offense and discovering what they had in Mudiay. Their investment in Harris made him a priority too, far ahead of Jokic in the pecking order.

Even worse, Nori would consistently mix up the "J-N" in Nurkic's initials for the "N-J" in Jokic's.

"Okay, this is you, Nikola, and I'm calling him Nurk," Nori said.

Neither Nori nor anyone else with the Nuggets knew what they had in Jokic. No one called any plays for him in Summer League because he was basically the ninth man in the rotation.

Jokic's job amounted to sprinting the length of the court—94 feet.

Now, in jest, Nori claims his early neglect was motivation. But Jokic hasn't let him forget his early coaching decisions. At least once a month, Jokic will text Nori a GIF of Forrest Gump . . . running.

It could be a congratulatory text from Nori or one just checking in. There was always a chance Jokic would reply, out of context, with Tom Hanks, jogging, on loop.

Harris, who'd shared a draft class with Jokic, knew a bit about Denver's overseas curiosity. And though Jokic's numbers weren't jarring in Las Vegas, Harris saw how polished his game was and how freely he moved within the confines of his position. His selfless attitude stuck with him.

"The game came so easy to him," Harris said.

Within that modest production was one double-double and a handful of moments that suggested an innovative feel for the game. Jokic's footwork and patience were already advanced, and his touch, as with every stop throughout his career, was sublime. He anticipated passing lanes, dissected the game in real time, and sought to elevate his teammates, even in Summer League. Those games are notoriously messy, with prospects eager to attract attention from NBA personnel. That allure didn't affect Jokic's approach. When he spotted a passing window, he got off the ball. When the game presented a 3-point look, he stepped into it without hesitation.

Even in 2015, he was WD-40: a multidimensional, offensive big who unlocked innumerable options on the court. If his spin move didn't yield a bucket for himself, then it drew another defender, which opened up a shot for his teammate. He played the game patiently and correctly. Though far from dominant, nothing seemed premeditated. Even accounting for the vast qualifiers of Summer League, the bursts of genius were evident.

Had Jokic not gotten into decent playing shape, perhaps he wouldn't have even warranted a look that summer. Upon arrival, Steve Hess, then Denver's ebullient strength coach, insisted Jokic had to lose thirty pounds. Humble and obedient, Jokic did as his new organization asked.

According to Arturas Karnisovas, Denver's assistant GM at the time, Jokic's typical playing weight in the Adriatic League was around 275. For Summer League, he'd dropped to 255, which, in retrospect, was too light. They found he wasn't able to physically overwhelm defenders as he'd done abroad.

His heft, paired with his skill, was an advantage. Why mitigate it?

Over the next two months heading into training camp, he climbed back closer to his ideal weight.

Hess laughed at the characterization of "ideal weight," since Jokic was still such an unknown commodity.

"No one thought he was going to play," Hess said. "Jokic was an afterthought."

CHAPTER 20

TRAINING CAMP

Nikola Jokic was not a natural candidate for paintball.

Large and somewhat plodding, he shouldn't have been good at evading the colorful pellets.

"He's sneaky," Darrell Arthur said.

"He's got soft feet, soft hands," said Wilson Chandler. "He's a big target, but he's light on his feet."

"Dude was a fucking assassin," said Steve Hess.

Heading into the 2015 season, Nikola's rookie year, Nuggets point guard Jameer Nelson held a team bonding week near his home in Philadelphia. Nelson, whose time in Orlando featured an NBA Finals run, knew the camaraderie incumbent of winning teams. When Nelson organized it in Orlando, it was called "Magic Week." Nikola's introduction to the Nuggets was, aptly, "Nuggets Week."

Which was how he found himself wandering the wrong side of a paintball field while his teammates were entrenched in a heated game of Capture the Flag. Jokic didn't quite grasp the concept—*capture the other team's flag without getting caught.*

Jokic was supposed to plant the flag in a certain spot, but instead he paraded on the wrong side of the line, flag proudly in hand.

"He didn't know the rules," Arthur said. "I shot him, he held his chest, he put the flag down and ran back to his side."

Harris wasn't keen on getting pelted with paintballs but distinctly remembered Jokic's indoctrination.

"Somebody lit his ass up," Harris said.

That somebody was Darrell Arthur.

Though he didn't grasp the specifics of Capture the Flag, Jokic was an asset.

Jokic shared a team with Hess and Chandler. They weren't interested in employing a free-for-all strategy, not with bragging rights and first impressions on the line. Together they devised a scheme of attacking Nelson's team from both sides.

If Jokic was going to compete, he wanted to prevail.

"He's a thinker," Nelson said. "His team always won."

Hess was smitten. He called up Nuggets GM Tim Connelly and gushed about the rookie.

"Bro, you've got a superstar," he told him.

"You watch him hoop?" Connelly replied.

"Fuck no," Hess said. "I just watched him play paintball."

Between paintball, golf, and dodgeball, it was the type of minicamp guys wanted to attend. For Jokic, it was ideal. A goofy, second-round pick from Serbia, Jokic was able to ingratiate himself with Denver's veterans. It was the perfect space to show how he didn't take himself too seriously, while establishing relationships with team pillars.

From 2013 to 2015, the Nuggets had no discernible DNA, had guys playing overlapping positions, and had little infrastructure as an organization. They were rudderless. Roles were fluid, and games were played but without purpose or direction.

"We didn't have a leader, we didn't have an identity," Arthur said. "We were trying to figure things out."

Jokic arrived the same season as coach Michael Malone, who'd been unceremoniously fired from his previous post leading the Sacramento Kings. There Malone had had success in building a relationship with tempestuous (and talented) big man DeMarcus Cousins. His savvy was in the bridges he could build with nearly any personality.

When he arrived in Denver, the culture was nebulous at best and nonexistent at worst. In prioritizing and drafting high-character prospects, Connelly was trying to establish what the Nuggets' identity would become.

The 2014 draft class was crucial, and Nelson's camp offered a fresh start.

"The one thing I noticed was his basketball IQ," Nelson said.

For a big man, to think and process like he did, was rare, Nelson thought.

"I don't really know the kid, but once he learns English well enough, he's gonna ascend to different levels than people actually think he can get to," Nelson said.

Nelson didn't even know how to pronounce his name. So, when he got a call from Connelly asking who looked good during their pickup runs, Nelson found an alternative route.

"The foreign kid," Nelson said.

Mike Miller was, by far, the eldest statesmen on that Nuggets squad. He couldn't—or wouldn't—pronounce his last name, stumbling over the soft *J*. To bypass the problem, he gave him a fitting nickname.

"Because he was a goofball and Jokic, Joker, and to be honest with you, the way he played the game was like that to me," Miller told the *Denver Post*.

"Again, that's why I fell in love [with his style] at his age, how much better he made players around him, how slow the game was for him, and how creative he was, not just scoring but passing the ball," Miller said. "That's where I gave him 'The Joker.'"

The nickname was a snug fit.

Prior to the camp, Darrell Arthur knew nothing about *the foreign kid*. In talking to Connelly, there was even some question whether he'd stick with the team that season. But in their pickup games, Arthur understood what Connelly and Karnisovas had seen the year before. He saw his skill, but skill alone would have undersold his talent.

He got anywhere he wanted on the court. He invented angles. He was stronger than he looked.

Most telling to Arthur, though, was how he played compared to other young prospects. When pressured, they tended to rush and panic. Under duress, Nikola stayed composed. He also noticed how Jokic kept getting to the rim with ease but would almost always spray out instead of taking the shot. Arthur saw a rare unselfish streak baked into the foreign kid's DNA. That wasn't how most prospects tried to establish themselves in the league.

The big men Arthur played with before arriving in Denver—Marc Gasol, Zach Randolph in Memphis—gave him context. And from body type to playing style, those two were halfway decent comparisons.

"I was just kind of in awe at Jokic's IQ at an early age," Arthur said, recounting their pickup games.

Chandler's first impression was equally as enlightening.

"Man, this guy's goofy as shit, but he's really good at basketball," he said.

Camp that season took place at the Olympic Training Facility in Colorado Springs, where the Nuggets got the benefits of training at altitude and had far more space than their second-floor practice gym allowed.

The whispers began inside that sprawling, gleaming gym a little more than an hour south of Denver.

"It was training camp," Harris said. "We were like, *yeah*, he might be the best player on this team."

As a twenty-year-old coming off an MVP campaign in the Adriatic League, Jokic could have had some semblance of entitlement when he got to Colorado for training camp. Instead, most of his teammates were unaware of the accolades he'd earned overseas. Jokic came humble, happy, and hungry.

Will Barton, who'd arrived via trade from Portland the previous season, remembered him performing rookie duties and grabbing waters for his teammates.

"Coming from where he came from, it probably was a dream to be there," Nelson said.

Arthur sensed nothing but gratitude from their unassuming Serbian rookie.

"I don't know if he ever thought that he would make it to the NBA," Arthur said.

That attitude went a long way toward unpacking Jokic's complex layers.

If none of his achievements were ever expected, what did he have to be cocky about?

That first training camp he was adjusting to a new country, a new language, with new teammates and a new coach eager to prove his coaching chops. With significant work to do on his body, everything inside Nikola's world was spinning except for the singular reason he was there in the first place.

"Basketball, for him, was easy," Chandler said.

CHAPTER 21

ROOKIE YEAR

Jameer Nelson knew better than to judge a player based on appearance.

"Look at me, five-eleven, stocky point guard, who everybody said I should've been a boxer or a football player," he said.

Nelson wasn't concerned that Nikola was skinny, goofy, and could barely speak English. He could hoop.

Veteran Wilson Chandler cited Kevin Durant, whose underwhelming bench press at the NBA combine famously predicted absolutely nothing about how his Hall of Fame career would transpire. Aesthetics and metrics didn't really matter. And it wasn't as if the Nuggets were on the verge of contention either. They were simply trying to right the ship.

"To be honest, at that time, I didn't want to be there," Chandler said. Going to work became much more enjoyable upon Jokic and Nelson's arrival ahead of the 2015 season. They breathed a fresh sense of joy into what had become a stale, uninviting space.

Even though the Nuggets weren't competitive, at least the energy of the locker room was changing.

On birthdays, part of rookie duties entailed singing "Happy Birthday" in front of the whole team. Arthur recalled Jokic participating, before adding his personal flavor to the celebration. Jokic sang and danced, then whipped his shirt off and jumped all around the honoree. His extra dose of levity always lifted the mood.

In huddles, Jokic was fond of tapping an unsuspecting teammate's shoulder before pleading ignorant when confronted. He was *always* messing around, teasing someone, talking trash.

"He's like a kid," Chandler said. "You look at him and you just like him."

Jokic's default was to enjoy himself. It wasn't that he didn't have the capacity to work hard; it was that while doing so, he wanted to smile.

"Joker, when he was having fun with it, would fucking kill it," Hess said, regarding his progression both on the court and in the weight room.

New to the team and to the NBA, all he wanted to do was hang out. When Jameer, Wilson, and Darrell went out for dinner, they invited Jokic to tag along. They viewed him as their Serbian little brother.

Jokic made himself more than comfortable.

With more than a decade's worth of NBA experience by that point, Nelson had his shower routine down to a science. That season, his $4.5 million salary afforded him the luxury of quality lotions and expensive soaps. His favorite of the bunch was a fifty-dollar bottle of soap he bought from Neiman Marcus. But too many times when he would go to shower, the bottles were lower than he'd left them.

Jokic.

"The dude would steal my soap," Nelson said.

Jokic walked around smelling like . . . *Nelson.*

One day he caught him, Neiman Marcus merchandise in hand.

"Yo, man, buy me some soap!" he quipped. But Nelson didn't have the heart to follow through with the lovable rookie.

On road trips, Arthur hung out in Jokic's room, the two killing count-less hours playing *FIFA.* It wasn't dissimilar to Jokic's childhood, when he and his older brothers competed for hours on end at video games.

"He said his brothers were crazy," Arthur said.

All three were wildly competitive, which meant the possibility of vio-lence always lingered around their battles. When Nikola would win, inev-itably, his brothers got mad. Once, according to Arthur, Nikola beat one of his brothers in *FIFA,* which prompted an outburst. The losing sibling took his controller and whipped it in Nikola's direction.

"Fractured his hand," Arthur said.

○

When Denver's strength staff first got Jokic, he struggled to even get into an athletic stance.

He was a seven-foot, second-round ball of clay, with few to no expectations. His flexibility and strength were equally dubious.

Wilson Chandler was among the hardest workers on the team. Whenever possible, Hess paired him with Jokic in the weight room.

Keep up with Wilson, Hess told him. And he did.

Wilson never viewed his relationship with Jokic as a mentorship, though that's what it amounted to. Wilson saw him as an equal and a friend. He simply enjoyed being around him. In the weight room, they became competitors.

On road trips, when rookies were assigned the first wave of workouts, Jokic protested while wanting to remain workout partners with Chandler. Jokic was committed. According to Hess, he was always there five minutes early and never missed a workout.

"He puts his trust in you," Hess said. "He married the weight room."

Their first Christmas, Connelly hosted a party with his wife, who was pregnant, and a few friends. Nuggets assistant coach Ogi Stojakovic was there with his young daughter, as was Strahinja. After dinner, Strahinja began peppering Connelly with questions about his younger brother's fitness.

"The other day we were wrestling, and his thighs felt very strong," said Strahinja, as if that was a normal observation to share.

Assistant coach Micah Nori gently reminded Jokic that he was more valuable to the Nuggets healthy than battered.

"When he was a rookie, his first few years, his brothers were living with him, he'd come with bruises to practice, and I'm like, 'What the hell happened?'" Nori said.

"Oh, we were wrestling," Jokic told him sheepishly.

In 2015, Nikola Vucevic was in his fifth season in the NBA, still on his path to becoming a future All-Star. The Montenegrin moved to the United States to complete high school, played basketball at the University of Southern California, and had been in the NBA since 2011. He understood far better than Jokic how the U.S. worked, and more specifically, how the league worked.

When the Nuggets faced the Magic, the two Nikolas met in the hallway where the elder Balkan big imparted whatever wisdom he could on the rookie. As a fellow big from the same part of the world, with similar playing characteristics, "Vooch," as he's known in NBA locker rooms, was eager to help.

"It's special for us, for everybody from the Balkans, regardless of which country it is," Vooch said. "When we come here, we get to share the biggest stage in the world of a sport we love to play. It's huge, and it means a lot to us."

Some of the secrets he shared with Jokic pertained to his physical fitness.

"I remember I talked to him a lot about the weight room," Vucevic said.

It helped Vucevic immensely when he was establishing himself in the league, and since it wasn't nearly as big a priority in Europe, he figured Jokic needed to hear it too.

By that point, Jokic was fully committed to the gym and invested in improving his body.

Vucevic also remembered specific encouragement he gave Jokic during those early years.

"You're super talented. Just be patient. Everything will come to you."

CHAPTER 22

DEPTH CHART

The first pick in Denver's vaunted 2014 draft class was another Balkan big man who had shown promise throughout his rookie season: Jusuf Nurkic.

Unlike Jokic, who spent one more year seasoning in Serbia, Nurkic proved he belonged quickly during that 2014–15 season. He started 27 games and finished with 6.2 rebounds per game—tied for third on the Nuggets—despite playing on a team stocked with big men. Nurkic had to contend with Chandler, Arthur, Kenneth Faried, J. J. Hickson, Timofey Mozgov, Danilo Gallinari, and JaVale McGee for boards. The roster construction wasn't conducive for development, and the defense was as porous as a water filter.

(Nurkic's potential undoubtedly played a role in Denver dealing both Mozgov and McGee midway through the season, opening up playing time.)

Nurkic stood out for his physicality, rim protection, and interior skills. His game was still raw, but the edgy Bosnian even flashed an ability to dissect a defense with his vision. For a team without a pecking order—or even much identity—his play was encouraging. His inaugural season earned him second-team All-Rookie honors, registering as a pleasant surprise and an early indication of Connelly's scouting acumen. Nurkic was a bright spot even if few people noticed.

Entering the 2015–16 season, Nurkic had a new coach (Malone), but the start of his year was marred by offseason knee surgery. Whatever momentum he built had faded. That cracked the door open for a relatively unknown rookie from Serbia.

Due to the dual trade departures of Mozgov and McGee, Jokic didn't have to contend with nearly as crowded a frontcourt as Nurkic had. And though it wasn't clear at all whether Jokic might threaten Nurkic's minutes, the injury allowed Malone to tinker.

Ten games into Jokic's rookie season, he sat stuck to the bench against an Anthony Davis–led Pelicans team that opted for small ball. In those scenarios, Malone believed, he was a liability.

The next night, November 18, the Nuggets were concluding a three-game road trip in San Antonio. A back-to-back, against the Spurs no less, was daunting. But the Nuggets were young, lacking cohesion and chemistry. As starters Danilo Gallinari, J. J. Hickson, and Emmanuel Mudiay managed to shoot 6-of-31 from the field, Malone turned to his bench, where a gangly, eager Jokic awaited.

He ran high pick-and-rolls with Jameer Nelson and Will Barton, finished softly on rolls toward the paint, and clawed for ricochets off the glass. The opposing frontcourt featured stars in Tim Duncan, LaMarcus Aldridge, and Kawhi Leonard. Even Boris Diaw, to whom Jokic had been compared during the draft process due to their shared shape and savvy, presented a challenge.

"I don't even know if he knows who those guys are, and maybe that's a good thing," Malone said.

Jokic was unfazed. Better yet, he was game. He dumped in 23 points and snatched 12 rebounds, adding in 3 blocks and 2 steals. On the bench, veteran Mike Miller stood and applauded at each basket, impressed by Jokic's growth. It was a superlative effort, even in defeat.

"I think it doesn't matter, really, because they scored 109 points," Jokic said. "That's too much. They had too many open shots. We must do better on defense. Offense will come."

Sean Elliott, the longtime former Spur, was on the San Antonio broadcast that night and was unabashed in his praise of Denver's rookie.

"He's looking like [Dirk] Nowitzki out there," he said.

Looking back on that game years later, Malone admitted the clues were there.

"Lightbulb!" Malone said.

Darrell Arthur had an inkling that Jokic was different from the preseason minicamp, but the San Antonio game validated what he'd seen.

Having been around Marc Gasol and Zach Randolph, Arthur couldn't ignore that Jokic's highlights were rarely solo endeavors. His approach, in facilitating for others and scrambling to screen for guards, was selfless and made the game easier for his teammates.

"It's weird saying that because that's what you [usually] see out of your vets," Arthur said.

Malone beamed at his young big man's skill and progression. He forecast a devastating tandem between he and Mudiay, that year's first-round pick. Behind the scenes, the Nuggets' depth chart flipped. He'd begun the season behind both Hickson and Joffrey Lauvergne.

Two nights later, Jokic earned the first start of his career.

O

The San Antonio game stuck with Chandler too.

In just his eleventh career NBA game, in front of the NBA's greatest head coach (Gregg Popovich) and the game's greatest power forward (Duncan), Jokic had popped. During the game, Jokic found a moment for a short chat with Duncan.

Do you shoot 3-pointers too? the Spurs legend asked him.

"So-so," Jokic responded modestly, having buried the first 3-pointer of his career that night.

In Duncan, Jokic had a role model, someone who dominated the game yet abhorred the spotlight. Chandler, who watched from the bench while hurt that season, remained endlessly curious about *the foreign kid.*

Yes, he marveled at his showing against the Spurs, but Chandler already knew that behind the scenes, in practices, Jokic was a menace. Chandler watched him, studied him, and tried to understand him.

"You could watch him score forty, and you'd be like, 'Man, I could guard that motherfucker,'" Chandler said.

And then he'd watch his lithe footwork in practice, or go back and watch game film, and it would start to make sense.

"I can't guard him," he conceded. "I was always joking with him, like, 'Man, I'll lock that shit up,' but I had no chance."

On the court, Jokic was content with whatever playing time he got.

In November, that meant a mere 18 minutes per night. There was no stewing.

When he did play, he thrived. With the ball in his hands, it was as if passing lanes appeared out of thin air.

Nelson became a staunch advocate. He wasn't ready to put a ceiling on Jokic's potential, but he told the front office he could be an All-Star. "They thought I was like bullshitting them," he said.

Connelly, who had seen every minute he'd played over the prior two seasons, watched curiously and felt he was holding back. He'd seen his wizardry in conjuring passing lanes in Serbia, or even in practices, and wondered why it wasn't translating to the NBA court.

"I'm like, 'Dude, be yourself, you were in Mega short-rolling, throwing it between your legs,'" Connelly told him.

Nikola replied, "Brother, in Mega, I could kick the ball and still play. Here, if I turn the ball over, I don't play so much."

The Nuggets were in the nascent stages of honing his brilliance. They needed to forge a balance between catering to his creativity while holding him accountable. The stakes were undeniably higher in the NBA than in the Adriatic League.

What differentiated Nikola, by virtue both of his demeanor and second-round status, was his lack of entitlement. As a kid, reaching the NBA was a pipe dream. It was a league he consumed, sparingly, through YouTube. The 3 and 4 a.m. tip times made it a chore to follow back home. When he queued up YouTube, there were highlights of Magic Johnson's passing, clips of Hakeem Olajuwon's footwork, and flashes of Michael Jordan's brilliance. That was his exposure to the NBA.

A world away, Nebojsa watched his godson's progression. When others would celebrate his scrap minutes, Nebojsa groused. He knew, even watching through the TV, that he was capable of handling more minutes and more responsibility.

Privately, he reinforced that belief: Don't settle for what they're giving you. Keep working and pushing for more.

In the locker room, Jokic was making believers of his teammates. The Nuggets weren't winning with any consistency, and losing streaks tended to spiral. Malone, still attempting to establish a foothold with his new organization, was searching. Arthur remembered a specific team meeting where Malone asked his guys a poignant question.

"Who are four other guys that you'd want to play with if you were starting?"

"I'm pretty sure ninety percent of the teams had Jokic on them," Arthur said.

CHAPTER 23

BALKAN BIGS

Nurkic returned in January after missing the first two months of the season following knee surgery. They tried to ease him back into the rotation, but in just his third game of the season, Nurkic recorded 15 points, 10 rebounds, and 5 blocks in just 22 minutes of work.

"It's fun, you know, always when you're back after a long time," Nurkic told reporters. "I can't wait to play."

Malone, still in his first year with the team, had a new piece to experiment with, a more traditional post presence. Jokic had started that night but was uncharacteristically quiet. In Nurkic, the Nuggets had a bruising, back-to-the-basket big man, just like what Malone had in Sacramento with DeMarcus Cousins.

"To be able to play through him on those high-lows and paint catches, he's so physical," Malone said. "Once he slows his game down a little bit—catch, gather, you don't have to flip that shot up, take your time, go up strong and finish."

Stylistically on offense, Nurkic was oil to Jokic's water. Defensively, he was more a traditional enforcer than Jokic. Nurkic was big and physical. Malone was adamant that they were better defensively when he was on the floor, clogging up the paint.

But his surgically repaired patellar tendon didn't cooperate. There were encouraging sequences and equally frustrating setbacks. His playing time, as with his conditioning, was inconsistent. In February he again posted a double-double of 16 points and 11 rebounds off the bench while Jokic, in the starting lineup, struggled.

"I'm happy for him," Malone said. "It hasn't been easy for Nurk. He had a great rookie season, but coming back from injury and then you have all of these other young bigs playing well . . . But I give him credit because he's come and worked very hard."

While Nurkic tried hard to establish consistency, there was a disconcerting trend developing between the two big men. Whenever Nurkic found a rhythm, Jokic struggled. And when Jokic erupted—as in a 27-point, 14-rebound game against the Raptors in early February—Nurkic was a nonfactor.

Raptors center Jonas Valanciunas looked helpless against Jokic as he weaved a seamless two-man game with Mudiay, then flashed an outside shooting ability against a center unwilling or unable to contest him. Jokic had mitigated Valanciunas's physical advantage with his transition play, range, and intelligence.

Malone was effusive in the aftermath, with perhaps his most bold public comments yet.

"Every time I think he's kind of maxed out for his rookie season, he finds a way to keep on impressing me," he told reporters. "You can talk about some of these other young bigs, who are all talented, and I wouldn't trade him for anybody in the world. He's a special young man and a special young talent."

That February, Jokic and Mudiay both took part in the NBA's annual Rising Stars game at All-Star weekend in Toronto. Fellow Hoop Summit participants Trey Lyles and Clint Capela were on the World team as well.

By the end of February, Nurkic had started stewing. He was averaging less than 15 minutes per game throughout the month, fewer than Jokic (21) and even Lauvergne (15.5). It was fair to wonder whether there was enough room in the frontcourt for all of them to develop.

"Nurk's not happy he's not playing, and I don't expect him to be," Malone said. "I'm not foolish."

Heading into the last week of the 2015–16 season, Jokic and Nurkic had shared the floor a grand total of 14 minutes together. One player was beginning to tap into his powers, which happened to elevate everyone else around him. The other was fighting to reclaim the foothold he'd had on the starting job before an injury robbed him of that status.

Any hope of the postseason had dissolved during a miserable first half of the season. With Connelly's blessing and encouragement, Malone needed to discover the potential of their roster. That meant experimenting, without consequences, before the season was over.

The Nuggets were committed to testing out a Jokic-Nurkic frontcourt.

"What, they called it the Balkan Bigs?" Harris said, laughing at the memory.

Beginning with an April game against the Spurs, the Nuggets trotted out their towering frontcourt, Nurkic at center and Jokic at power forward. By virtue of his size, Nurkic drew the Duncan matchup, leaving Jokic to guard veteran forward David West.

Perhaps sensing the moment, Nurkic seized on the opportunity to showcase his skills. He scored a season-high 21 on a season-high 18 attempts. He buried jumpers from the midrange and found paydirt playing through Duncan's chest inside. No one doubted Nurkic's ability to score when he was featured in the offense. There *was* a valid question whether his success came at the expense of Jokic's.

Against the Spurs, whose starters rested outside of Duncan, Jokic managed just 8 points but snatched a season-high 15 rebounds. Between the two of them, the Nuggets could be devastating on the glass.

But was that fair to Jokic—and fair to the rest of the guys who preferred playing with him—to play him out of position?

Denver's roster construction was already unique in that its strength was in the frontcourt, with multiple skilled big men. Amid the NBA's 3-point revolution, they had a choice to make: chase the latest trend—pace-and-space—or lean into their best attributes.

The Nuggets started Jokic and Nurkic together for the final two games of the 2015–16 season with mixed results. In their penultimate game, Jokic logged another double-double, his 15th of his rookie campaign. His scoring came within the flow of the offense, in transition breaks, off dribble penetration, and even via a clever find from Nurkic. There was nothing premeditated about his effort. Even playing out of position, he was an effective offensive hub.

Nurkic forced the issue against Utah's Rudy Gobert with quick-hitting shots in the paint or deep, inefficient twos. It didn't work. His 2-for-11 shooting performance wasn't helping the pair's case to coexist, but the duo was still learning their new roles. On the final day of the regular season, an inconsequential loss to Portland, both players secured double-doubles, though Nurkic's line was marred by 8 turnovers. Even though both played at least 35 minutes, Jokic's plus/minus was a team-high +4 to Nurkic's team-worst –19.

It was still early, Denver's coaches and front office members told themselves. If nothing else had been accomplished, at least the franchise had film of their experiment. Individually, Nikola finished third in Rookie of the Year voting behind Kristaps Porzingis and Karl-Anthony Towns. His season had been superb. However, the Balkan Big experiment was far from over. There was a commitment—and a plan—to see it through.

After the season, Connelly asked Jokic how he felt his rookie season had gone. There was a new country, with new teammates, a new language, and a new coach. Ever appreciative of even reaching the NBA and always self-deprecating, Jokic was blunt with his boss.

"Honestly, brother," Jokic told him, "I can't believe how well I played."

CHAPTER 24

OLYMPICS

The red, yellow, and green tie-dyed shirts leapt off the Olympic podium, as if some middle schoolers had crashed the global games.

The newly independent Lithuanian national team had only secured funding for the 1992 Olympic Games in Barcelona thanks to a donation from the Grateful Dead, who were both hoop heads and generous philanthropists. The Lithuanian players' only responsibility was to wear the dunking skeletons with the accompanying psychedelic (tie-dyed) shorts.

They did so, proudly.

The fanny pack Arturas Karnisovas wore after Lithuania won the bronze medal, knocking off the Unified Team of post–Soviet Union states, did not appear to be Dead-sponsored. Karnisovas just had a knack for fashion.

The Nuggets' assistant GM had forged a path to his current position that was unlike anyone else's in history.

After enduring a tense three days in Moscow, where his basketball future rested in the hands of the KGB, the eighteen-year-old was given clearance to become the first player from the Soviet Union to play college basketball in the United States. That was in 1989. Karnisovas spent the next four years at Seton Hall University in New Jersey, teaching himself English, becoming a scholar-athlete, and leading the Pirates to the NCAA tournament each season.

Karnisovas was a sophomore in college while vying for a spot on Lithuania's Olympic team, its first since declaring independence from the Soviet Union. The opportunity, on a global stage, was overwhelming. His reward for making it to Barcelona in 1992? A matchup against Charles Barkley, the leading scorer on perhaps the greatest basketball team ever constructed: the Dream Team.

Part of the reason the Dream Team, with Michael Jordan, Magic Johnson, and Scottie Pippen, was ever assembled was the U.S.'s underwhelming bronze-medal finish at the prior Olympic Games, in Seoul in 1988. There the Soviet Union, featuring numerous Lithuanian stars, prevailed. Yugoslavia, with Drazen Petrovic, Vlade Divac, and Toni Kukoc, earned silver.

In Barcelona in 1992, the United States dismantled Lithuania in the semifinals, just as they'd done to every other opponent en route to the gold medal. Karnisovas fouled out amid the blowout, but before the game was over, he sat starry-eyed on the sidelines, snapping pictures of his iconic opponents. He wasn't ashamed at all. The gulf between the rest of the world and the United States' surplus of future Hall of Famers was the same as the distance from Kansas to Kaunas.

Karnisovas lived a colorful life owing to his decorated basketball career. Ahead of the 2016 Olympics in Rio de Janeiro, Nikola felt a similar sense of pride at the prospect of representing Serbia on the global stage.

"Oh my gosh," Jokic told reporters. "I would be really honored to play for my country."

To the countries of the former Yugoslavia, basketball was religion. The NBA wasn't accessible to the basketball-mad region. What mattered was how teams performed on a global stage, with national pride at stake.

Karnisovas knew as well as anyone with the Nuggets what an Olympic berth meant to Jokic, who'd dreamed of playing for his national team as a child.

He hadn't represented Serbia the previous summer at EuroBasket because the Nuggets wanted him to prioritize Summer League and acclimate his body to the NBA. But a sensational rookie season opened the door.

"I think it's very emotional for him to play for his national team," Karnisovas said. "He really cares about his country."

But the irony, of who Jokic was on the court, wasn't lost on Karnisovas.

"All the Olympic slogans, he's not that," he said. "Faster, stronger, higher is not what he does, but then you're surprised when he just snatches the rebound and throws a pass across the whole court or leads the break."

Karnisovas said the desire to play was always there for him. The Olympics just needed to align with his professional priorities.

In 2016, they did.

Aside from Jokic, who was just twenty-one at the time, Serbia had NBA talent on its roster. Current Atlanta Hawks sniper Bogdan Bogdanovic gave them 3-point spacing and Milos Teodosic, later a guard for the Clippers, was a wizard with the rock in his hands. But as Bogdanovic explained, Olympic basketball was an entirely different animal than the NBA or EuroLeague.

"National team is completely different basketball," Bogdanovic said. "It's only a few games, and you have to give your max in these few games."

Despite establishing himself in Denver, Jokic hadn't yet proven anything with the national team.

Like most of Jokic's path, his route to the national team was atypical. Because he'd been discovered late, he wasn't a fixture in their pipeline. Even at the U-19 tournament in Prague in 2013, Jokic was a complementary piece and not a star. But ahead of Rio, and throughout Olympic qualifying where he won the MVP, Jokic was too good to ignore. This iteration, however, was very much the veteran Teodosic's team.

"The most memorable thing for me is still what happened at his first training session with the national team, where he needed literally two minutes to adopt and understand the principles and actions that we created in previous years with the [coach Aleksandar] Djordjevic," Teodosic said.

What Teodosic saw was his intuition on the court and the snap decisions he made to facilitate the game for others.

In the preliminary round, Serbia took on a U.S. team brimming with talent. Kevin Durant, Kyrie Irving, Paul George, and other All-Stars littered the roster. Inside, DeAndre Jordan, Draymond Green, and DeMarcus Cousins gave Team USA heft in the paint.

Jokic gave all three of them problems, working Green near the basket and stretching both Jordan and Cousins far out of their comfort zones near the 3-point line. He and Teodosic shared the same unselfish philosophy on the floor.

If they didn't have the talent to compete with the Americans, they at least had the chemistry.

In Jokic and Teodosic, the Serbians had two pass-first playmakers to keep defenses spinning.

"We have similar visions," Teodosic said. "He sees the game in a great way, feels the game, and can predict what will happen during the game with a great sense for assists. But there is another reason why we clicked, and that is we used to play video games online. We're usually on the same team, and most of the time it was *CounterStrike*."

In the preliminary stage, Jokic scored a game-high 25 points to complement Teodosic's game-high 6 assists. The Serbians fell, narrowly, to the Americans, 94–91.

"Does he play that well for Denver?" Team USA head coach Mike Krzyzewski asked *Denver Post* columnist Mark Kiszla. "He played with the poise of a much older player."

The Serbian squad was unusually close that summer. Jokic was the youngest on the roster but ingratiated himself to his teammates like he always did.

"Especially after a couple beers, he gets very creative," Bogdanovic said of his propensity to keep the mood light.

One night while they were drinking, Jokic got a hankering for McDonald's and asked his teammates whether they wanted anything. The next thing Bogdanovic remembered was Jokic hauling food for the whole squad.

"He came back with six, seven bags of stuff from McDonald's," Bogdanovic said.

But there was one significant wrinkle to the story, according to Teodosic. As the captain of the team, he wanted to test Jokic.

"I sent him to go get food for the whole team at McDonald's, and he did it without any problem or opposition, and that was very important for me in forming my opinion about him," Teodosic said. "He showed that he is a good boy, and that he understands [the team aspect] of the Serbian national team."

In the gold medal game, the U.S. again ran into Serbia, though the Americans were far more prepared for Jokic the second time around.

"We kicked their ass," DeAndre Jordan said of the 30-point rout. "Then I got a gold medal."

There wasn't any dejection on Jokic's face as he stood to receive his silver medal in the aftermath of the beatdown. There was sheer pride at the hardware he'd won.

"It's really cool," he told reporters. "I don't know how many people in the world have a silver medal. Maybe a thousand?

"This is a big thing for us," he said. "It's a big thing for the whole nation. I don't know, but I think all my friends are waiting for us to come back home. Serbia is now, like, crazy."

Jokic was younger and less accomplished than some of his teammates but the emotion upon returning to Belgrade and then Sombor was palpable. His voice cracked as he addressed his countrymen in Sombor. Making Serbia proud meant more to him than anything he'd done individually.

"This medal is all for me and my family," he said, beaming despite the defeat.

Serbia, core of the former Yugoslavia, was accustomed to basketball success. Before its dissolution, Vlade Divac (Serbian), Drazen Petrovic, and Toni Kukoc (both Croatian) led Yugoslavia to the 1990 FIBA World Championship.

The national team's success often superseded whatever individual triumphs a Serbian achieved in the NBA, which is why Jokic's participation was always a contentious topic. But Bogdanovic said he understood how taxing a commitment it was.

"My body hurts, and he played almost double [the minutes] I think," he said.

Still, the national team was what every kid dreamed to represent.

During the Balkan Wars, a deadly conflict of racial and ethnic tensions among neighboring states that preempted the dissolution of Yugoslavia, sports became a healthy distraction. Basketball, already revered in the region, was a sanctuary.

"[Players were] like someone who you can look up to, during the wars, during a lot of bad stuff in the country," Bogdanovic said. "As a kid, every parent wanted to navigate their kids through sports and positive things."

In claiming the silver medal at the 2016 Olympics, Jokic gave his countrymen even more reason to feel pride. Basketball in Serbia was akin to football in Argentina, according to Bogdanovic. Fans were knowledgeable and passionate. Their team's success meant they could walk a little taller. At just twenty-one, Jokic was overwhelmed with the impact upon seeing his countrymen rejoice.

"He realized what he did," Bogdanovic said.

Meanwhile, Denver's front office gushed at the performance. Their burgeoning star hadn't blinked against a team of NBA All-Stars. Jokic regarded the Americans as the latest iteration of the Dream Team. The knowledge that his slow, savvy approach to the game worked against them was invaluable. It was one more tool in his arsenal.

"I play against them," he told Kiszla. "I know them. They are just players."

Connelly was proud but not necessarily surprised. Everything he excelled at—leverage, footwork, touch, confidence—translated to the Olympic stage.

He was a guy they could construct a team around.

Jokic's talent was being validated, his work ethic starting to pay dividends. Like an addiction, Connelly saw his competitive drive start to spark.

"The snowball had started rolling," Connelly said.

Upon his return, Jokic gifted Connelly his Olympic jersey. Then he teased another one of his bosses.

"He goes, 'Hey Arturas, want to see the silver medal? Because I know you've just got a bronze,'" Connelly recalled.

Karnisovas was always quiet and reserved, offering a pensive balance to Connelly's enthusiasm. Even he started to let himself dream a little bit.

"The Olympics was like . . . he might figure it out," Karnisovas said.

CHAPTER 25

FINCHY

The Nuggets tried to bring Chris Finch to Denver a year earlier than he actually arrived.

Finch, now the head coach of the Timberwolves, was an assistant in Houston during the 2015–16 season when the Nuggets attempted to nab him. The Rockets blocked the move, but he was fired a year later. It was Michael Malone's second season at the helm when Finch was added to the staff.

Finch had worked with Karnisovas in Houston and knew Connelly from their shared basketball trails in Europe. He spent more than a decade coaching in England, Belgium, and Germany before he got his break. The Rockets plucked him out of relative obscurity. They hired him to coach their G League squad, which turned into an offensive incubator.

In Europe, Finch blended both NBA and European concepts. However, his philosophies were most informed by his time at college. At Division III Franklin & Marshall, Finch was a two-time All American.

"We played a lot of high-low, motion offense through the bigs," Finch said.

As his coaching career progressed, he continued to tinker. He wasn't scared to incorporate new ideas or to experiment. His approach yielded a four-out offense, with ample floor spacing and room to cut.

When Finch was hired to run the G League's Rio Grande Valley Vipers, Houston's boundary-pushing executive Daryl Morey wanted him to expand what a traditional offense looked like. His first season they won the championship, finishing second in the G League in 3-point attempts. The next season, 2010–11, they reached the finals, again, while taking nearly 200 more 3-pointers than any other team in the league.

They wanted him to incorporate corner principles—an analytic-friendly concept—that mirrored what the Rockets were running in the NBA.

A career's worth of theories, coupled with experience at all levels, distilled into a few basic tenets. He wanted to play through big men at the top of the floor, and he wanted them to facilitate. They could operate in more basic dribble-handoff situations, or, if skilled enough, they could create and open up lanes on their own. But the goal was to space the floor and encourage movement. Dragging a big man out of the paint was a core element. In Finch's mind, he called for freedom on offense and accountability on defense.

Connelly maintained the hire was serendipitous, though there was probably some intent of pairing a progressive offensive coach alongside two big men with both the ability and willingness to distribute. Under Finch's directive, there would be fewer play calls, more fluidity, and an adherence to the right shots and the right cuts.

"When I first came into the league, getting people to cut was one of the hardest things to do," Finch said.

Cutting was mostly sacrificial. One player's effort opened up space for another. Convincing NBA players on this particular front was a chore. Besides, most players grew up with the ball in their hands. They didn't make it to the NBA on the strength of their movement away from the ball.

But in Finch's vision, with big men serving as conductors from the top of the arc, the effort could pay dividends. With great passers, and willing passers, cuts took on a different value.

"Now there's a prize for cutting," Finch said.

Gary Harris might have been the first to reap those rewards. A slashing two guard, Harris recognized the attention Jokic mandated and made a concerted effort to read him.

"I knew how good of a passer he was just because that's how I used to get my points," Harris said.

Harris credited Finch for establishing those cutting principles. Within them, the Nuggets' offense eventually blossomed. What were Harris's marching orders?

"Basically, dump it to Nikola and cut early off of it," Finch said.

The offense was never premeditated, but there were concepts based on where the ball went early in a possession. There were guidelines, not necessarily rules. The other advantage was that an offense guided through a big man didn't require a traditional point guard. In the summer of 2016, the Nuggets were ecstatic when Jamal Murray fell to them at No. 7 in the draft. They never expected him to last that long.

Ironically, current Nuggets GM Calvin Booth was then in Minnesota, serving as the director of player personnel. The Timberwolves sat on the No. 5 pick, and the young, fiery guard out of Kentucky caught Booth's eye. He believed his shooting would translate to the next level and was high on him heading into the draft, a person familiar with Booth's thinking told the *Denver Post*.

The Timberwolves scouted Murray heavily, but Tom Thibodeau, who'd become their head coach and president of basketball operations only a few months earlier, preferred older, more established prospects. Bucking conventional wisdom, the T-Wolves drafted twenty-two-year-old Kris Dunn out of Providence. Two picks later, the Nuggets nabbed Murray.

A point guard, though not in the traditional sense, Murray was a hunter. He could disrupt a defense from deep, run tandem offense with a big man, or stretch a defense as an off-ball threat. Murray was far more ingrained in the offense than a traditional initiator.

Getting off the ball early invited movement. Beyond that, guys could be themselves instead of pigeonholed into traditional roles.

The rules were cut, space, probe for gaps or mismatches, and open up the bottom of the floor. Those baseline cuts were intended to be scoring cuts. They also emphasized turning the corner and pivoting from dribble handoffs to the paint. In Harris they had a player who excelled off the ball. In Kenneth Faried they had a dunker to roam the baseline.

Finch saw how smoothly Jokic grasped the concepts. Beyond that, the schemes allowed Jokic to improvise and manipulate. His processing speed was often the difference between an assist and a turnover.

When Harris came around for a dribble handoff, Jokic excelled at bypassing the initial dump-off, only to whip it late to Harris once the defense relaxed. It was a natural read that empowered Jokic's playmaking and catered to his intelligence.

The Nuggets morphed from a set-heavy offense to one that relied on principles and instincts. To Malone's credit, he blended those concepts with his preferred sets. During the 2015–16 season, Denver's offense ranked just 17th in the league and lacked any discernible identity. They had ample room to grow.

They also had a generational distributor waiting to be tapped.

"It's one thing identifying that, then you have to formulate well, 'How do we use this?'" Malone said.

He cited what transpired in Houston, as Steve Francis came around on the benefits of Yao Ming.

"Oh, shit," Malone said. "He's going to make my life easier."

There was a blueprint to follow within former Rockets coach Rick Adelman's corner offense. Just as he did in Sacramento with Chris Webber and Vlade Divac, Adelman implemented the action built around passing big men.

In Jokic, the coaching staff had an endless runway to experiment. They tinkered with the spacing around him and the shots that they could create for him. He was a three-level scorer and a constant threat, from anywhere on the floor, to thread an assist.

The default thinking at the time was that a stretch big had to *shoot* to stretch the floor. Finch was insistent that Jokic's playmaking—his vision and ballhandling—had the same effect on a defense. Wherever they plopped him, like a queen on a chessboard, gravity followed.

Jokic had a knack for exploiting opponents' vulnerabilities.

"Like water seeks a certain level," Finch said.

What the Nuggets intended to do that year wasn't groundbreaking by NBA standards. They recognized a player's superpower and sought to burnish it.

"It's always about how do you make your best players great," Finch said.

CHAPTER 26

THE SWITCH

At the beginning of the 2016–17 season, the Nuggets' depth chart was as sturdy as a Jenga tower.

They had blossoming centers (Jokic and Nurkic), numerous talented forwards (Gallinari, Faried, and Chandler), and a surplus of guards (Mudiay, Harris, and Murray) whom coach Michael Malone had to vet.

The starting lineup, throughout the first quarter of the season, was a potpourri of varying combinations. Their only consistency came in the frontcourt, where the Nuggets were committed to size.

More specifically, they had to decide whether a Jokic-Nurkic pairing could work.

The first eight games of the season saw Malone play Gallinari alongside the two Balkan big men.

"Obviously, the trend [in the NBA] is going away from what we do, but we're not worried about what the trends are," Malone told reporters after Denver's season-opening win against New Orleans. "We're going to do what we think is best for us, but within our game, you'll see a lot of different lineups."

The early returns weren't encouraging. Denver began the year just 3-5, with a middling offense and one that led the NBA in turnovers per game (18.4). In a nod to their size, they also led the league in rebounding, but it wasn't translating to wins. The same problem plagued Nurkic. He was playing well, averaging 12.5 points per game and 8.6 rebounds, but his success wasn't correlating to team success.

Coming off a sterling rookie season and an encouraging Olympic run, Jokic was . . . fine. He hovered around his rookie averages (10 points, 7 rebounds) despite playing out of position.

"It just wasn't meshing right," said Darrell Arthur, one of the many forwards who littered the roster.

Malone himself had a nagging suspicion about Jokic's play.

"He had an unbelievable rookie year playing the five," Malone told reporters. "I told him I feel like I've done him a disservice almost, exploring playing big. There are some good things with that, but I took a kid who had a great year last year, changed his position on him, and it hasn't been easy for him."

He conceded that the ploy, with Nikola at the four and Nurkic at the five, wasn't working. Worse, it was handicapping their best player and ultimately, Nikola felt, hurting the team.

"Coach, please, I can't do this," Jokic told Malone.

He asked to come off the bench.

Inside Malone's cramped office, it was obvious how heavy the decision weighed on Jokic. His face was expressive, his eyes were tearing. It was a raw, candid conversation, far from the light ones they'd shared in that same office.

The move was guided by Jokic's preference to play center.

"He's not a four," Malone said.

But it was also a selfless act.

Jameer Nelson had seen other guys volunteer to come off the bench before, but never anybody that young. Nikola was in just his second year in the NBA, trying to establish himself with the Nuggets and within the league as a whole.

Connelly had a sense of how good he was already, and didn't want him backing up anyone. But for the time being, Jokic had changed the equation. Even though the Nuggets hadn't formally made a decision on Jokic versus Nurkic, Connelly was bullish enough on Jokic to shun any trade inquiries.

The Clippers noticed Jokic's unique impact early. They offered a trade package involving multi-time All-Star Blake Griffin for Jokic, according to a source. The deal was intriguing, but the Nuggets weren't ready to cash in their Jokic ticket quite yet even if it meant landing a marquee forward.

The trade offer and subsequent rejection was an early referendum on Jokic's rising potential.

Nurkic remained in the starting lineup for the first 25 games of the season. The team, mired in losing streaks and the business end of blow-outs, fell to 9-16. Off the bench, Jokic was playing better than he had as a starter. He was averaging 11.6 points, nearly 8 rebounds, and 3.4 assists per game in 24 minutes a night. The freedom to roam, to create, uninhib-ited, off the bench at his natural position was liberating.

There was another unforeseen benefit to Jokic's selfless act. In vol-unteering to come off the bench, Jokic was building the backbone of his relationship with a precocious rookie: Jamal Murray.

The dribble handoffs were there from the start. It was the easiest ac-tion for Jokic to share the ball with Murray while simultaneously creating space for him going downhill. But that was day-one stuff. Soon Jokic was searching for Murray on the perimeter with his diagonal, crosscourt feeds. Then they started running more complicated sets for the pair, where de-coys would come off screens and Murray would follow with a secondary curl that yielded space and time to shoot.

Murray already had a hunter's mentality. He was more than happy to indulge Jokic's generosity.

When he wasn't stationed on the perimeter, Murray caught the cutting bug too. As long as he made himself available, the ball would be there. Those were the options afforded to Jokic *before* he asserted himself offen-sively and began searching for his shot. The dual threat opened up untold options, as long as they remembered where to deploy him.

It got to the point where Connelly would rib Finch for underutilizing him in the paint.

"He was so good at the top of the floor, we forgot about putting him on the bottom of the floor," Finch said.

Jokic, a center in name only, preferred to pass. Murray, technically a point guard, preferred to shoot.

"It was a perfect match," assistant coach Micah Nori said of the bud-ding duo.

On December 12, the Nuggets were finishing a grueling six-game road trip—long, even by NBA standards. They'd already lost to Utah, Brooklyn, and Washington and were wrapping up that evening in Dallas. The game was out of hand by halftime, meaning Jokic and Murray were in line for extended looks.

Living almost exclusively in the paint, Jokic scored 23 of his 27 in the second half. Murray had 8 points and 3 assists after the break. Early in the fourth quarter, after Jokic found Murray for a layup, the local broadcast began searching for silver linings.

"Look for the chemistry between Jokic and Murray," Altitude's Scott Hastings, a member of the Bad Boy Pistons, remarked.

It was an astute assessment from a basketball lifer. The starters were mostly an afterthought. Jokic finished with 27 points and 11 rebounds—his fifth double-double of the last six games.

In an otherwise meaningless game, for a team that was struggling with its identity, Connelly was encouraged by how Jokic and Murray finished the game.

"The fourth quarter looked like real basketball," he said.

Whatever we do, Jokic and Murray need to be featured, Connelly thought.

Beyond that, it was emblematic of the style of play the organization was trending toward. There was flow and rhythm and improvisation. It was unselfish basketball that proved difficult to guard. It was also infectious—an unpredictable brand of basketball that appealed to those running the sets.

As a veteran on the team, Jameer Nelson was consulted and gave his opinion of the situation. He was fond of both Jokic and Nurkic but one was better for the system they were trying to implement. Some of the coaching staff shared that opinion. Others were less convinced.

The way Denver wanted to play was free-flowing and positionless basketball. When Jokic played point-center, the Nuggets could flip the court upside down, running inverted pick-and-rolls with Jokic decoying as a guard.

With Nurkic, they looked like a traditional NBA offense, with a big man rolling toward the rim and offering an imposing post presence. Nurkic was a good passer, though not elite. He wasn't the shooting threat that Jokic was either.

No one in the league had a center like Jokic. Offensively, the possibilities were limitless. Because of that, he could almost always compromise opposing centers, or entire defenses.

"In the halfcourt, if you want to play him straight up, he's gonna give you forty," Nori said. "If you want to double him, he'll pass it every single time."

After the Dallas game, there was a growing sense that a change was imminent.

"What are we doing here?" said Finch, sharing a collective belief about the swap.

When Malone drove home that night, he was muttering to himself about his predicament. Jokic made first-team All-Rookie *as a center*. He was about the right things, he was unselfish, smart, and made everybody better.

"What am I doing?" he asked himself.

On December 15 against the Blazers, Malone filed a brand-new lineup card that featured Jokic in the starting lineup and Nurkic on the bench. There was no telling what the decision would yield, but it amounted to a seismic shift in the franchise. Not only had Malone made the decision to ride with the curious second-year center who seemed to galvanize the young group, but the rest of the organization followed suit.

"We all hitched our wagon to him," Nelson said.

CHAPTER 27

ROAD DOGS

Jokic had already convinced management that his talent was worth out-fitting, but who he was as a person solidified the organization's intuition.

"It was magnetic, his personality," Connelly said.

His smile was as ubiquitous as his jokes.

Jameer Nelson became close with Jokic over shared car rides to and from the airport. On every road trip for Jokic's first two years, Nelson was the driver.

"He was my Serbian little brother," he said.

Most of the conversation was about life, not necessarily basketball. On the way to the airport, Nelson was always plotting where he could secure a beer upon arrival in the upcoming city. Jokic was always invited but would respectfully decline.

Coming home from a road trip, Nelson preferred watching film before diving into an assessment of a game. That left plenty of time to con-verse. Nelson understood that basketball was secondary to, or at least a by-product of, the relationship.

A few years ago, after Nelson retired from the NBA, he caught up with Jokic on a call when the then-superstar surprised him with his honesty.

"He said, 'Hey, man, I wanna thank you for keeping me straight and not exposing me to the bad stuff,'" Nelson recalled.

Nelson deflected, "'Nah, man, you did the work.'"

But inside, Nelson knew he'd done his job as a veteran. Besides, it was easy to lead guys who wanted to be led.

As good as he was becoming, there was never any sense of entitlement. That made coaching Jokic a pleasure. Finch noticed it from the start. Out-side of the game itself and the work he put in off the court, he didn't take anything seriously. What resonated with Finch was how much the veterans respected him.

"I mean they loved him," he said.

They, of course, appreciated how unselfish he was and the fact that he consistently found them open looks.

During timeouts, while Malone commanded the huddle, Finch used to steal a knowing glance at Mike Miller, who was always thinking the same thing about Jokic.

How good is this guy?

Jokic's bond with assistant Micah Nori was built on humor. If Jokic didn't understand English slang, he wasn't embarrassed to ask. That might have meant a word or phrase from the locker room, or maybe something he heard while binge-watching *Friends* or Kevin Hart stand-ups. His sly, observant sense of humor was always there.

"He loves sarcasm where you say something to someone, and he catches it, but they don't," Nori said.

Nori used to stand between Jokic and Wilson Chandler in the locker room and was privy to their dynamics.

The Nuggets had the Kings on the schedule, which meant a heavy dose of DeMarcus Cousins in the paint. Jokic had been entrusted with the starting center position, and Chandler was paired alongside him, the starting forward in the frontcourt. Because of Nikola's defensive limitations, Chandler drew the Cousins assignment despite being undersized.

Jokic leaned over to Chandler's locker room stall and deadpanned his remorse: "Sorry."

There was a rotating cast of starting-caliber forwards, from Chandler to Gallinari, to Kenneth Faried to Darrell Arthur. Even rookie Juancho Hernangomez drew a few starting nods that season.

Chandler recognized the unique way Jokic's presence spaced the floor and understood the multidimensional offense he unlocked. Still, at one point during that season, Chandler was starting alongside numerous guys who could score and felt he'd have more room to operate if he was coming off the bench.

Almost immediately he regretted his decision.

"Fuck, why did I do that?" he said. "I wanted to play with him."

Jokic made the game easier, but Chandler learned it wasn't that simple. In order to optimize Jokic—and himself—he needed to think like Jokic thought. He realized he had to make himself presentable and, therefore, accountable. When there was a cut to make, he had to seize it. He had to learn to read the floor like their conductor.

Jokic was among Chandler's biggest advocates. A slashing, shooting big man, he offered the potential of a lethal four-five combination.

Chandler recalled one team meeting where Malone asked each player to define his role. That wasn't such a simple task with the evolving nature of the team, not to mention the overlapping skill sets of Denver's bevvy of forwards.

Chandler's attitude was laid-back. He wasn't eager to say much, or even worse, say too much. He tried to downplay his role, even though he was in the midst of a career year. Jokic didn't let him get away with it.

"Joker was like, 'Nah, nah, you're way better than that, what are you talking about?'" Chandler said.

There was young, budding potential in Jokic, Murray, and Harris but that talent needed to be nurtured. The Nuggets' veterans taught their young core how to be professionals even when the losing started to snowball and fans remained indifferent.

"They all helped us grow up," said Harris, citing the veteran examples of Nelson, Miller, Gallinari, and Chandler. "We were all young and didn't necessarily know what the fuck was going on."

CHAPTER 28

SAVANT

The date—December 15, 2016—took on special lore as the Nuggets galvanized around their unquestioned leader. In Jokic they had a selfless, playmaking center who always put the team ahead of himself.

Whatever he accomplished on an individual level was inconsequential to the team's success.

Tim Connelly and Michael Malone had no idea what was to come, but if nothing else ever materialized around their curious experiment, at least the Nuggets could play as they'd envisioned. In Jokic, Denver would have structure, a quality NBA teams search for years to achieve. Players understood their roles and responsibilities. There was a pecking order and a maturity to their approach.

Jusuf Nurkic struggled with the changing dynamics as he racked up DNP-CDs, basketball parlance for "did not play—coach's decision." The Nuggets won their first three games after the swap with an offense that teetered on devastating. It was so good—their lowest score of the winning streak was 117—it almost rendered their defense immaterial.

The only thing that undermined Jokic's full assumption of the offense was his fouls. He had a habit of picking up unnecessary, ticky-tack fouls that were born of laziness more than intention. He picked up five fouls in each of his first two games in the starting lineup, which kept his minutes in check.

In the third game, against a familiar opponent, Dallas, Jokic authored a resounding showing. It was an emphatic validation of the switch. He dominated mismatches and exploited the paint. He picked-and-popped, finding his shots within the flow of the offense. He finished with a career-high tying 27 points. He owned the glass with 17 rebounds—eight more than the entire Mavs' starting lineup combined. And when he wasn't imposing himself in the paint, he was creating for his teammates. He finished one assist shy of his first career triple-double.

"It doesn't really matter," he said after the win. "The game is more important than your name."

With just one foul, he kept his emotions in check.

"[Malone] told me he was going to beat me if I made more stupid fouls," Jokic said. "I listened."

A few weeks later, with international soccer stars Thierry Henry and Per Mertesacker sitting courtside, the Nuggets steamrolled the Pacers in one of the league's showcase games in London. The lopsided 140–112 win was a harbinger of what the Nuggets were becoming—an offensive juggernaut.

"Nikola looked like an offensive savant," Connelly said.

He diced Myles Turner (another of the elite prospects from that 2014 Hoop Summit showcase), then outlasted Indiana's defense with incessant, unrelenting pressure. Any time the ball was in his hands, he was liable to pick the Pacers apart. As soon as Indiana scored, it was vulnerable. Jokic whipped a full-court pass to Harris with 2.7 seconds left in the first half before any of the Pacers' players crossed halfcourt. He was an all-encompassing offensive nightmare, with another near triple-double on an international stage. Under Jokic's direction, the Nuggets' offense rose to an improvisational art form.

According to Nori, Jokic had a unique brand of unselfishness.

"He will pass to the open jersey," he said, as opposed to feeding a specific teammate—a standard players espouse though rarely reach.

In making the right pass, players came to expect the ball from Jokic as soon as they were open. The effect of bypassing the *right* play was potentially costly. Next time, a teammate might not expect a pass, a miscommunication leading to a turnover. Worse, what if a player second-guessed his confidence?

Jokic's process was far simpler. The right play was the easiest to spot. His approach elicited an up-tempo, exciting brand of basketball.

"He reminds me of Magic Johnson," Hall of Fame point guard Isiah Thomas said during the Nuggets' international broadcast. Jokic's flair and his joy were palpable.

Malone grew up in gyms alongside his father, former NBA coach Brendan Malone. What he saw, even at Jokic's size, were shades of Showtime.

"You could see there was something special about Nikola," Malone said. "You see Magic Johnson."

In early February, amid an uptick in wins, Jokic finally secured the first triple-double of his career. The landmark assist came via another full-court heave, this time to Faried, before the Bucks had recalibrated on defense. At the time, his 20-point, 12-rebound, 11-assist line was a novel achievement and something worth celebrating. Malone retrieved the ball before Jokic had his teammates all autograph it.

In the middle of the locker room, Jokic crossed one more frontier when he embraced Malone.

"I was naked and I hugged him," Jokic said. "That's true."

In the two months since Jokic started conducting Denver's attack, the Nuggets' offense became elite. They had the second-best offensive rating and were second in the NBA in assists over that span. The only team ahead of them, in both categories, was the vaunted Warriors. Their averages before tailoring their offense around Jokic were 17th and 19th, respectively. Even their 16-15 record with Jokic as a starter was encouraging.

"It was a defining moment for us," Nuggets wing Will Barton told The Athletic's Nick Kosmider. "It hit right away. It just freed everyone up. It allowed everyone to play the way we needed to play to be successful."

Less than two weeks before the trade deadline, Jokic erupted on one of the league's most hallowed stages.

"I remember that time he had forty in the Garden," Harris said. "I was like, 'Oh, shit.' That's when they had Porzingis and Melo."

During the Nuggets' lone visit to Madison Square Garden his rookie season, Jokic had a modest impact in 19 minutes. One year later, he destroyed New York's frontcourt with an array of spin moves and floaters that left the Knicks' big men swiping at air. His dominance was even more debilitating because it came within the flow of Denver's offense. Of his 17 made field goals that night, 10 were assisted by his teammates. In a game featuring former Nugget stalwart Carmelo Anthony and highly touted European forward Kristaps Porzingis, Jokic was by far the best player on the court.

Malone, a proud native of Queens, felt the performance signified Jokic's arrival.

"The Garden is a special place," Malone told reporters. "When you do it here, you kind of cement yourself in terms of the NBA and being a real player."

Jokic's ascendance gave the Nuggets a sense of direction.

In establishing a culture, Connelly needed guys who wanted to be there and supported the direction they'd chosen. Nurkic saw the writing on the wall.

"I believe you can develop guards together. But two centers? No way," Nurkic said to *Sports Illustrated*. "I was never on the same page with the coach and the front office. It just came to the point where I needed to go. My career was on the line."

Connelly was reluctant to trade him, but the situation was untenable. The Nuggets had a defined future, and Nurkic wasn't a part of it. The Nuggets reached a deal to send the disgruntled center and a first-round pick to Portland for Mason Plumlee, an athletic playmaking big man.

After their failed "Balkan Big" experiment, there was even some discussion that Plumlee might be able to pair alongside Jokic in the frontcourt.

"It's never fun to trade anybody," Connelly said.

CHAPTER 29

SUPERSTAR IS BORN

Plumlee had been impressed with Jokic during their prior matchups but didn't realize how overwhelming his impact was until he arrived.

Like a stock gaining momentum, "the league still was figuring out how good he was," Plumlee said.

Plumlee saw quickly what the rest of the league would come to realize: everything came easy to Jokic.

His lines—19 points, 16 rebounds, and 10 assists, for example—didn't seem to require much exertion. Plumlee wouldn't monitor stats throughout the game, yet when he checked the box scores after games, he was dumbfounded.

"It was amazing to see," he said.

And the numbers never told the whole story. Often it was the context within those numbers that was more interesting. Plumlee enjoyed watching how Jokic manipulated a matchup, or how he distorted a defense that prioritized stopping him. Nothing seemed preordained. His success was always a matter of process.

Still vying for the postseason late in March, the Nuggets were hosting the defending champion Cavaliers. Jokic was matched up against Cleveland big men Tristan Thompson and Kevin Love most of the night before he drew a fortuitous matchup against LeBron James late in the third quarter.

James, admittedly undersized against Jokic, was physical with the second-year center and did his best to swarm him. Jokic faked left then swung back to his right hand, burrowing James deeper and deeper into the paint.

"Joker just kept going and getting to his hook, and the arena was going crazy," Plumlee said.

He turned and lofted a short hook shot over James's outstretched hand that dropped gently through the net. The Nuggets won, convincingly, over Cleveland, and Jokic's seminal highlight was secured.

"I'm sure Nikola will be showing that to his grandkids many years from now," Malone said after the game.

In the postgame locker room, Jokic was nonchalant about the moment.

Cross-matched against the smaller James, Jokic wasn't being patronizing to arguably the game's greatest player as much as he was acknowledging the size discrepancy between the two.

"That's a mismatch for us," he said, without an ounce of arrogance.

He wasn't belittling James, but the remark did reveal an inner confidence that Jokic had brewing. He wasn't intimidated by anyone.

Two and a half weeks later, as Denver flirted with the Western Conference's No. 8 seed and a playoff berth, Russell Westbrook effectively ended the Nuggets' season.

Only minutes after Westbrook broke Oscar Robertson's NBA record for most triple-doubles in a season—Westbrook's 42nd of the season drew a standing ovation from the Nuggets' crowd—the league's MVP drained a 36-foot buzzer-beating prayer to extinguish Denver's postseason chances. It was a devastating sequence, featuring an improbable fourth-quarter collapse on their home floor.

Amid the bedlam, Jokic picked up a dubious flagrant foul against Westbrook that underscored the dynamics between the established star and the plucky center. Leveled with the penalty, Jokic smirked.

In the stands, Nikola's oldest brother, Strahinja, seethed. Security intervened before he could confront the official who'd called the questionable foul.

As swiftly as the end of the season came, the gains the Nuggets made were undeniable. They had a newfound identity built around a selfless, fearless playmaker, which was more than they could say a year earlier. In entrenching himself in the starting lineup, Jokic also finished second to Giannis Antetokounmpo for the league's Most Improved Player award.

Jokic's flashes were compelling. His competitive spirit, in only his second season, was equally as alluring. Asked by the *Denver Post*'s Mark

Kiszla whether he felt he could become a superstar, carrying a similar burden as other franchise pillars, Jokic demurred.

"I don't think so, to be honest," said Jokic. "I mean, look at the guys who are superstars: LeBron James, Kawhi Leonard. I don't know if I can be a superstar."

Through his thick accent, Jokic honed his dry, biting sense of humor, which often deliberately clouded his intent. During the same conversation, Jokic claimed he wasn't scared of anybody in the NBA.

"Why be afraid? I am playing a game of basketball," said Jokic. "I am scared of only one person in my life. That's my brother. Have you seen him?"

CHAPTER 30

WES UNSELD JR.

Wes Unseld Jr. arrived from Orlando in the summer of 2015 on the eve of the Nuggets' first Summer League practice.

He was getting settled on Michael Malone's coaching staff just as Nikola was learning what life in the NBA entailed.

"Nothing special," Unseld recalled of the gangly, second-round pick.

Unseld's job was to help Summer League coach Micah Nori; neither viewed Jokic as a priority. Unseld saw him as a traditional big, a plodding, screening, rolling center who might be able to take up some space. By no means did they plan to call any plays for him.

But because he was a rookie coming into Denver's system, Unseld, later the head coach of the Washington Wizards, naturally intended to spend more time with him. What he found was a self-deprecating, down-to-earth guy with a quirky sense of humor. Like Will Ferrell in *Elf*, everything about the real-world NBA astonished him.

According to Unseld, Jokic couldn't believe he had access to the facilities any time he wanted.

Then there were the more mundane realizations that are customary in professional sports.

"He was just amazed about how much food we had," Unseld said.

Jokic always sat in the front of the bus with the coaches, either out of habit or because, Unseld surmised, there was an external motivation. After shootarounds, there was always a spread waiting for the players back at the hotel.

Jokic wanted to be first off the bus.

"So he could get to the omelet station," Unseld said.

Early in his career, it was hard not to find Jokic's childlike nature endearing.

One morning, Malone was fed up with his team and didn't like the energy they'd brought to shootaround. Worse, they were scheduled to face defending champion Golden State that evening.

Malone, who could be every bit as emotional as Nikola, kicked the entire team out of the gym.

"I said, 'Fuck this, balls in, you guys get the fuck out of here, go home,'" Malone said. "'You guys don't want to be here, you're not ready to play, we're gonna get our ass kicked tonight.'"

Jokic didn't know if Malone was serious.

"The look on Nikola's face . . ." Unseld said.

He was dumbfounded.

"What do we do?" he asked.

"I'm like, 'Go home,'" Unseld replied.

Later that night, the Nuggets knocked off the defending champions.

The relationship between Unseld and Jokic developed naturally. Both were cerebral about basketball, preferring to indulge the topic from an intellectual standpoint. But oftentimes the more engaging conversations revolved around family or politics. In Jokic, Unseld discovered a laid-back, curious, and intelligent twenty-year-old. In Unseld, Jokic discovered a humble, hardworking assistant.

When it came to Denver's defense, which Unseld was responsible for, the discussions became organic. The weakest point in Jokic's game became an avenue for exploration.

"I was always on him about his perceived lack of defense, even to his own admission," Unseld said.

Jokic wasn't a rim protector, but there were ways to mitigate his defensive vulnerabilities. They just had to discover them. Within those film sessions, Unseld began to see things through Jokic's perspective. Inevitably, their relationship deepened.

Unseld came to believe that Jokic had a "special" quality that could potentially change the Nuggets' trajectory. Every few games, there'd be moments that stuck.

The big-to-big passing wasn't normal, Unseld thought. *Neither was Jo-kic's comfort level while ball-handling in the open court. The full-court passes weren't unlike the ones Unseld's dad, a Hall of Famer, used to throw.*

The Nurkic decision wasn't easy, though behind Jokic, he believed Denver's ceiling was higher.

In the 57 games the Nuggets played after inserting Jokic into the starting lineup during the 2016–17 season, they had the most prolific offense in the NBA. Simultaneously, they had the league's most porous defense. It was a boom-or-bust strategy. Denver's 114.4 points per game barely outpaced the 112.2 it was allowing.

That summer, Denver's coaching staff did a full audit of its defensive approach. They studied the top defensive teams in every area, including pick-and-roll, catch-and-shoot, post-up, etc. Just as the Nuggets' front office was now able to ask germane questions about a player's efficacy alongside Jokic, the coaching staff was able to scheme with him in mind.

At the time, teams tended to guard the pick-and-roll with drop coverage—planting the big man deeper down the floor so as not to be exposed on the perimeter off a switch. But Jokic felt vulnerable with a guard charging downhill toward him. Guards had space to maneuver, and that alignment allowed the offense to dictate its level of aggression.

The only chance Jokic felt he had was to play up in the pick-and-roll and suffocate the ball handler. The onus was on him to squeeze the action, which catered to his length, anticipation, and intelligence. Of course, that took energy and stamina that most big men wouldn't, or couldn't, exert.

The overriding conclusion was that the Nuggets couldn't sit back and let teams exploit him. If Jokic could get there, he could read the ball handler, deflect a pass, and interrupt the sequence.

"We need to be more aggressive, because it suits Nikola," Unseld determined.

They wanted to put the ball handler under duress and force him into earlier decisions. Behind the play, the Nuggets' defense needed to be connected, rotating to the space Jokic had vacated. The scramble-and-help situations the Nuggets played before left their defense compromised, especially from the 3-point line.

Heading into the next season, they prioritized asking more of guys individually, while implementing the fundamental pick-and-roll change.

That decision, and those discussions, were born of Jokic's relationship with Wes.

On off days, Unseld used to be in his office, breaking down film and preparing game plans for the team's next opponent. More often than not, after Jokic came into the building and got his work done, he would drop into Unseld's office and just sit there. For hours.

Why?

"Just to try to annoy the hell out of me," Unseld said.

CHAPTER 31

OGI

Before he became an assistant coach in Denver, Ogi Stojakovic ran a basketball academy in Belgrade.

His energy and personality were infectious. Connelly hired the fellow Serbian a year before Jokic reached the NBA.

Ogi didn't know Jokic personally, but he was aware of the multifaceted, rising star at Mega. He also knew about his habits in the gym.

"He wasn't a hard worker," said Stojakovic, whose job it became to turn him into one.

Ogi's father was a weapons engineer, whose thinking and tinkering trickled down to his son. When Jokic arrived, talented and stubborn, Ogi was presented with a shapeless ball of clay waiting to be molded.

It was his job to reach him, push him in uncomfortable ways, test him, and develop him. Their relationship, which permitted that growth, came first.

Ogi first connected with him during the summertime, before Jokic had even come to Denver. He made it a point to get to know him.

"I had a vision about him," Stojakovic said. "He didn't have that vision."

Hardly anybody did. But when Stojakovic watched Jokic in Belgrade, he saw wisps of Marc Gasol's passing and glimpses of Dirk Nowitzki's touch. For an atypical athlete, Ogi tried to establish how to maximize his impact on the game. The first tweak came within Jokic's shooting motion, raising his elbow ever so slightly.

"Our main thing, he was naturally good at his touches around the rim, and then we start to build all his technique and all his skills according to his talent," he said. "He's a great passer, right, so in order to be a great passer, you need to be a great shooter. You need to connect defense."

If passing was Jokic's superpower, then, Ogi thought, they needed to optimize it. By raising his elbow on his jumper, that dragged opposing centers a few more inches outside of the passing lanes that he could then exploit. They wanted to force defenders into longer closeouts that would further destabilize opponents.

Then, recognizing his unique touch, their focus turned to his floaters. Using either hand, Jokic could devastate a defense with his timing and feel. As if playing on a Pop-A-Shot machine, Jokic would float the basketball in from untold angles.

"His floater was so unique," said Karnisovas, who delighted in watching his early flashes. The floaters in particular left Karnisovas wondering whether anyone had honed his unique touch or whether it was just innate.

While Ogi explored what he had in Jokic, the stubborn rookie groused.

"Like all the shots I kinda make, I'm doing that since my Day 1 here," Jokic told the *Denver Post*. "I was mad at him, like, 'Why I'm doing this? I'm never going to shoot like this.' All the floaters, all the one legs, all the midranges. I never thought I'm gonna be a midrange guy because I thought I'm just gonna roll, floater, and I'm gonna maybe shoot a couple threes."

But Ogi didn't let him settle. He had a vision beyond what Jokic had for himself.

Forward Darrell Arthur was privy to that blueprint. During pregame or before practices, Arthur took part in their shared workouts.

"Him and Ogi used to bump heads a lot," Arthur said, acknowledging Jokic hated the pregame workouts.

Early on, Jokic felt there was a ceiling to what he could accomplish. After all, this was a prospect who was simply happy to be in the NBA.

"I hated him," Jokic said. "We argue, we fight all the time. Beginning of the third year, I was young, and I was just not . . . I didn't know what I'm gonna do, but he always knew. He always wanted me to be the best I can."

Once, when Jokic arrived a few minutes late for a workout, Ogi told him that was it and they were finished for the day.

During another early workout, Ogi noticed Jokic's energy was low. He tried different drills to engage him or different shooting competitions to spark his interest. It wasn't translating.

"I was like 'Okay, we're done,'" Ogi said, ending the workout before it even got started. If he wasn't mentally there, Ogi had no interest in coddling him.

"Both of us we get mad at each other," Ogi said. "We barely spoke for two weeks."

Given what Ogi knew of Jokic previously, there was a personal mandate to build good professional habits. In doing so, he taught Jokic about accountability. After two weeks, the two stubborn Serbians were back in the gym as if nothing had happened.

Unfazed by the friction, Ogi deemed it normal. Jokic's talent, coupled with his intelligence, fostered a sense of inflexibility in his approach. He believed his way was the right way, which wasn't necessarily the worst perspective. Without that resolve, Ogi said, Jokic wouldn't have been the player he was in the first place. Ogi's job was to shape that conviction.

"He has that stubbornness," Karnisovas said, which was frustrating when the Nuggets tried to negotiate with him but a positive attribute for a competitor. Without any hope of changing him, Karnisovas rationalized that the competitive aspect to Jokic was something they could work with.

Ogi viewed it from a different lens.

"You want to have those kinds of players because it's challenging for you as a coach how to enhance them," he said.

With a player as smart as Jokic, he tried to keep their workouts interesting and challenging. If his last workout was low-energy, Ogi would begin the next one with a new drill, or maybe a soccer drill. Anything to change the routine.

"He's always thinking about, like, today, we were doing something different than yesterday," Jokic said. "He always tries to put something new to give us different perspectives of what we can do in some kind of situations."

Ogi also learned that he needed to be as honest and straightforward with Jokic as possible. He was too smart to be anything other than direct. There were plenty of moments Jokic didn't want to hear Ogi's coaching. But after a few days of consideration, he would inevitably come around to Ogi's vision.

That was the start of their rocky relationship. Over time, it smoothed into a bond as close as any Jokic has outside of, or maybe including, his family.

"He's like a big brother, like a mentor, father, he's like a really good friend," Jokic told the *Denver Post*. "He's really everything."

O

Part of Ogi's offseason routine involved traveling to Sombor for more intense, focused work with Jokic.

After Jokic's second season, in 2016–17, Ogi was there, in the town's rickety practice gym, alongside Jokic's two brothers, his godfather, Nebojsa, and Jokic himself. It was just the five of them, working in solitude, to sharpen what was already a devastating skill set.

"We worked *real* hard," Stojakovic said.

There were two sessions per day, each lasting an hour and a half to two hours. The emphasis that offseason was on stretching his range from the 3-point line. His strength down low, and his touch in the midrange, already were elite *before* accounting for his passing. As a 3-point threat, Jokic had the potential to be unstoppable. His second season he took only 1.9 3-pointers per game, converting less than a third of them. It was a weakness, although one they intended to correct.

By the end of his third season, Jokic was shooting nearly double the 3-point attempts at close to a 40 percent clip. But those results began with the work inside that run-down, crimson and beige practice gym in Sombor.

The court's white 3-point line was far short of an NBA 3-point line, so he honed his perimeter shot from a full step outside the demarcated lines.

With tucked-in shirts and a foam blocking stick meant to replicate the reach of an NBA center, the crew worked tirelessly inside the paint and on his midrange. There was ballhandling and finishing through contact and the type of sweat equity that fans, especially of Jokic's, rarely saw.

In red Nike shoes and matching red shorts, Jokic honed his touch around the restricted area as his brother, Nemanja, leapt with the blocking stick in hand. He finished off the right foot, then the left, then lofted soft floaters, at odd angles, from both hands. He spliced in left-handed floaters off his right foot, and vice versa. The funky finishes that became customary in the NBA weren't happenstance.

The fadeaways were reminiscent of one of Ogi's archetypes for Jokic. The way he tilted back and released from an unguardable angle looked like vintage Dirk.

Shown a picture of their workout, Gary Harris said it reminded him of someone else: Larry Bird.

The shots that Jokic once couldn't see were becoming second nature to him. As a seven-footer with a guard's intuition, they honed his handle in the pick-and-roll, with the goal of making him a threat from *everywhere*. Over time, and with the advent of his playmaking, Ogi added one more piece to Jokic's NBA profile: Steve Nash. He didn't play at Nash's break-neck pace, but his decisions were as precise as the two-time MVP's.

"That's how I mentally projected him," Stojakovic said. "Now I can say he's unique."

From the start, Ogi's goal was to enhance his foundation. Jokic was talented enough to decide how to wield his gifts.

"My job is to show him the notes," Ogi said. "He creates his own music."

Denver's strength coach, Steve Hess, was in Sombor that summer as well. No one, at least from the team's strength staff, had any idea what type of equipment Jokic had at home.

"The gym is backwards," Hess said. "The facilities are like backwards."

But what stuck with Hess was how tight the family was. Strahinja and Nemanja Jokic attended—and participated in—all the workouts that Nikola did. If they went to the track to work on speed and agility, the brothers were there. The same thing happened when they flipped tires in a field. For two to three hours every single day, they pummeled Nikola's body and built it up.

The support Hess saw, and the camaraderie he felt as part of the Jokic clan, were unparalleled. To decompress, the crew took a boat out on a canal and jumped in. Sombor was Jokic's sanctuary, and the river, no matter if he was fishing, swimming, or dining beside it, was his space to rejuvenate.

O

When he was on walks with his wife, Ogi's mind used to wander.

"Okay, stop talking to Nikola," she'd tell him in a stern, irritated voice.

But the line between player and coach had already faded. They were attached at the hip. Fortunately for Ogi, so were their families.

"How much he helps me on the court, he helps me off the court just to get out of the basketball," Jokic said. "We hang out, for real. When we have a day off, my family is always with his family."

They routinely traded—and still do, to this day—dinners at each other's homes since dining in public became a hassle. Together they could talk about books, or politics, or "normal" things as Ogi liked to say.

Ogi's favorite moments with him weren't from a game, or even from the countless hours refining his technique in the practice gym. They were from the conversations, with beers in hand, as two regular Serbians who happened to be linked through basketball.

During shared family dinners, they tried not to talk about their job, but inevitably, one would ask who was playing that night and the other would check the TV listings.

"We always get back to basketball, which sucks," Ogi said. "And then our wives get mad."

Jokic has intentionally kept his circle small. Only a few people have any idea what drives him or what he's like behind his reluctantly public persona. After initially butting heads, Ogi became one of them.

What people underestimated, according to Stojakovic, was his competitiveness. When Nikola took on one of Ogi's daughters in a kids' game, he didn't want her to win.

"She's like six years old," Ogi said.

It was the same playing spikeball, volleyball, or Ping-Pong. He hated to lose. And the emotion he showed when he did, according to Ogi, was evidence of how much he cared.

His makeup—their makeup, really—was a product of how they were raised in Serbia and informed the type of player, and competitor, he became in the NBA.

"Either you're a colonel or you're dead," Stojakovic said, invoking a phrase stemming from the Balkan Wars.

It meant either you're a winner or a loser, with no in-between, and it roughly defined Jokic's ethos. It didn't matter how he won, as long as he did.

"I think at the end of the day, it's competition," Karnisovas said. "Winning drives him. He always mentioned winning. . . . That said, he still wants to do what he wants to do."

Competition was his fuel. And within that, the team was celebrated, not the individual.

The other principle Jokic was taught growing up aligned with his humility.

"In our culture, when you talk about yourself that you are good, that's bad," Stojakovic said.

Culturally, he learned that nothing else mattered other than winning or losing. And once he learned to win, his natural inclination was to deflect. By virtue of his upbringing, Jokic was unlike any other rising star in the NBA.

CHAPTER 32

FOUNDATION

As Jokic refined his doughy frame and fashioned fadeaways in homage to Dirk, the Nuggets' front office landed their biggest free agent in franchise history.

In signing Paul Millsap to a three-year, $90 million deal, the Nuggets acquired a player they hoped would expedite their growth into a playoff contender. Millsap, who came to Denver on the heels of four consecutive All-Star appearances in Atlanta, was a playmaking veteran who would, in theory, stabilize a reeling defense. Offensively, the Nuggets felt a frontcourt pairing of Jokic and Millsap would be devastating and similar to the impact Millsap made playing alongside Al Horford.

"We feel in Nikola and Paul, we have the most talented, most unselfish, best playmaking frontcourt in the NBA," Nuggets coach Michael Malone said.

Millsap, a second-round pick in 2006, was another low-maintenance, high-character player the Nuggets coveted for years. That he chose Denver—historically not an NBA destination in free agency—validated their direction. The Nuggets felt that in Jokic, Jamal Murray, and Gary Harris there was a young, talented core worth cultivating.

"Paul Millsap was the grown-up that helped the young kids to grow up," said Nuggets assistant and future Nets coach Jordi Fernandez.

Even as Millsap helped the Hawks become perennial playoff contenders in the East, he took notice of Jokic's unique impact in the West.

"He's definitely a big part of why I came here," Millsap said of Jokic. "The things that he's able to do I think will help my game. And I think the things that I'm able to do and the experience I have, I think I'll be able to help his game."

In Jokic, Millsap, and Wilson Chandler, the Nuggets had excellent positional size. In Harris they had a budding two-way guard recently signed to a lucrative extension, and in Jamal Murray and Emmanuel Mudiay they had healthy competition at point guard. Will Barton provided scoring off the bench, and Juancho Hernangomez and Malik Beasley offered young depth. Beyond some roster imbalance at forward (Kenneth Faried wasn't happy about his relegation to the bench), there were outlines of a roster fashioned around Jokic.

"He's the type of player we want to build around, and the type of guy we want to build around," Connelly said at the time. "His unique skill set allows us to look for certain types of players to complement his brand— cutters, guys who make quick decisions, shooters."

A season after narrowly missing the playoffs, there was palpable buzz about a return to the postseason. But in a new role, playing next to an All-Star forward and serving as the face of the Nuggets' renaissance, Jokic took a moment to find himself. In the season-opening loss, he made just three shots. In their next game, a blowout win over the Kings, Jokic didn't score in 30 minutes (though his +21 was a game high).

"If I don't score, who cares?" Jokic said afterward. "The more important thing is that we win. I'm here to help my team win. That's it."

His relationship with statistics was never complicated.

When told he was still the team leader in rebounds and assists, according to the *Denver Post*'s Gina Mizell, Jokic "made a fist, pulled it down to his chest, and whispered 'Yes!'"

A few weeks later, with his initial scoring malaise behind him, Jokic erupted for a career-high 41 points against the Nets.

If there was one game that embodied the exhaustive offseason work Jokic had done with Ogi, his godfather, and his brothers, it was this one. His shooting touch (16-for-25) was astonishing, his array of shots unparalleled. The floaters, like the ones he buried over his brother's foam stick in Sombor, or the midrange looks he never felt he needed, were all there.

"Obviously, the way he's been shooting the ball from 3-point range this year has been magnificent," Malone remarked, alluding to his dedicated summer work beyond the arc.

When Jokic checked out of the game that night, the jubilant Pepsi

Center crowd showered him with "MVP" chants. Unaccustomed to the adulation, Jokic called it "funny."

It was one good game, Jokic said—his stock answer for when he had a good game. When a reporter pushed back, insisting the crowd was being serious, Jokic tried to deflect again. In his best impersonation of his namesake, Jokic cracked, "Why so serious?"

CHAPTER 33

JUANCHO

Juancho Hernangomez arrived from Spain as a spry twenty-year-old, eager to prove he was worthy of a first-round pick.

Hernangomez was part of the 2016 draft class, a sweet-shooting forward whom the Nuggets took eight picks after Jamal Murray. His selection was the latest example of Denver's international bent. As a rookie he shot 40 percent from the 3-point line and showed good instincts as a rebounder. But on a roster loaded with veteran forwards, Hernangomez's opportunities were limited.

As fellow Europeans, Jokic and Hernangomez gravitated toward one another. Jokic had gone through the same growing pains as Hernangomez only a year earlier. He knew what it was like to arrive in the NBA a foreigner without any bearings. Jokic had his two brothers; Hernangomez had his, Willy, though he was trying to establish himself with the Knicks.

Their similarities, in valuing family and cherishing basketball, built the foundation for their friendship.

"It was like family," Hernangomez said. "Probably he was my best friend basketball-wise in [the] NBA, for sure."

By the 2017–18 season (Jokic's third, Hernangomez's second), Jokic was cemented as the franchise cornerstone, while Hernangomez was struggling to crack the rotation of an ascendant team. As a first-round pick, he felt pressure to live up to the franchise's investment in him.

When that weighed him down, Jokic was there. He offered advice, support, and a model for how to succeed. Despite Jokic's success, Hernangomez saw how a good game didn't elevate his friend's mood, just as a poor performance didn't leave him downtrodden. The separation Jokic established helped protect him mentally and gave him a blueprint to share with Hernangomez.

"I finished the game playing bad, and I was probably getting home really mad," Hernangomez said. "Next day, [I felt like] I gotta work even harder. He was like, 'Next game.'"

If Hernangomez was emotional, Jokic was steady.

"He always told me to be ready," Hernangomez said.

Juancho's minutes came and went, his 3-point shot proving as difficult to master as his emotions. But he was a proficient cutter, with good size. Naturally, Jokic turned him into a viable, better player.

"He probably got me my second NBA contract because I play really good with him," he said.

As teammates, they became inseparable. As competitors, they were dogged.

Nikola and Juancho played Ping-Pong at least three or four times a week. Jokic won, according to Hernangomez, about 60 percent of the time, which was still a better winning percentage than most enjoyed against him.

They'd humor the team's longtime and beloved equipment manager, Sparky Gonzales, but he was just table-tennis chum.

"Sparky was terrible," Hernangomez said.

Jamal Murray was an upgrade but still wasn't among the team's elite.

"Jamal tried to be the best, but no way," Hernangomez said.

Their games—anything from soccer to simply tossing a football— underlined Jokic's competitive streak.

The ease with which Jokic navigated practices grated on Hernangomez. For average NBA players like him, they had to put in a lot of extra hours studying film or working on their craft.

"He did everything so easy," Hernangomez said.

According to Hernangomez, Jokic's talent and his brain differentiated him among his peers.

"You tell him one play, and he remembers it all year," he said.

When they played against other teams, Hernangomez said, Jokic knew what plays they'd be running.

His intelligence and his lust to win were what truly defined him. And his humor.

Jokic got little value out of the practices and shootarounds since he already grasped the concepts they were running.

"At least early, I don't think this is the case now, but early, the game came so easy to him, and he wasn't as interested in practice," Mason Plumlee said. "He was getting triple-doubles, playing so well, so it was like, 'Why am I gonna come in to practice and bust my ass?'"

More often than not, he coasted.

"He didn't really play for real in practice," Nuggets point guard Monte Morris said. "And when he did play serious, it's a wrap."

As such, Jokic always found ways to entertain himself and his teammates.

"He was like, 'Who am I, who am I?'" Juancho said, making his teammates guess which one he was mocking.

Plumlee was a career 56 percent free-throw shooter, and Jokic found ample ground to tease Plumlee about his abrupt shooting form. Jokic found similar fodder in Trey Lyles's mechanical free throws. The same went for Torrey Craig, whose brutish drives to the basket were rarely graceful. If you'd been playing a selfish brand of basketball lately, it only increased your chances of getting mocked.

"It would be the funniest thing," Plumlee said.

"He was always doing some shit, like missing or [reenacting] turnovers," Juancho said.

Jokic would walk like his coaches, talk like his coaches, before zeroing in on the easiest, most emotional target: Malone.

"He would do me," Malone said, crossing his arms and staring skyward in disbelief like Joe Pesci in *My Cousin Vinny*.

"Oh, fuck," Malone groused, imitating Jokic's impression of himself.

It was one of the clever ways Jokic regulated the locker room.

On road trips, Juancho was part of Jokic's international supper club. Aside from those two, Vlatko Cancar (Slovenian) and the team's two Brazilian strength coaches, Felipe Eichenberger and Claus Souza, would always dine at Fogo de Chao, a Brazilian steak house. The routine became the group's family away from family. Basketball was rarely the topic du jour, and the dinners became an escape from their professional obligations or their rigorous travel schedules.

"Don't mess around, get the nice ribs," the two Brazilians, affectionately deemed the "Brazilian Mafia," told them.

The regulars knew the routine, but Jokic gently reminded any newcomers of his preference: don't be on your phone. Dinner was about enjoying one another's company.

"Be present," Eichenberger said.

Hernangomez cherished the moments and the camaraderie. Since entering the league, Jokic had looked out for him, mentoring him until they became inseparable.

"I was there at nineteen, no English, no nothing, don't know shit about life and finished with everything," Hernangomez said.

When Jokic invited Hernangomez over for a homemade meal on January 7, Serbian Christmas, he received hospitality afforded to only those whom Jokic held dear. Ogi's family was there, along with Felipe's, rejoicing with Nikola's immediate family. The group prayed and then feasted for a long, satisfying dinner, toasting liberally to health and happiness.

"I remember during my four years there, I was probably the most happy person ever," Hernangomez said.

CHAPTER 34

PATIENCE

In mid-November 2017, twice within a week, Jamal Murray showed why the Nuggets were so bullish on the feisty guard out of Kentucky.

Against the Magic, he lit up the perimeter with six 3-pointers en route to a career-high 32 points. Though he snatched 17 rebounds and whipped 9 assists, Jokic didn't need to be the offensive plug. He was more than happy to supplement Murray's momentum with deft passes and timely screens.

Their shared intuition was merging.

Two games later, Denver erupted for 146 points against the Pelicans, which was the high-water mark across the entire league. As Murray hung 31, Jokic took only five shots. The team's 37 assists were one shy of their season high.

"When everybody touches the ball and we get a lot of open looks, we're really hard to guard," Murray said afterward. "It's great team basketball."

Within their construct, Denver had a glut of unselfish, playmaking big men who could set Murray up with driving lanes or shooting windows. When Paul Millsap, Denver's flashy free agent signing, suffered a wrist injury that sidelined him for months, it only heightened their need for a willing scorer.

Murray wasn't shy.

"You're just seeing him kind of grow up in front of our eyes," Nuggets coach Michael Malone said after a 38-point Murray masterpiece against Portland in January.

His confidence brimming, Murray was pushing the boundaries of his capabilities. The two-man game with Jokic was becoming instinctual. There seemed to always be space when they utilized one another on screens, or dribble handoffs. The actions weren't complicated, but the two relished the cat-and-mouse sequences that left defenders scrambling.

"When he's aggressive like that and he starts making shots like that, he's one of the best guards in the league," Jokic said.

Connelly had a knack for projecting such things.

A summer after burying arguably the most clutch shot in NBA history, clinching the Cavaliers' historic 2016 championship, enigmatic point guard Kyrie Irving requested a trade out of Cleveland. That same summer, the Pacers traded Paul George to Oklahoma City, and on draft night, the Bulls traded Jimmy Butler to Minnesota.

The Nuggets, beginning from the previous trade deadline up until that summer, had a shot at each of the aforementioned All-Stars had they been willing to part with Murray, who was then coming off a promising rookie season, multiple sources said.

But according to Connelly, forsaking their foundation wasn't enticing.

"It wasn't that tempting to me at all," Connelly said of breaking up the Murray-Jokic tandem.

How come?

"Because when you get really good players, who are really good guys, you put them on a different shelf," Connelly said.

Stylistically, there were arguments against acquiring one of the league's uber-talents because of how the Nuggets constructed their roster and envisioned playing. If Jokic was the fulcrum, any addition had to coexist in his sphere, not the other way around.

What did Irving's trade request say about him as a team player? Beyond his attitude, did his penchant for one-on-one play align with Denver's stated intention of moving and sharing the basketball?

While a notoriously hard worker, Butler was an inconsistent and unreliable 3-point shooter. The spacing, with Murray, was ideal for cutters. Moreover, Denver's front office had to consider locker room dynamics and whether Butler's blunt approach would mesh with their young core.

In Murray, they had a young, hungry scoring guard (still on a rookie deal) whose play complemented Jokic perfectly. Who he was as a person—competitive and tough—made the decision to rebuff any inquiries easier. Though those decisions weren't unanimous within the front office, and

Irving was particularly alluring, Connelly decided to wager on Murray. The partnership, between Jokic and Murray, was "just about optimal," Connelly said.

○

The hackneyed marketing ploy was supposed to gin up excitement between the Nuggets and Bucks, a matchup that already pitted two rising international stars against one another.

"Salute to the Olympics" night in Milwaukee was an unnecessary nod to Giannis Antetokounmpo (Greece) and Nikola Jokic (Serbia), and the type of silly promotional event that Jokic didn't appreciate, anyway.

Nonetheless, Serbian flags dotted the crowd when Jokic and the Nuggets visited in mid-February.

Little did his fellow countrymen know that they were about to witness history.

There wasn't anything too remarkable about the 16 points Jokic scored in the first half; his bevy of interior baskets landed off his pillowy touch and adroit footwork. A few of his 11 rebounds were the result of sound positioning, while he snatched a few more due to his remarkable ability to read the ball's trajectory. His quick-twitch reactions always belied his drowsy aesthetic.

When Wilson Chandler buried a corner 3-pointer with 1:54 remaining in the second quarter, it marked Jokic's 10th assist—and cemented the fastest triple-double in the NBA over the prior two decades.

"It just seemed like I made a lot of passes, so that's why I got that many assists," a garrulous Jokic said, before pointing out that he also finished two turnovers away from a quadruple-double.

Monte Morris was on the bench that night, watching in awe at the subtle ways he dominated the game.

"I was like *uhh, he's different*," Morris said.

Jokic's influence taught Morris, then a rookie, a lesson.

"It just shows basketball isn't all about how strong you are, how high you can jump," he said. "It's really just knowing the angles, playing at your own pace."

Jokic ended the night with 30 points, 15 boards, and a career-high 17 assists in dispatching the Bucks. The Nuggets still weren't whole, but they were in the thick of the playoff race, eyeing their first berth of the Jokic era. The win placed them in a temporary tie for the No. 6 seed amid a logjam in the Western Conference.

Gary Harris saw the offense galvanizing around Jokic in real time.

Move, and he'd find you. If not, a cut would open up a pocket for someone else. Behind their leader, the Nuggets were buying in to Jokic's selfless brand of basketball. The onus was on the players; coaches preferred not to stymie the offense with play calls.

"That shit was just popping," Harris said. "It became automatic."

The core was young, but didn't know what they didn't know. They believed they were postseason bound behind their transcendent talent.

"No one in our organization takes it for granted," Nuggets coach Michael Malone said. "We feel we have the most dynamic, best facilitator, best playmaking young player in the NBA."

CHAPTER 35

GAME 82

Egalitarian by nature, Jokic struggled with authority.

Like every coach in his colorful basketball history, there were times when he drove his coach crazy.

Nuggets coach Michael Malone was no exception.

Early on Jokic was stubborn, and he was always opinionated, about practices, plays, drills, whatever. He was a constant conundrum with an elusive drive.

Malone remembered Nuggets GM Tim Connelly encouraging him to get on Jokic. He could take it, he would tell him. He was tough, he was Serbian.

"It's not that simple," Malone would say.

There was a fine line to walk between coaching him and circumnavigating him. Malone was adamant that he was going to be himself, which meant holding him accountable. But there was a price to pay.

"You gotta understand that when I coach him hard at times, it's gonna be two weeks before he's back to being regular Nikola," Malone told Connelly. "And I go, 'Can we afford those two weeks?'"

It wasn't that Jokic was being malicious.

"He was immature," Malone said, which was a significant distinction.

Malone tried to place himself in Jokic's shoes, a foreigner, speaking a new language, tasked with the responsibilities incumbent of a franchise cornerstone.

"That's a lot to ask of a guy that was picked No. 41," Malone said.

But if the Nuggets were going to entrust the franchise to Jokic, he had to mature. He couldn't lose his temper when he disagreed with officials.

He had to accept coaching. He had to work harder. He needed to be patient with teammates who didn't grasp concepts as quickly as he did.

In what was a constant source of frustration for him, Jokic didn't handle it well when his teammates missed a read or failed to identify a mismatch.

"That is part of the curse of being a genius," Malone said.

If he was to be the face of the team, all eyes would eventually settle on him.

"After year one, after year two, my exit interview, it wasn't, 'Hey, Nikola, I want you to go home and work on your lefty jump hook,'" Malone said. "It was that, 'You have to grow up.'"

Adversity was inevitable as Denver began its steep march toward relevancy. To get there, his intangibles needed to improve.

"We all gotta grow up," Malone said. "I gotta grow up."

Occasionally at a loss, Malone used to consult Will Barton and Mason Plumlee, two of the team's elder statesmen, about how to reach him.

When dealing with the personalities of eighteen distinct players, Malone needed every advantage he could find.

"Hey, Mase, you sit next to Nikola in the locker room," Malone recalled. "What do you see?"

Once, Plumlee recalled, Malone kicked Jokic out of shootaround and he responded with a career-high 40 or 50 points that night. Later that season, with Jokic struggling, Malone sought the pair's advice.

"Man, I just don't know how to get through to him," Malone confided in them on the team plane, according to Plumlee.

"Me and Will are like, 'Coach, the last time you got on him, he had damn-near fifty,'" Plumlee said.

But when Malone challenged Jokic, thinking it might elicit the same response, it backfired.

"And Joker was like, 'Oh you think you can just yell at me and I'm gonna score fifty points,'" Plumlee said.

Instead, Plumlee recalled, he opted not to shoot the next game.

After practices, every player would step to the line, concluding the sessions with free throws. Barton once relayed a story to Plumlee about Jokic's penchant for deception.

"Joker's funny in his own way," Plumlee said. "He's what, an eighty to ninety percent free-throw shooter?"

As his players shot, Malone would wander around the gym engaging guys for individual conversations or quietly observing the proceedings. When he got to Nikola, Jokic sensed his presence.

"Joker would just miss every free throw on purpose," Plumlee said.

It was a window into their relationship—an authority whom Jokic respected but couldn't help antagonize.

"It was hard at times, because sometimes Nikola would do things just to poke the bear," said Nuggets assistant and future Wizards coach Wes Unseld Jr., who acknowledged Jokic's stubbornness frustrated Malone. "Once you knew that that's what he was doing, it took the sting out of it."

Staring at the final six weeks of the season, the Nuggets needed to catch a wave in order to reach the playoffs. Millsap returned after a three-month absence, which meant a reintegration that would cost valuable time Denver could ill afford.

Naturally deferential, Jokic stopped shooting as much upon Millsap's return. For four consecutive games, Jokic took single-digit shot attempts, and the Nuggets suffered as a result.

"Nikola is still the focal point of our offense," Malone said following a month where Jokic averaged almost 22 points, shot 56 percent from 3-point range, and finished an assist shy of a triple-double average.

"I don't want Nikola thinking that he has to play second fiddle to anyone," Malone said.

The dichotomy of Jokic's game was often confounding, a riddle Malone had not yet solved.

"Nikola can't take seven shots a night for us," Malone said. "Granted, he is unselfish, he makes the right play and I love all that. But Nikola needs to be aggressive."

Getting him to accept that—essentially asking him to rewire his approach—wasn't an easy conversation.

As assistant Wes Unseld Jr. astutely reminded him, "For us to be good and take that next step . . . you being selfish is the most selfless thing you could do for us."

With that in mind, Jokic and the Nuggets faced a grueling seven-game, fifteen-day road trip at the end of March that would all but determine their playoff future that season.

An ignominious start—the Nuggets lost to the Grizzlies, who snapped their own 19-game losing streak—prompted Connelly to grab a stiff drink with colleagues.

"That's probably a wrap," he thought, his team falling further behind Minnesota in the chase for the No. 8 seed.

But the Nuggets did just enough to survive the road trip, including a gripping overtime win at Oklahoma City, to precede a do-or-die home stand at the beginning of April. When they rallied from an 18-point, fourth-quarter deficit against Milwaukee to win again in overtime, it was fair to believe in their resolve.

"Every win right now is huge," Malone said. "I think it speaks to the growth of our team."

As the winning streak continued and optimism started to balloon, Denver seized control of its destiny. Win and in. The six-game winning streak the Nuggets strung together to close the regular season vaulted them to the edge of the postseason. All that stood between their first playoff berth since 2013 was the Minnesota Timberwolves, who could also snap a fourteen-year playoff drought with a win.

Over the prior frenzied month, Denver's future crystallized. Jokic heeded Malone's message and averaged 23 points, 11 rebounds, and 6.5 assists. He conducted an offense that averaged over 115 points per game throughout their final 17 games. Murray, only a second-year player, averaged over 19 points per game during the run.

Mason Plumlee had been on teams who'd packed it in when their playoff futures looked bleak. The Nuggets' tenacity was a testament to their "character," he said. Collectively, they'd decided to play through what amounted to de facto playoff games for weeks.

Asked about their belief entering game 82, Malone was effusive. "It's as high as it can be," he said.

Even against veterans like Jimmy Butler and Taj Gibson, Jeff Teague and Jamal Crawford, the Nuggets were game. They'd already, improbably, extended their season as Murray and Jokic proved undaunted by the pressure in the most crucial games of their career.

Game 82 was no different. Jokic's modest 13-point first half wasn't enough. In the third quarter, Jokic dropped 17 points alone, including 3-for-3 from outside the arc. There was zero hesitation within his looks and an unambiguous willingness to compete against Karl-Anthony Towns and Minnesota's veterans. The same was true for Murray, whose 9 fourth-quarter points forced overtime.

In a tense, physical environment, both burgeoning stars were unafraid of the stage or the consequences, which wasn't the case for all of their teammates. When the Timberwolves pulled away in overtime, it was the most devastating loss of the current regime's era.

"I can't even think right now," Will Barton said after the game. "I'm so disappointed that we lost."

Despite the emotion, their willingness to engage spoke volumes about their competitive fortitude and the direction they were forging. The scars Jokic, Murray, Harris, and Barton endured were necessary if this group was going to mature in the NBA.

Connelly was emboldened by what his young core, and specifically their two pillars, had displayed.

"They weren't scared of the moment," he said.

The sting of the loss couldn't shroud Malone's brimming excitement at the future.

"Both those guys balled out," he said.

To Wilson Chandler, who didn't score despite playing a game-high 48 minutes, Jokic's 35-point effort was a testament.

"He's a big-time player," Chandler said of what the night proved. "He's not scared of the spotlight."

On the flight home that night, still smarting from the sting but emboldened nonetheless, Jokic walked the plane and thanked his teammates. His performance on the court spoke for itself, but his actions in the quiet moments after the loss marked an assumption of responsibility. In just his third season in the NBA, this was unequivocally his team.

"He had no reason to be taking ownership of that game," Chandler said.

Assistant coach David Adelman saw another first from Jokic that night. When he got to the coaches' section of the plane, Jokic acknowledged he was in the zone.

"Man, I was cooking tonight," Adelman recalled him saying, a rare acceptance of his scoring ability.

He had a big grin draped across his face.

"It was the first time I'd seen him look at the game and say, 'I have to score,'" Adelman said.

Beyond that acknowledgment, Jokic seemed to grasp what he was capable of.

Sitting among the coaches, there was also an immediate reflection that spoke to Nikola's growing maturity.

"I vividly remember him talking about, 'If we just would've won this game in January, in February . . .'" Adelman said. "We all got in our cars that night after we flew back from Minnesota and it kind of hit us. We have an all-time player here."

As painful as the loss was, assistant coach Wes Unseld Jr. found a silver lining.

"Had we won that game, made the playoffs, probably got knocked out in the first round, I'm not sure they would've come back with the same level of intensity and purpose," he said.

Micah Nori, an assistant and one of Jokic's confidants, wouldn't be along for the ride.

"I made the decision to go to Detroit, which Nikola still reminds me was the dumbest decision I ever made."

CHAPTER 36

$147 MILLION

Whatever doubts lingered about Michael Malone's job status in Denver following game 82 were quickly extinguished by Connelly.

"There's improvement across all levels of our team," Connelly said. "I guess [questioning whether he'll be back is] the unfortunate narrative of professional basketball, but Mo's done a fantastic job."

The more interesting question pertained to Jokic, who had made barely $4.1 million across his first three seasons in the NBA. During the 2017–18 season, Jokic had made about $100,000 *less* than Tyler Lydon, the Nuggets' first-round pick who played in two minutes of one game that season.

By virtue of his second-round contract, the Nuggets had a team option for his fourth season. Had they picked it up, (thus severely underpaying Jokic for another season), he would have become an unrestricted free agent the following summer. They also could have declined his option, making him a restricted free agent and paving a path to offer him a massive deal worth $147 million.

Connelly and Karnisovas met with Strahinja and Nemanja Jokic at the Thirsty Lion in downtown Denver. They discussed Nikola's unique predicament. Only, from the Jokics' perspective, there wasn't a predicament at all.

Nikola's value, trajectory, commitment, and performance had proven his worth about 147 times over. Nothing could be made official until free agency commenced. However, Strahinja made their position unambiguous.

"What do you think about this offseason?" Strahinja asked.

Connelly explained the vastly divergent options, to which Strahinja responded in a way that left zero room for negotiating.

"Timmy, you are family now, but either we get married this summer, or we get divorced next summer," Strahinja told them.

Connelly trusted the conviction in Strahinja's eyes. There would be nothing to negotiate. Jokic's stance was shared with Malone and ownership before the Nuggets could officially commit once free agency opened on July 1.

Connelly wanted to celebrate the partnership and a potentially fruitful future for the franchise as soon as possible. He planned to visit Serbia, but only for twenty-four hours. He flew to Belgrade, where Nemanja Jokic was waiting to pick him up ahead of their two-hour drive. The single-lane roads to Sombor stretched for miles.

There was a handshake and a hug that was worth as much as any signature. The Nuggets always wanted to do right by Jokic.

That night, Nikola and Natalija were headed to the theater, but the show was in Serbian.

"Brother, do you want to come?" Nikola asked.

Connelly passed.

Nemanja was going to a concert in nearby Novi Sad and invited Connelly. The Nuggets' president declined.

Finally, Strahinja and Nebojsa, Nikola's godfather, decided they would go to a friend's farmhouse. The plan was for one pivo—one beer—but when Strahinja showed up sporting his favorite sartorial accessory, rings, Connelly had a sense they were in for a different type of night. At the farmhouse, Connelly spotted Darko Milicic, the former No. 2 overall pick who also happened to be a friend of the Jokic family and a former teammate of Nemanja's.

One pivo bled into one rakija, a potent Serbian brandy, which bled into another. Soon the group was taking rakija shots out of a plastic Gatorade bottle, which was proof, he could be sure, that the spirit was homemade and had aged for decades. By the third or fourth shot, Connelly found himself drinking on a tractor.

Amid the festivities, Connelly phoned Nuggets governor Josh Kroenke to include him in the celebration. The crew made its way to a local bar, where Connelly asked the bartender for an address. He'd had enough partying for one night.

"Brate"—brother—"no Uber," he was told.

"Brate, no taxi."

Connelly realized he was going to need to shepherd the crew home. Not typically a coffee drinker, Connelly started pounding caffeine while the revelry continued. Late that night, they eventually made it back, safely, to Sombor.

When Connelly woke up, Nikola came to greet him.

"I thought my brother was taking care of you," he joked.

They took a long walk, stopped for ice cream, and dreamed about what the future entailed.

"He's got this irreverent view of the world that I think we probably share," Connelly said. "We don't take things too seriously. I think both of us try to prioritize fun. He and I challenged each other quite a bit, don't take it too seriously."

That attitude was even more amazing because of the deal both sides reached; the max contract Jokic received that summer was the richest in franchise history.

"I've never seen a guy less enthused about a contract this big, and I say that in a positive sense," Connelly said after the deal was signed. "Everything is secondary to him to basketball and family. . . . Beyond that, he doesn't care."

CHAPTER 37

TEMPTATION

On the verge of the postseason, the plan for building around Jokic was obvious.

The Nuggets were always on the hunt for shooters and floor spacers and cutters with good size. They especially coveted intelligent players who could augment Jokic's game. That summer, they were armed with the No. 14 pick—the last in the draft lottery.

There were a few polarizing prospects near the top of the draft, including Michael Porter Jr., the former top-rated prospect whose college career had been thwarted by back surgery. Were it not for that injury, which limited him to only three games at Missouri, Porter could have been the top overall selection.

The closer it got to the draft, the more his medical history became a red flag for most teams.

But heading into draft night in 2018, Denver's initial target wasn't Porter. There were two other names on their draft board that were circled, one within their range and another that could only be accessed via trade. The first was Shai Gilgeous-Alexander, according to multiple sources. With some luck, there was a chance he could fall to No. 14.

The other, according to multiple sources, was a precocious teenage Slovenian from Real Madrid named Luka Doncic.

At 6'7", Doncic, like Jokic, had a preternatural feel for the game. The Nuggets felt they had a genuine chance to land him on draft night. They envisioned pairing his skill set with Jokic's, merging two elite distributors into an already potent Denver offense. Their unique ability to dictate games at their own pace could have compounded to disassemble defenses.

Sacramento, whose front office was led by Serbian Vlade Divac, had the second overall pick in a draft with Doncic, Trae Young, Jaren Jackson, and Gilgeous-Alexander. The Nuggets, according to a source, knew Divac and his staff weren't high on Doncic and tried to exploit it.

The Nuggets offered Gary Harris and two first-round picks in exchange for the No. 2 pick, a source said.

In the moment—and moments tended to crawl on draft night—there appeared to be at least some traction toward a deal.

"For thirty seconds . . . we thought we had Luka," according to a person with knowledge of the deal.

After a few tense, exhilarating beats, Sacramento declined and selected Marvin Bagley, a forward out of Duke. Divac's explanation for passing on Doncic was that he didn't want him to impede De'Aaron Fox's development. But the Nuggets' most willing trade partner had passed.

There had been a brief discussion about including Murray in the proposal, a source said, but that notion was quickly squashed, owing to how much they valued him internally.

Doncic landed in Dallas via a draft-night swap with Atlanta, and the Nuggets, despite some drama, stood pat at No. 14. Gilgeous-Alexander was off the board at No. 11.

Nuggets owner Stan Kroenke and his son, Josh, had both gone to Missouri. They were strong advocates of drafting Porter, whose injury concerns saw him drop that night. The Nuggets' core was already teeming with talent, and Denver's front office rationalized it could be patient with Porter. At No. 14, they believed the potential reward was worth the risk.

When healthy, Michael Porter Jr. was an ideal floor spacer. Paired alongside Jokic, defenses wouldn't stand a chance. He, not Luka, was Denver-bound.

CHAPTER 38

GARY HARRIS

Gary Harris had a sneaky, wry wit that differentiated him among his teammates. He was quiet but confident, humble yet talented. He was one of the backbones of Denver's locker room.

Among the Americans, he was also one of Jokic's closest teammates, and that had little to do with their on-court synergy.

When coaches had difficulty reaching Jokic, they'd come to Harris and ask if he'd be willing to get in Jokic's ear. Harris, though, knew better. If Jokic didn't feel like doing something, nothing Harris said would change his mind.

There was already solidarity between the two *before* Harris traveled overseas that summer to participate, with Jokic, in an NBA-sponsored Basketball Without Borders event in Belgrade. Harris's willingness to go was an investment in their relationship. Jokic's willingness to later show him his hometown, which he treasured fiercely, said even more.

Sombor was Jokic's own personal bubble, a world away from the hassle and spotlight of NBA obligations. In Sombor, he was generally able to be himself. When Harris was invited into that world, it was a nod to their friendship.

"They don't treat him like Nikola Jokic the superstar, they treat him like Nikola the little kid, just eating fruit and walking around, barefoot, going to see the horses," Harris said.

Harris saw how simple and easy his life there was, a world away from the glaring and constant scrutiny of the NBA. It opened up a new perspective on Jokic that made sense. He knew who he was, in part, because of where he came from.

In their strolls through the town center or eating Sombor's traditional dish—a fish stew with notes of paprikash—alongside the river where Jo-kic grew up, Harris gained so much more than the knowledge of how best to play off Jokic.

He understood why he was so grounded.

Given the caliber of player he'd already become by 2018, Harris joked there was no reason he shouldn't have a signature shoe or a reel of featured commercials.

"That's not him," Harris said. And though both perks eventually came, Jokic never let material opportunities undermine who he was.

What Harris marveled at, more than anything, was his authenticity. The games, while important and a means of living, didn't define him. When Harris thought about Jokic's career ending, he didn't need to con-jure an image of the horse stables he would retreat to, or the river where he'd pass Sombor's sun-soaked days. He saw it, firsthand.

"He's gonna go back to Serbia and live a great life. . . . He already does," he said.

Harris appreciated how Jokic lived according to his own doctrine. He was a different kind of superstar, who knew who he was and was unwilling to let the money or fame change him.

"A lot of people think that's for show, that it's fake," Harris said. "No, that's just who he is. . . . He's running his own race, and bringing other people along with him, not just as a basketball player but as a person."

The example Jokic set, Harris said, was a powerful one.

"That's my brother from another mother," he said.

The serenity Jokic enjoyed in his quaint hometown served in stark contrast to the chaos of Belgrade. There, Harris said, he got hounded for photos and autographs. The group's bodyguards, better known as Jokic's brothers, served as protection.

"Nobody's fucking with them," Harris said.

CHAPTER 39

MISSTEP

Jokic had yet to make an All-Star team before he started getting peppered with MVP questions.

It was early in the 2018–19 season, and the Nuggets, on the heels of their game 82 heartbreak, were cooking. The pain of the prior season had dissipated and turned into motivation. On the strength of Jokic's shoulders, the Nuggets ripped off a 9-1 record to start the year.

"I'm just playing my game, so if that's gonna make me MVP one day this year, next year, in next whatever years, yes, but I think it's still silly," Jokic said. "I love it because it just makes me laugh."

He knew it was a compliment, but he also knew how ludicrous the notion was. At that point, it was easier to laugh at the hypothetical than indulge it.

The other issue with the MVP talk was that it was antithetical to who he was. In order to win the award, he felt, there was an element of selfishness.

"That's an individual thing," he said. "It happens, it happens. I cannot affect that."

He, of course, *would* affect that, whether he cared to or not. And maybe Jokic didn't need to accept it quite yet, but he was the face of an upstart team whose stock was rising. And when a momentary controversy struck, Jokic didn't know how to respond.

During an early visit to Chicago, Jokic was asked, innocuously, his thoughts on then–Bulls center Wendell Carter Jr. Late in his answer, he slipped in a slur he'd picked up in the locker room.

"No homo, he's longer than you expected," Jokic said.

In the moment, none of the reporters around Jokic even registered the remark. A week later, a social media clip of the interview circulated, prompting the NBA to issue Jokic a $25,000 fine.

"He was legit mad," Mason Plumlee said, because none of his teammates had explained the implication to him.

In the locker room, his teammates laughed at how flustered he was.

When the Nuggets played in Memphis that night, Jokic was a shell of himself. He bypassed open looks and neglected to shoot the basketball until there were only three seconds left in the game. Jokic's bizarre night was over after his potential game winner drew back iron, and the Nuggets lost.

In the locker room, Jokic circumvented any interviews by telling reporters that any questions would yield a "no comment" from him. It was as uncharacteristic a night as he'd ever had, likely with equal parts irritation and embarrassment. Later, one theory emerged over his reluctance to shoot. By not scoring, Jokic ensured he wouldn't have to speak with the media.

"I don't know what it does to our offense," Malone said. "Obviously, we'd like him to take more shots, but right now he's not shooting the ball, and we'll have to figure out why."

Whatever his agenda was—and his unselfishness afforded him some cover—the outcome reinforced how Jokic couldn't defer.

"A lot of our offense is through him, so he has to take the initiative to take shots," Plumlee said that night.

The game left his teammates confounded but also aware of how much control he wielded. Jokic was going to operate how he saw fit.

A prior conversation with legendary Spurs coach Gregg Popovich ensured it.

Popovich was in Belgrade for the same Basketball Without Borders event that Jokic and Gary Harris attended. Popovich, whose father was Serbian, had a deep and healthy respect for international basketball. The litany of foreign players on his teams was a testament to his appreciation for basketball abroad. He frequented Belgrade as often as possible.

Within Jokic's emergence, a friendship developed between the two.

"I was talking to him a little bit more," Jokic said. "He's the one who makes basketball really simple. When someone like that [compliments] you, it means a lot just because someone appreciated what you're doing, someone who knows basketball. I appreciate it a lot. I don't need to speak about him. He's probably the best coach in the world right now."

Popovich described Jokic as "pudgy," and acknowledged he couldn't jump high or run fast. But his intelligence, as "one of the smartest players in the league," rendered those other skills less relevant. As for deeming Jokic a revolutionary talent on the verge of reinventing basketball, Popovich went full Popovich.

"When I think of revolutions, I think of people like Che Guevara, Vladimir Ilyich Lenin," Popovich deadpanned. "I don't really think of Jokic as far as revolutionary, so I think you're a bit hyperbolic there. But he is one heck of a player."

CHAPTER 40

MARIO KART

The max contract Jokic received in the summer of 2018 meant he'd finally be paid commensurate to his value.

"He used to joke with me, 'Mase, when my first check clears, I might go home,'" Mason Plumlee recalled. "'You know how far a million dollars goes in Serbia?'"

While adhering to his day job, Jokic found ways to entertain himself.

That season, numerous guys bought Nintendo Switches—video game consoles that were ideal for road trips. On the countless plane rides NBA teams took, guys would sync their devices and compete. The Nuggets' game of choice? *Mario Kart*.

The teams were Jokic and Juancho Hernangomez against Plumlee, Malik Beasley, and Tyler Lydon. A season later, Vlatko Cancar joined the chaos.

It was Europeans versus Americans for bragging rights. Races were heated, with insults hurled across the aisles and bananas strategically strewn.

"Every time we beat them, the losers had to do something," Hernangomez said.

That was how Lydon, at Jokic's request, wound up in a "binky dress," according to Hernangomez. According to Lydon, it was more a crop top that Jokic had been gifted as a joke. Lydon's punishment was a picture in the attire alongside a beaming Jokic.

NBA flights could be as long as four hours in the air to some coastal cities. If the Nuggets had a late-night TNT game, a midnight takeoff was likely.

Nikola Jokic's first Serbian basketball membership.
Credit: Isidor Rudic

After the 2012 regional championship, the light danced radiantly off just one player's medal: Nikola's. *Credit: Isidor Rudic*

Nikola Jokic's attendance at practice was a constant conundrum. Jokic (eighth row, No. 14) only attended practices prior to games, demarcated with a star in this image (right). Without any games on the schedule, Jokic didn't mind disappearing. *Credit: Isidor Rudic*

Nikola Jokic alongside his best friend, Nemanja Pribic (white shirt). *Credit: Nemanja Pribic*

Nikola Jokic visited Nikola Tesla kindergarten in Belgrade to play basketball and hang out with some kids (right and below). *Credit: Goran Cakic*

Nikola Jokic stands next to Ratko Varda (far right) before a game during the 2013–'14 season at Mega. *Credit: Basketball club Mega Vizura*

Nikola Jokic looks on as head coach Dejan Milojevic conducts a huddle. *Credit: Basketball club Mega Vizura*

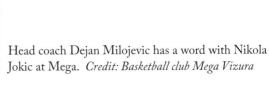

Nikola Jokic and Dejan Milojevic sit for a press conference while at Mega. *Credit: Basketball club Mega Vizura.*

Head coach Dejan Milojevic has a word with Nikola Jokic at Mega. *Credit: Basketball club Mega Vizura*

Nikola Jokic with Nuggets
scouting director Jim Clibanoff and
international scout Rafal Juc.
Credit: Jim Clibanoff

Nuggets director of scouting Jim Clibanoff was sent
on a special assignment to bond with Nikola and his
family in Santa Barbara. *Credit: Jim Clibanoff*

Nikola with Isidor Rudic, the first coac
he bonded with in Sombor.
Credit: Isidor Rudic

Nikola Jokic perfected his one-legged fadeaway from the free-throw line. *Credit: Ognjen Stojakovic*

Nikola Jokic's touch wasn't an accident. He honed his arcing floaters over his brother's outstretched hand. *Credit: Ognjen Stojakovic*

Nikola Jokic works on his off-hand finishing with assistant Ogi Stojakovic and his brother Nemanja. *Credit: Ognjen Stojakovic*

Back home in Sombor, Nikola Jokic works on his ball-handling while Nuggets assistant coach Ogi Stojakovic monitors. *Credit: Ognjen Stojakovic*

During COVID, a trim Nikola Jokic occupied his time by river. *Credit: Sparky Gonzales*

Nuggets equipment manager Sparky Gonzales hosted a BBQ for the team's ballboys, and an unexpected guest showed up. *Credit: Sparky Gonzales*

Nikola Jokic and his brother, Strahinja, trying out all the team's apparel after telling equipment manager Sparky Gonzales, "I want to look like Allen Iverson." *Credit: Sparky Gonzales*

Nikola Jokic showed up at associate head athletic trainer Jason Miller's house for his son's birthday party, where Joker took a picture with Batman (below). *Credit: Jason Miller*

Associate head athletic trainer Jason Miller (above) with Nikola Jokic at the NBA All-Star Game in Cleveland. *Credit: Jason Miller*

Nikola Jokic and Juancho Hernangomez pose with the Nuggets' training staff. *Credit: Juancho Hernangomez*

Nikola Jokic with reserve forward Tyler Lydon (below), who wore the tank top as punishment for losing in Mario Kart. *Credit: Juancho Hernangomez*

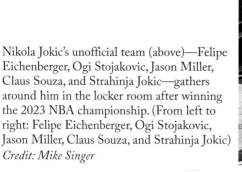

Nikola Jokic's unofficial team (above)—Felipe Eichenberger, Ogi Stojakovic, Jason Miller, Claus Souza, and Strahinja Jokic—gathers around him in the locker room after winning the 2023 NBA championship. (From left to right: Felipe Eichenberger, Ogi Stojakovic, Jason Miller, Claus Souza, and Strahinja Jokic) *Credit: Mike Singer*

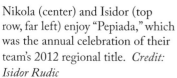

Nikola (center) and Isidor (top row, far left) enjoy "Pepiada," which was the annual celebration of their team's 2012 regional title. *Credit: Isidor Rudic*

"But Me, Nikola, Mason, and Juancho were up grinding," Lydon said proudly.

It turned into a routine. While smarter teammates slept, they tore through the tracks.

"It goes to show the type of guy Nikola is because he can go out and have 40 and 20 and 15 and the next thought in his head, in my opinion, is 'I'm just gonna relax now, hang out with the guys and play *Mario Kart*,'" Lydon said.

They played the grand prix series, which combined the scores from several races and yielded a winner.

"I was Yoshi, and I was driving a bike," Nikola said.

A video game specialist, Jokic was by far the most dominant.

"I remember wanting to throw my game," Plumlee said. "Like, this dude won *Mario Kart* every time."

At the beginning, Jokic torched Team America.

"Two weeks go by, and we're like, 'How the fuck is Nikola always winning?'" Lydon said.

"Joker's honestly one of the best at that game," said Malik Beasley. "Him and Juancho were always winning. I was in the back of the pack. . . . I just did it for the camaraderie."

The Americans were helpless. When Jokic would win, it prompted jubilant outbursts of "Europe! Europe!" on the team plane. And when he'd win, it wasn't just by a car length or two. He'd obliterate the field by a half, or sometimes a whole lap.

"After like the second trip, I was like, 'Bro, why you always winning?'" Beasley asked him.

"He was like, 'I know the courses.'"

It wasn't until a conversation with assistant coach David Adelman that Team America learned what was happening. Adelman played *Mario Kart* at home with his kids. What Jokic knew, and they didn't, were the hidden shortcuts tucked inside the races. Adelman knew you could research the secret paths online. Jokic was also a savvy drifter.

"Come to find out later, [Jokic] studied the maps, and he'd study the boost-ups," Plumlee said.

Hernangomez knew there was something suspicious about their wins. "He knows everything!" he said. "He got the fastest car."

Jokic wasn't pleased when he learned Adelman tipped his teammates off. His cover was blown.

"Joker would just beat the hell out of you and never tell you about all the extra ways to be better," Plumlee said.

Jokic tried to be modest about his margin of victory.

"I think they were not really good, and I was decent," he said.

The Switches kept head-to-head records of all the races. Lydon's and Plumlee's consoles have been lost or given away, but Jokic still had his. His records indicated somewhere between 250 and 300 wins.

"So that's a lot," he said.

There was no arguing Jokic's dominance. Lydon offered the only real competition, since Plumlee could never master the drift.

"Mason was definitely dead last," Lydon said. "He was terrible."

CHAPTER 41

TYLER LYDON

Not long ago, Tyler Lydon's mom called the former Nuggets forward with an odd question.

"Why the hell do you have a boxful of Nikola Jokic fan mail?" she asked Lydon, who'd spent two injury-riddled seasons with the Nuggets from 2017 to 2019.

Lydon could only laugh. After he was drafted 24th overall, he'd been granted prime real estate within the team's locker room; his stall was next to Jokic's.

Before practices and after games, Lydon picked Jokic's brain every chance he got. Over time, a friendship developed between the two laid-back big men.

When Nuggets superfan Vicki Ray passed candy to each member of the team as they jogged off the court following their pregame shooting routines, Jokic's stash ended up in Lydon's drawer.

"My drawer would be overflowing," Lydon said.

Even though his Nuggets career was short, Lydon grew close to Jokic. On road trips, he'd join Juancho and Nikola on their frequent jaunts to Fogo de Chao, where dinners were always lively and conversation never revolved around basketball.

Lydon grew to understand how Jokic was wired. Family mattered more to him than anything.

Jokic had international fame and generational wealth, yet Lydon noticed how none of it materially changed him. And Lydon saw him at a time when *everything* was changing for him, from his notoriety to his bank account. On the floor, he was unstoppable; the moment he was off it, he checked on his horses and his people.

"It made me grow more in touch with my family," Lydon said.

Lydon knew it sounded weird, but basketball, for Jokic, was almost an "afterthought."

Years after he stuffed candy in his drawer, Lydon said he could Face-Time Jokic on a whim and the two would catch up as if they were still teammates. On random occasions, they will.

"It says a lot about him, especially as a player—MVP, NBA champion," Lydon began. "That's very, very hard to come by in the NBA because everybody's ego kind of blows up a little bit, and guys get too good for other people. All the shit that everybody kind of knows to be true, is true about the NBA, but for him, he really did not care."

Lydon's mom was sorting through a box of his old NBA stuff—a type of take-home bag players leave with at the end of the season. In it she found troves of fan mail for Nikola Jokic. According to Lydon, Jokic was among the few players who were actually good about signing autographs and responding to fan mail, but he couldn't get to all of it.

Before Lydon left Denver, Jokic stuffed the overflow in his teammate's bag, a joke to be savored years later.

CHAPTER 42

POETRY IN MOTION

Midway through the 2018–19 season, by virtue of his MVP profile, Jokic was on the verge of becoming a first-time All-Star.

Individually, Jokic was averaging over 20 points and 10 rebounds per game. His 7.7 assists per night ranked 8th in the NBA behind a list of, exclusively, point guards. There was no similar profile in the NBA; his 12 triple-doubles ranked second only to Russell Westbrook.

Jokic was an unguardable enigma. One night he'd surgically dismember Utah's defense with 16 assists, the next he'd pummel Portland's frontcourt (and old friend Jusuf Nurkic) for 40 points. His combination of touch, range, intelligence, and vision yielded a ceaseless array of outs.

After one transition dunk sparked a January win over Charlotte, Jokic gracefully deemed himself "poetry in motion."

His self-deprecating attitude was infectious around the locker room. As long as he refused to take himself seriously, no one else was allowed to either.

"He's goofy all the time," said Jamal Murray, who struggled to get through an interview as Jokic danced, unapologetically, by himself to Serbian rock music after a game. "He's just a happy guy, that's what makes him so good. He's deceptive, the way he looks, the way he acts, the way he talks, the way he moves. . . . Dancing, oh my god, don't even get me started."

Monte Morris confirmed his musical taste stretched beyond the Balkans.

"When he tries to rap songs, he doesn't know how to rap at all," Morris said. "Lil Wayne, he knows 50 Cent. He loves 50 Cent."

Jokic was at ease. And, much to his liking, his success was translating to team success.

Through the first four months of the season, the Nuggets were 39-18, trailing only the Golden State Warriors in the standings. By the All-Star break, simply making the playoffs would've been an underachievement.

On the verge of becoming the Nuggets' first All-Star since Carmelo Anthony in 2011, Jokic admitted it wouldn't define his season.

"If it doesn't happen, I'm not gonna die," Jokic said.

Naturally, when it finally did, his family showed more emotion than he did.

"My girlfriend started to cry, my brothers started yelling and screaming at me," he said. "I was like 'Guys, come on.'"

Because of their record, Denver's coaching staff would be joining Jokic in Charlotte for the All-Star Game. It was a Nuggets affair, where the league would "get to know us," according to an opportunistic Michael Malone. That Jokic had been drafted by Team Giannis—and not Team LeBron, which Malone was coaching—didn't dampen the mood.

"I think it's better that way," Malone joked. "I'm sick of coaching him, he's sick of playing for me."

At the NBA's car wash of All-Star festivities, Jokic got his due. TNT's Charles Barkley raved about Denver's budding core before his colleague Kenny Smith gave Jokic his flowers.

"For me, he's like every New York player that plays in the park," Smith said. "Little overweight, can't really jump. . . . Just know how to play basketball. It was a guy in my neighborhood called Fat Ike. Five-foot-eleven, power forward and we played pickup, and everyone picked him because he knew how to play basketball. And that's him. He's my Fat Ike."

Aside from the All-Star exhibition itself, Jokic was also invited to participate in the skills competition on the Saturday night of the weekend. The timed dribbling, passing, and shooting event included guys like Jayson Tatum, De'Aaron Fox, and Luka Doncic. Though skilled, Jokic was out of his element. After he got eliminated by Tatum in the second round, he was asked what the hardest part of the event was.

"Running," he said.

No one doubted his sincerity.

In the All-Star game itself, Jokic was concerned with how Team

Giannis, filled with international players like Joel Embiid and Nikola Vucevic, would communicate.

"How we gonna speak together?" he deadpanned.

There was a twinkle in Jokic's eyes with everything he did that weekend, a joy that was childlike and unmistakable. Jokic never envisioned he'd be standing side by side among the world's best players.

"I never think about NBA," Jokic said during a press conference that weekend when asked if he ever thought he'd be in this position. "I never think about All-Star."

No one doubted his sincerity.

Assistant coach Wes Unseld Jr. was there that weekend as a part of Denver's coaching staff. After the event, he confided in Unseld how out of place he felt standing alongside LeBron James, Giannis Antetokounmpo, and Steph Curry.

"I remember him telling me, he felt like he didn't belong," Unseld said.

Jokic still maintained an element of disbelief at his astonishing rise. He tended to disguise it with humor. When Malone's Team LeBron won the exhibition—"a rousing halftime speech," Malone quipped—Jokic managed one more jab before the regular season resumed.

"Yeah, I didn't shake his hand at the end," Jokic said. "Not today, buddy."

CHAPTER 43

HEAVY IS THE HEAD

In early March 2019, the Warriors bombarded the Nuggets with a not-so-subtle reminder of their supremacy.

With the No. 1 seed at stake, Denver drowned under a deluge of Steph Curry and Klay Thompson 3-pointers. Despite the duo's thirteen triples, the Nuggets actually fared *better* this time around than a January clash that saw Golden State dump 51 points on Denver . . . in the first quarter.

The Warriors were still the class of the Western Conference. Whatever the Nuggets thought they were, or thought they could become, wouldn't materialize until the playoffs.

"They are a better team than us," said Nuggets coach Michael Malone, stating the obvious after the blowout.

"Monte [Morris] had a lot to do with [the bench success], running our team, actually getting us into an offense, which is a novel concept for a point guard to do," Malone said.

Denver was entrenched in the playoff race, but it became a question of how greedy the Nuggets wanted to be. Were they simply content reaching the playoffs for the first time together, or was there more for them to achieve?

"We need to kind of think about where we want to go, and that's it," Jokic said.

Isaiah Thomas joined the Nuggets in free agency but didn't debut until February, when his surgically repaired hip allowed. Before his injuries, Thomas was an MVP candidate in Boston. His path was turbulent, but his passion for the sport remained steadfast. To Thomas, Jokic was an anomaly.

"I never seen a superstar that low-maintenance," Thomas said.

Every day he clocked in, got his work done, then clocked out, Thomas said. He wasn't driven by accolades or by being great. His motivation was singular: winning.

"He just figured the game out," Thomas said.

Thomas's favorite memory from his proximity to Jokic came at half-time of a tense game. Thomas peered over from his locker room stall and saw Jokic playing a game on his phone.

"I think it was a dogfight too," he said. "It was at halftime."

Thomas remembered Jokic sitting cross-legged, absorbed in some kid's game. Thomas couldn't comprehend how his level of dominance appeared to be so effortless.

"That describes him," he said with equal parts awe and disbelief. "You don't see guys like that around the league."

With less than a week left in the season, the Nuggets did what every team in their position would do: jockey for seeding.

Having already wrapped up home-court advantage, at least for the first round, the Nuggets opted to sit Jokic, Millsap, and Murray for a game in Portland. Only Jokic, who'd missed one game all season, protested the decision. Unless he was hurt, Jokic wanted to play. The decision to rest, for any reason, didn't compute.

A loss that night, however, was potentially advantageous. The Nuggets were eyeing the No. 2 seed, but a loss to Portland kept the Blazers in the hunt for the No. 3 seed. Perhaps most importantly, that engineering helped trap the Rockets into the No. 4 seed, thus delaying a potential series against Houston.

Malone vehemently denied any chicanery.

"There's this crazy—I don't know where it's coming from, I really don't—story out there that we rested guys because we're trying to avoid Houston," Malone said during a shootaround in Utah, ahead of their pen-ultimate game of the season. "We're not trying to avoid anybody. We're not scared of anybody. . . . [Any notion is] very wrong, very erroneous reporting."

There was already tension in the arena *before* the game started. Denver's traditional starters were back in the starting lineup against Utah, but Jokic wasn't himself. In 16 minutes on the floor, Jokic scored a season-low

2 points. He grabbed 5 rebounds and dished 2 assists before, unconscionably, fouling out.

The Nuggets lost in a game they theoretically had wanted to win.

In the postgame locker room, Malone was more blunt than he'd ever been with Jokic. He hadn't played against Portland and produced a dud against Utah. The playoffs were imminent, and Malone was fuming.

"Next time you don't want to fucking play, tell me, and I won't play your ass," Malone said in front of the whole team.

He was livid at how he'd gone through the motions. He continued.

"Heavy is the head that wears the crown," Malone said, according to a teammate who was there.

There was an example Malone expected him to set, especially while fully rested. He was the cornerstone of the team.

"Okay, so why'd you wait until game 81 to say something?" Jokic snapped back, according to multiple teammates.

Jokic had been excellent all season, with a team that flirted with the No. 1 seed. His engagement and production levels were almost unimpeachable. That year, Jokic finished fourth in MVP voting behind Giannis Antetokounmpo, James Harden, and Paul George. Beyond that, Jokic refused to be belittled, and certainly not publicly.

"It was a very tense moment," said assistant Wes Unseld Jr.

As they went back and forth at each other, still in front of the team, neither was making any headway, according to Malone. They brought it in for a huddle, uncomfortably pausing the confrontation.

Malone was as competitive as his players. He hated losing more than he savored winning.

The timing of the exchange was the most alarming aspect. The Nuggets had yet to secure their playoff seeding and had one game left in the regular season. This was uncharted territory.

Still in the locker room, Millsap and Harris gathered around a reporter's phone to watch the end of Houston versus Oklahoma City. The Rockets' loss momentarily took the sting out of that night's game and the subsequent postgame drama.

Will Barton hinted at something else.

"I don't feel like we're at any liberty to be trying to pick who we're playing against or pick the seed because if we go out there and we're not playing the right way, anybody can beat us," he said. "I try to lend my advice but we're going to have to go through some things," Barton said.

The Nuggets flew home that night ahead of their regular-season finale against Minnesota the following day. There was no time to address what had happened, and emotions were still raw.

Malone deemed the two of them "coexisting."

Mason Plumlee was keenly aware of the tension.

"Hey, Joker, have you talked to coach?" he asked, sitting next to his stall in the locker room.

"Nope," he replied.

Before the game, Plumlee asked another assistant, Jordi Fernandez, whether they were going to address what happened. Fernandez said he suggested Malone should speak to Jokic and bury it.

"They're both stubborn," Plumlee said.

Once the game started, it was readily apparent that they hadn't spoken to each other. In the huddles, they weren't so much as interacting, Plumlee recalled.

"It was like we won a game despite ourselves," Plumlee said of Denver's 99–95 win that clinched the No. 2 seed and a date with the San Antonio Spurs.

Back at home in the postgame locker room, guys were drained from the comeback victory. But when the team went to put their hands in the middle of the room, as was customary after wins, Plumlee noticed Jokic was still sitting in his chair. Plumlee told Jokic to get up and bring it in with the rest of his teammates.

"I was like, 'Are you good?'" Plumlee asked Denver's franchise center. Jokic affirmed he was.

"Coach, are you good?" Plumlee asked Malone.

"Yeah, I'm good," he said.

"You guys are our leaders!" Plumlee said in front of the team. "We can't go into the playoffs if y'all aren't talking to each other."

Plumlee's intervention had to happen, but both knew they were lying through their teeth.

"We're both full of shit, because we're not all right," Malone said on the precipice of the postseason.

Jokic's problem wasn't so much with authority as it was with condescension. He could take criticism.

"If it's respectful, if it's something that makes sense to me, I'm gonna accept it, but even if I talk bad to you, I think I can be respectful," Nikola said when reminded of the incident and asked about confronting authority.

"As soon as you cross that line, I can cross that line," he said. "It's not that I'm feeling offended, it's just that I don't need to take that."

Besides, if someone really wanted to trade barbs with Jokic, they likely wouldn't register. He was adamant that he'd been his harshest critic.

"The things that I said to myself, nobody else said that to me," he said.

The Nuggets had the Spurs in their crosshairs, their first postseason series as a unit. Malone and Jokic were still "coexisting."

There was a practice day before the series started, and Malone ventured to the team's second-floor facility, where he found Jokic shooting free throws on the far end of the floor about thirty minutes before the team convened.

He grabbed him by the shoulders and asked, "How you doing?"

Jokic was flippant.

"Fine," he told him.

"No, no," Malone pressed. "How you *doing*?"

He had Jokic's attention.

"I said, 'Nikola, I want you to know something,'" Malone said. "'I love you, I care about you, and I'm going to coach you. You're not always going to like me. But it's important for you to know that I do care about you.'"

In the moment, Malone heard his dad's wisdom. He remembered a story that had been passed on of former Knicks coach Jeff Van Gundy laying into John Starks in front of the whole team.

The lesson, Malone said, was that *those* conversations needed to happen behind closed doors and not publicly. Undressing a player in front of his peers only served to embarrass him, which wasn't the point.

"Because now, he's not hearing what you're saying," Malone said.

Malone was unabashedly emotional and stubborn, not unlike Jokic. By that point, their relationship had roots. "Coexisting," wasn't an option when theirs was a shared investment.

"Hopefully what he's always respected is that I've always been myself," Malone said. "This is who I am. I've tried to improve who I am, I've tried to become a better version of myself."

In the aftermath of their incident, which was the last time they'd really locked horns, Plumlee said something to Malone that was worth jotting down.

"Leadership is lonely," he told him.

Plumlee understood that calling out the team's best player wasn't easy but was sometimes necessary.

"Hey, Coach, that was great," Plumlee said, according to Malone. "We all appreciate that."

CHAPTER 44

PLAYOFFS

Nuggets assistant Ogi Stojakovic knew a matchup with the Spurs was more than just an inaugural postseason debut for Jokic.

"Why did Nikola play at the beginning [of his career] such great games against San Antonio?" he asked, knowing the answer.

It had to do with the reverence Jokic had for Gregg Popovich and the respect he had for San Antonio's entire organization. With Serbian roots, Popovich was the gold standard in coaching, preaching ball movement and selflessness.

"It's more than a game," Stojakovic said of Jokic's clashes with Popovich. There was personal pride at stake.

And back when the best access Jokic had to the NBA was YouTube, he found a certain power forward captivating. He studied Tim Duncan's footwork, and once Jokic got to the NBA, he grasped how Duncan leveraged his positioning, enhanced angles, and opened windows with his screens.

"Just watching him you can learn a lot," Jokic said.

Two seasons later, after the comparisons between him and Duncan had even more merit, Nikola savored the cerebral aspect of his approach.

"I can just imagine him in his prime," Jokic said. "I think he knew it in every moment what he's going to do on the floor, how he can manipulate the defender or whatever. He's a good guy to look up to."

It was fitting, then, that Jokic's first playoff test came against San Antonio. Duncan had retired, but LaMarcus Aldridge and DeMar DeRozan were still the figureheads of the steady, professional Spurs.

In Game 1, in front of a frothing home crowd, Jokic diced San Antonio for a triple-double, featuring 14 assists but only 10 points. His two-man game with his guards—Jamal Murray, Gary Harris, or Will Barton—was unstoppable. Yet Murray missed a wide-open elbow jumper that could've given Denver the game, and the Spurs quickly wrested home-court advantage away from the playoff newbies.

"He was wide-open, I think it's a great shot for us," Jokic said. "He didn't make it, I'm good with that."

The Spurs sent a barrage of double teams to harass Jokic, but his line, again, fostered questions of his *ideal* aggression.

"I'm fine with [dishing to] the open guy, he's wide open, so I don't have any problems with passing the ball," Jokic said. "If I force it, maybe it's a bad shot, so I'm just going to pass it to [an open shooter], and that's how we're supposed to play."

As if to show how amused he was by the pretense of the playoff stage, Jokic concluded his press conference by leaning into the microphone, unwittingly declaring how insignificant one loss was.

"My voice is really funny in this," he offered to no one. *"Nuhh, nuhh, nuhhh,"* he mused before walking off.

Down 19 points with four minutes and change left in the third quarter of Game 2, the Nuggets' season hung in the balance. They hadn't won in San Antonio since 2012. An 0-2 hole likely would've been a death knell and a premature exit for a fledgling playoff team.

Jokic ignited a furious rally with a 3-pointer from the top of the arc, and the Nuggets stormed back with clutch shooting and suffocating defense. Facing their first real postseason pressure, Denver responded. And though Jokic was more aggressive, finishing two assists shy of another triple-double, the fourth-quarter seizure belonged to Jamal Murray.

He poured in 21 points on an array of dagger 3-pointers and fadeaway jumpers that suggested a level of confidence bordering on irrational. It was the type of showing that hinted at what might be possible under Jokic and Murray's watch.

"Everybody knows when I get in the zone," Murray began. "I just kind of go crazy. I have a lot of fun. I love the game, play with passion. I was hot."

The series now en route to San Antonio, the Nuggets had life thanks to their pugnacious point guard. But Colorado's own Derrick White embarrassed Denver's defense in Game 3. His shifty drives and timely pull-ups made a mockery of Murray's defense. Denver dropped Game 3 and was once again in a must-win situation heading into Game 4.

The losing streak in San Antonio had reached 14 games—long enough to seep into psychological territory. The Nuggets knew they were going to have to win on the road to advance. In Game 4, Jokic set an assertive tone, hunting for openings in the paint. Whether he was willing to admit it publicly or not, the more aggressive he was, the better the Nuggets fared.

Murray once again met the moment in a hostile environment. Jokic fed him for a backdoor cut through the heart of San Antonio's paint and Murray elevated for a vicious jackhammer jam that drew a satisfying sneer from the Canadian. Denver smelled blood.

Both stars were unfazed by the pressure in the biggest moments of their careers. Jokic dictated the pace and tempo of Denver's offense, while Murray redeemed himself after White undressed him. For Jokic, twenty-four, and Murray, twenty-two, the moments were invaluable.

"I just feel like we've seen it all at a young age so far," Murray said after their convincing Game 4 win. "Going to the playoffs is a big experience for us, and we're all learning on the fly."

Jokic was eager to shine light on his counterpart.

"He's our point guard, he's our leader on the floor, he's our general, so when he has great energy, we just follow him," Jokic said.

So, you guys go as he goes, a reporter asked?

Jokic released a contemplative moan ("*mhmm*") into the microphone, decided he found the noise funny, then moaned some more ("*mhmmm*") for effect.

As much as he loathed individual attention, Jokic knew exactly how to command a press conference. He was disarming and quirky, yet insightful when a question piqued his interest—which was rare. He didn't mind being goofy, since that meant being himself. His press conferences became appointment viewing.

"Joker's not your typical young guy," Paul Millsap said. "If you asked me what age he is, I'd think he's thirty. But then when you have a conversation with him and you watch him with his video games . . ." Millsap trailed off. "He knows what this moment is about."

That was another beautiful incongruity about him. As serious as he took the game of basketball, Jokic was a child at heart. A tall, talented one but a child nonetheless.

The children of Nuggets staffers would line the hallway as players ambled from the court back to the team's locker room. Jokic loved interacting with all of them, a big, friendly giant in high-tops. After innumerable high fives and bear hugs, Jokic would take Wes Unseld Jr.'s son and sling him over his shoulder. This routine became routine, an inside joke that was worth maintaining because it delighted Unseld's son. His stroll through the children's canyon was a part of his game-day tradition, win or lose. That they were indifferent to the outcome no doubt appealed to the kid inside him.

During a press scrum ahead of their crucial Game 5, Jokic wandered into the middle of dozens of cameras and recorders and pleaded, "No dumb questions!" After five minutes he left smiling, pleased with the media's effort.

"Only one questionable question," he mused.

In front of a raucous home crowd, the Nuggets dismantled San Antonio to stake a 3-2 lead. Jokic was overwhelming. For the fourth time in five games, he flirted with a triple-double. The Nuggets were a different animal when the non-Jokic shooters were connecting from beyond the arc. The threat of a 3-pointer forced the Spurs defenders to stay home rather than sink off onto Jokic. It yielded an offensive assault that thrust Denver to the verge of its first playoff series win since 2009.

"We were just playing the game, and obviously San Antonio's a team that started that many years ago, the beautiful game," Malone said.

Ironically, Malone never would have been in position to knock off the Spurs had Popovich not endorsed him years earlier. In 2005 there was a Basketball Without Borders camp in Argentina, and there, indulging in the region's best wine, Malone worked his way into Popovich's orbit.

"I just had a feeling about the guy," Popovich said. "He had a quick knowledge of the game, understood people, and had a real competitive spirit about him, that kind of thing. The friendship just kind of grew."

When former San Antonio assistant Mike Brown landed the head-coaching job in Cleveland, coaching a transcendent talent in LeBron James, Popovich vouched for Malone, who settled as an assistant.

"He said to me one time, he goes, 'Malone, I have no idea why I help keep getting you jobs because you've never helped me win a damn game,'" Malone said. "And I said, 'I can't figure it out either, but don't stop helping me out.' . . . Me, my wife, my girls, we have a little shrine for Coach Popovich in the house."

Even though the respect ran deep, in the throes of a playoff series, none of the pleasantries mattered.

Jokic's 43-point eruption in Game 6 wasn't enough. The Spurs were desperate, and Denver's defense didn't travel. It was a dispiriting outcome for a team that tried to trick itself into believing they were facing elimination and not the other way around. For most of them, this series marked their postseason debuts. If they were to unearth a killer instinct, it would have to come at home in Game 7.

By virtue of their home-court advantage and No. 2 seed, all the pressure was on Denver to hold serve. But before the game, Juancho Hernangomez walked around the arena with a reassuring message on his shirt: "Keep calm, we got Nikola Jokic."

The mantra turned into a prescient bit of marketing: Jokic's Game 7 triple-double was the foundation of Denver's gripping win.

The Spurs chipped away at Denver's double-digit fourth-quarter lead, whittling it to two with 52 seconds remaining. That's when Jokic fed Murray for a fading, floating prayer from the elbow that sealed the Nuggets' first series win in a decade.

Earlier, Malone described the chemistry of Jokic and Murray as "almost romantic." The bedrock of the Nuggets' foundation was a cerebral Serbian and a gutsy Canadian.

In their first playoff run, they'd won in near-desperate circumstances, endured on the road, and survived elimination. Murray's clutch shooting was a tantalizing development, while Jokic's dominance was astonishing, averaging 23 points, 12 rebounds, and 9 assists.

"And win," Jokic interjected after a reporter rattled off his jarring stats from the series but neglected to mention the only one that mattered to him. "[Are the numbers] something I live for? No, it's just really good stats."

CHAPTER 45

HEARTBREAK

The San Antonio series didn't surprise Portland star C. J. McCollum. He was well aware of Jokic's capabilities *before* the playoffs started, and braced for the havoc he intended to wreak against his frontcourt in the second round.

"He's the leader of the orchestra, in terms of when he wants to score, when he wants to rebound, when he wants to playmake," McCollum said. "I think it's just a sign of greatness."

The respect was well established, but now the Nuggets had tangible playoff experience. They'd grown immensely throughout their first seven postseason games, and had new confidence to show for it.

McCollum knew you couldn't guard Jokic one-on-one but also accepted that sending double teams left the defense vulnerable. When accounting for his touch, range, and the "one-leg stuff," McCollum was at a loss for how to defend him.

"It's obvious that he's a basketball savant," he said years later.

Malone reached a similar conclusion as McCollum, his confidence brimming at Jokic's indefensibility.

"If you watched the San Antonio series closely, they stopped doubling him for a reason," he said. "He picked people apart. . . . After that, you could tell, they said, 'We're going to play this guy one-on-one,' and he had 43 points. Good luck. Do whatever you want to do."

Jokic backed up Malone's open invitation when he made light work of Enes Kanter, dousing him with 3-pointers and floaters for 37 points and a Game 1 victory.

"I consider him like Tom Brady," said Paul Millsap of his teammate's ability to process and exploit. Jokic didn't refute the comparison.

"I think I can read everything," Jokic said candidly. "I just need to know what they're going to do, you know?"

In Game 2, Portland varied up its defensive coverages, harassing Jokic with an array of big men. The physicality, specifically from Zach Collins, made Jokic work. Behind McCollum's 20 points, the Blazers seized Game 2 and home-court advantage. Beyond the win, there was disdain brewing between the two division rivals.

Both teams had generational players—Jokic in Denver, Damian Lillard in Portland—and were clawing for relevancy in the cutthroat Western Conference.

What was a playoff series without some feistiness and a little blood?

Malone's father, Brendan, was an assistant on the "Bad Boy" Pistons, who only achieved NBA supremacy after surviving two brutal series against Michael Jordan's Bulls. There was a level of tenacity baked into the younger Malone's DNA.

"Listen, both of these teams are trying to get to the Western Conference finals," Malone said. "It's gonna be hard-fought, it's gonna be physical, but there's nothing dirty about that and I respect that."

The lessons the Nuggets were learning—about playoff physicality, playing through injuries, and fighting exhaustion—were invaluable. In their Game 7 triumph over San Antonio, Jokic played 43 minutes. When questioned about his fatigue, he scoffed, as if he had any choice but to endure.

"It's Game 7," he said. "You gotta do what you gotta do."

Nothing they'd experienced collectively could have prepared them for what awaited in Game 3.

Early in the fourth quarter, the game within two possessions, ESPN's broadcast suggested fatigue would play a role as Jokic's minutes approached 35 for the night. What they couldn't have known was that Jokic would play 30 *more* minutes than he already had.

With a jersey so soaked the shade of blue was darker than the rest of his teammates', Jokic played 65 minutes, smashing his previous career high by nearly 20 minutes. The marathon thriller turned into just the second quadruple-overtime game in NBA playoff history.

Despite Jokic's triple-double and the handful of chances Denver had to snatch Game 3, the Blazers survived. McCollum, among the most balanced and unpredictable scorers in the league, torched Denver's defense from the midrange. While Jokic's minutes accumulated, his decision-making faltered, no doubt a result of exhaustion.

There were diminishing returns the longer he dictated the offense, yet his presence was a testament to his impact. The Nuggets *needed* him, if not to score then to facilitate and command attention. It was as grueling a physical test as the Nuggets had ever been a part of, and it ended in disappointment. Jokic said he didn't register the unfathomable court time he'd played.

"They're always talking about I'm not in shape," Jokic said. "I'm in really good shape. I don't know what they're talking about. Even when I came here, I was just maybe a little bit chubby?"

He paused for effect.

"There's no difference right now."

Jokic's humor was indefatigable.

"Defeated?" Will Barton asked, questioning a reporter's word choice. "Definitely not. [We're] disappointed."

When their heads hit the pillows well after midnight and the emotions subsided, their reality remained unchanged. Down 2–1, it was the exact same place they'd been last series.

Malone encouraged his team to completely detach the following day. There was no need to relive the emotional roller coaster.

"I woke up ten thirty," Jokic said. "I went to the breakfast, then I went to the massage, then I went to treatments, then I walked on the treadmill a little bit. Have a nice lunch, rested, didn't do nothing. Watched a couple episodes of a TV show."

When the Nuggets rebounded in Game 4 some forty hours later, it reflected a resiliency within one of the youngest playoff teams in NBA history. Jokic authored *another* triple-double—his fourth of the postseason—and Jamal Murray sank 34 points, the latest act of his breakout postseason. Murray drained 6 clutch free throws in the final 13 seconds to seal it.

"It feels good knowing that the game is basically in my hands if I make them or not," Murray told the *Denver Post* that night.

When Murray took the scoring lead, and Jokic served as the central nervous system of the offense, both players resorted to their natural comfort zones. Their shared focus, in seizing a road win in Portland, illuminated a steely resolve—and one that Jokic had no interest in indulging.

"Everybody write this down right now, so no extra questions about Jamal and me," commanded Jokic with a sardonic tone.

He then reeled off a laundry list of attributes that worked between him and Murray, heaping praise on his competitive nature.

Another question began before Jokic interrupted.

"Did you write that down?" he said, his timing upon delivery as precise as his bounce passes.

Buoyed by their series-shifting win in Portland, the Nuggets pasted the Blazers in Game 5 to stake a 3–2 lead. Jokic was sensational, finishing with 25 points and 19 rebounds. Almost all of his damage came inside, where the Blazers were helpless against his size.

"The good thing with Jok is, he makes the right play, every play," Barton said. "I don't know if [there has] been a player in NBA history that does that. Like, every play he makes the right play. . . . I'm serious."

In Game 6, Lillard (32 points) and McCollum (30) held serve to force another Game 7, the Nuggets' second of the postseason. *This* series came with all the drama and spice associated with a brewing rivalry. There were shoving matches, wayward comments from each locker room, and at least one middle finger aimed at the Nuggets' bench. Ahead of Game 7—Mother's Day—all those stories became subplots.

The Nuggets were one game away from reaching the Western Conference Finals for just the fourth time in their history.

But the Nuggets' 17-point first-half lead evaporated beneath a flood of slippery McCollum drives, and Portland clamored back by the fourth quarter. Due to fatigue, inexperience, or the stakes, the Nuggets got tight on their home floor. Possessions petered out and McCollum, the only NBA player to come from Lehigh University, fleeced the Nuggets' rangy defenders. Jokic and Murray provided the lion's share of scoring in the fourth quarter, serving as one last reminder that the moment wasn't too big for them, that the pressure wasn't overwhelming.

On Mother's Day, the Blazers seized Game 7. Jokic's 29 points and 13 rebounds had lifted his team to the threshold of a conference final against

Golden State, yet his two assists were indicative of a team that couldn't buy a bucket.

In the sober postgame locker room, Jokic took the blame, even though it wasn't his to take. One late missed free throw wasn't why they'd lost.

"They look at me as a leader, they look at me as their best player," Jokic said. "I feel responsible. I missed a lot of other shots, and I'm supposed to make some of those."

What occasionally presented as apathy from Jokic wasn't accurate. That was more a disguise than anything, or perhaps a defense mechanism. He cared, deeply, about lifting the franchise that had invested so much in him.

Back in the locker room, with front-office members and coaches all present, Jokic took more responsibility.

"I think Tim, I, and Malone, some coaches are there, and he comes in sobbing and he starts apologizing," said GM Arturas Karnisovas.

They all looked at each other bewildered.

"We're like, 'Dude, what are you apologizing for, you got us here,'" Connelly said.

According to assistant David Adelman, his tears were because of the internal pressure he put on himself. He felt he was the reason why the Nuggets won or lost, why the coaching staff and his teammates succeeded or not. In the moment, it didn't register how far they'd already come.

"He felt a huge responsibility," Adelman said.

The moment was one more tell on who he was as a teammate.

"It just showed you how much he cared," Connelly said.

It was in those painful, raw moments that Jokic's façade was lifted. He couldn't bury his supposed indifference under a joke. Regardless of how he acted most of the time, his tears suggested there was always an underlying motivation that most would never see. His emotion stemmed from the burden of a franchise. He knew it was his to lead.

"I knew it would be a time when this would come for him," Nuggets veteran Will Barton told the *Denver Post*. "When your role changes and you become that guy, you're almost forced to care. Not saying that he never did, but now it's just, it's more. He knows we come and go as he goes."

CHAPTER 46

FELIPE

What was once a fifteen-minute escape has dwindled to ten or sometimes, depending on the night, only an eight-minute reprieve before tip-off.

For years, in the quiet moments before games, Jokic has sought refuge in Felipe Eichenberger's office. There, he's far from the prying media and invasive cameras.

"We laugh a lot," Eichenberger said.

A creature of habit, Jokic's routine illustrates where Eichenberger, the team's head strength coach, fits into the superstar's hierarchy.

No one within the Nuggets' organization was more influential in Jokic's development than Felipe, a soft-spoken, burly Brazilian.

Felipe's impact, on his body and his belief, was nothing less than profound. What began as a traditional coach-player relationship morphed into something more akin to family. Without Felipe's incessant encouragement and ceaseless friendship, Jokic wouldn't have blossomed in the same transcendent way.

Like a quality performance trainer, Felipe remembered the humbling bar Jokic set upon arrival in Denver. He couldn't hold a plank for thirty seconds. His body, built on greasy Balkan pastries and liters of Coke, didn't look like most NBA players.

"We noticed that his body was not well developed," Felipe said. "Not just like overweight or anything. He hadn't really lifted or was doing stuff to keep his body healthy for a long period of time."

What commenced was a complete physical overhaul.

Felipe, then the assistant strength coach, oversaw Jokic's development in the weight room and his nutrition. Jokic was naturally strong, but Felipe saw a frame capable of much more with the proper oversight. From a dietary perspective, Jokic deferred to Eichenberger to order for him when they went out to eat. In Denver, Felipe would deliver healthy food options to his apartment, or teach him to make protein shakes as part of his regimen.

Jokic was curious and, Felipe sensed, committed.

Felipe's São Paulo accent is still prominent, but his command of English, after playing college basketball in Oklahoma, has become excellent. In 2015, Jokic's grasp of the language was tenuous at best. They bonded over the shared experience of being a foreigner in a new country, each trying to establish himself in the NBA.

When Jokic had questions, about nutrition or the science behind an exercise, Felipe saw him struggle to express himself. Given his personal experience, Felipe was patient and understanding. Jokic's desire to improve gave Felipe even more reason to encourage him.

Well before Jokic became an unequivocal part of Denver's future, Felipe watched practice daily and saw how he imposed himself in the post, how he *already* appeared to be the best player on the court.

"He was just different," Felipe said.

But at that point, there were no guarantees Jokic would even be the backup center, let alone one day a starter. Climbing the depth chart was the goal. Whatever future he had was nebulous.

"He was hungry for more," Felipe said. "He knew that he had a very slim opportunity to make it happen."

Under Felipe's guidance, he was intent on seizing it.

Felipe was part of the Nuggets' traveling party that visited Jokic in the summer of 2017, along with head strength coach Steve Hess, assistant coach Ogi Stojakovic, and coach Michael Malone.

What he discovered was an environment in Sombor wholly unfit to build a superstar.

"We couldn't do anything on the treadmill because the treadmill didn't work," Felipe said.

Of the dumbbells available, one was black and one was white. Both claimed to be 25 kilograms, but Felipe was skeptical.

"I don't think they're the same weight," he said.

Initially they improvised, making the best of what they had. But as the summers went on, and Felipe continued his annual trek to Sombor, the environment improved drastically. Jokic purchased the heavier machinery, then invested in a gym space that was available to him anytime he wanted. Sometimes Felipe stuffed extra equipment in his luggage to bring over.

That first trip, though, laid the foundation for their friendship. It was then that Eichenberger could show Jokic how invested he was in him as a player but also as a person. If Sombor was where Jokic preferred to spend his summers, then the Nuggets were going to accommodate him.

When Malone left Serbia, Eichenberger stayed longer, allowing him to witness Jokic in a different light. While Malone was there, Felipe said, Jokic tried everything to accommodate his head coach. Even if Jokic appeared to be a foundational piece of the Nuggets moving forward, there was still a different dynamic when the head coach was around.

"It's okay, you can take a break," Felipe told him once he was the lone team representative remaining. Felipe sensed an appreciation from Jokic that he could drop his guard.

They darted to and from practice in Jokic's little red car, lovingly nicknamed the "Red Bullet." Eichenberger, roughly 6'7", and Jokic, a seven-footer, couldn't help but laugh at their ride. They crammed six people into a car that could only comfortably accommodate three.

"It was awesome," Eichenberger said.

Within that trip, the trust settled between the two of them. A ten-year age gap melted amid their shared investment.

One night, among Jokic's friends, Felipe learned exactly what it meant to be outgoing in Sombor. He generally doesn't drink, but the environment was too tempting, the mood too much fun.

The details remained hazy, but the group made a handle of Jack Daniel's disappear, then found themselves at a bar, shotgunning beers as fast as they could. Eichenberger was astounded at the congenial bartender, who was quick to facilitate the drinking games for the rowdy group.

"It was a good night," Eichenberger said.

The trust Jokic showed in dropping his guard with Eichenberger was being repaid as the team's strength coach embraced Jokic's crew. It was a legendary night among Jokic's friends, and one they still reference to this day.

Eichenberger still remembers a drink they had to start the night, something they called the "Blue Frog." Years later, he still had no idea what they consumed.

"You can spit fire right after it," he said.

CHAPTER 47

TOM BRADY

Felipe was careful with the messages he brought to his players' attention.

He was sensitive to overwhelming them, or worse, for his message to be construed as "fake." There was an art to picking and choosing what to share with Nikola, or any other player for that matter.

He was delicate, until he found something he truly believed would help a player. And then he doubled down.

He wasn't self-indulgent enough to think that *he* was the reason Jokic prioritized improving his body, and he firmly believed that Jokic would have succeeded in any environment, on any team.

But, early on, Felipe's confidence in Jokic was steadfast. When he sent a picture of seven-time Super Bowl winner Tom Brady to Jokic's phone, the message was unambiguous. The image was one Brady shared on Instagram of himself wearing his NFL draft combine shirt, a reminder that he was a sixth-round selection of the New England Patriots.

"This is what they said about me then," the caption read, before listing off a handful of critiques about his physique and his skill set.

Brady was the NFL's equivalent to Jokic, a Hall of Famer overlooked for myriad reasons. A second-round pick, like Jokic, was roughly the equivalent of a sixth-round selection in the NFL draft.

"I said, 'Man, listen, just a reminder,'" Eichenberger told the *Denver Post*. "A guy that can't jump or can't do this, they're saying all these things about this guy, and look at where he is now, just like you."

Felipe also knew the message would resonate.

"He really liked to watch the Patriots play when they had Tom Brady," Eichenberger said.

Felipe watched as Jokic's confidence blossomed. The more experience he got in the NBA, the more he began to believe in himself. Felipe saw it firsthand as he honed his endurance, then molded his body into a tree trunk.

"He saw the opportunity and he took it," Felipe said, emphasizing how hard Jokic worked every single day on the practice court and in the weight room.

Since Felipe's daughter was a one-year-old, Jokic has made it to every one of her birthday parties. Felipe knows he's often tired and battered, but that's never stopped him. His attendance serves as a testament to what Eichenberger and his family mean to Jokic.

"He never loses that [perspective] and I don't think he will," Eichenberger said.

"He's my family," Jokic told the *Denver Post*. "I'm really honest with him. He understands me. He knows when I'm lying. It's funny. . . . We're not hiding nothing from each other."

The proximity of their families, not to mention the bond between the two men, could have infringed on their professional relationship had Felipe ever let it. But from the beginning, long before Jokic ever made his first All-Star team, Eichenberger was honest with him.

When his diet was trash, he called him on it. When his workouts were underwhelming, he let him know.

"Even if he was mad, I told him, 'I'm not here to be your friend. I'm here to make you better,'" he said. "We can be friends after."

Which was precisely why their friendship deepened. Eichenberger never needed anything from Jokic, as others did. Instead he was available as a trainer and, when necessary, a friend. He challenged him to maximize his potential, refusing to let him settle for anything other than great. There were no shortcuts in the weight room and no lapses when Jokic's body hurt.

"Brother . . ." Jokic's plea would begin, before Eichenberger insisted on completing a set.

In the moment, Jokic might have been irritated at Eichenberger's resolve, but he craved accountability. And no one held him to that standard like Eichenberger.

"If you soften up around him, I think he loses respect for you a little bit," Felipe said.

CHAPTER 48

THERAPEUTIC

The car rides to Denver International Airport could last anywhere from thirty to forty minutes, which was plenty of time for Jokic to vent or laugh, depending on the mood.

For years, he and Eichenberger made the drive together, the Rocky Mountains splayed out like a postcard in their rearview mirror. Eichenberger came to know Jokic's body language so well that those drives could take on all kinds of formats. Eichenberger knew when he was upset or could read when he needed a friend. If there was a family matter such as impending fatherhood, with Eichenberger, it could be addressed.

He conscientiously never forced conversations. If a topic needed addressing, they'd inevitably get to it. When Jokic needed a pick-me-up, Eichenberger had the stories and the recall to elicit a laugh.

"You can call it therapeutic, or you can call it a friendship," Felipe said. Often it was one and the same.

There was an inverse correlation that Felipe came to recognize: as Jokic's fame soared, fewer people seemed to understand him, or were willing to challenge him. Felipe never had that issue. He shared his opinions, whether Jokic wanted to hear them or not.

There was one opinion that Jokic *really* didn't want to hear.

"Man, you can win MVP," Felipe told him during one of their dozens of car rides.

Felipe always believed in the talent Jokic harbored and knew better than anyone how dedicated he was.

"'Brother, I can't, it's just selfish,'" Felipe recalled Jokic saying. "'I'm a passer,' this and that."

But Felipe had more conviction than Jokic had excuses.

"I don't care," Felipe told him. "You're gonna be MVP."

Jokic started getting animated with Eichenberger. He couldn't believe that he really thought it was possible. Furthermore, Jokic resented the implication of the award.

"He thought I was calling him a selfish player," Eichenberger said.

That, of course, would have impugned his reputation and wasn't Eichenberger's intention at all. Eichenberger vehemently believed it was possible and wanted Jokic to see it for himself. Meanwhile, Jokic stewed.

"He lost it and didn't talk to me for a week," Eichenberger said.

Later, once the temperature cooled, Eichenberger broached the topic again. Only this time, he offered a carrot. Felipe vaguely recalled that MVP winners earned a Kia car and some prize money.

"How much money do I get?" Jokic asked him.

Felipe didn't know the exact number, but made up an amount—$100,000—on the spot.

"I was like, 'You can buy a new horse with that,'" he told Jokic.

"He was like, 'Oh, wow. Okay, that's interesting.'"

CHAPTER 49

THERMOSTAT

Following a disappointing (and short) summer, Jokic began the 2019–20 season in one of *those* moods.

Despite Jokic's participation, Serbia had finished fifth at the FIBA World Cup in China that summer. His underwhelming play seemed tied to his conditioning.

He arrived back in Denver out of shape and far from rejuvenated. His fluctuating weight raised concern among team officials.

"He got, I think, to 305, 310, which I've never seen him that heavy," said the team's GM Arturas Karnisovas.

He'd been so impressive during his inaugural postseason that he'd almost set unrealistic expectations moving forward. One off shooting night bled into a couple of lethargic performances—which was all it took to set off alarm bells.

When Jokic's aggressiveness or his production fell off, there was usually a reason. He was so good, and so consistent, that there almost had to be. (It was long past the point where simply playing in the NBA, against the best players in the world, served as a viable explanation.)

Jokic returned to the States bigger than he'd left them. Never one to move swiftly, he seemed to be plodding at an even slower pace than before. His size offered one explanation, but his engagement was curious as well.

"I don't think he is, in terms of people thinking he's checked out or not playing hard," Malone said a couple of weeks into the season. "I don't see that as the case at all."

Malone, who again had to talk with him about his assertiveness, kept defending him. The message was always the same.

"When he's aggressive, he takes everybody with him," his coach reminded him. "And the same way, when he's not aggressive, he takes everybody with him."

Eventually, Malone settled on a perfect description for Jokic's regulatory ability: he deemed him the thermostat.

Jokic's influence was so overwhelming that his funk could be debilitating.

As Jamal Murray explained, "When you're open and you don't shoot it, that's kind of the offense."

Jokic appeared to be mired in one of his confounding riddles, which prompted some level of reckoning from those around him.

"I have a good idea of how to read Nikola, get through to him, push the right buttons, and he knows me," Malone said. "And he reads me as well."

A thermostat, indeed.

Jokic temporarily turned down the temperature when he buried consecutive game-winning shots, first against Philadelphia and then two nights later in Minnesota. Against the Sixers, his deep jumper came off a broken play where he happened to find space amid a thicket of Philadelphia arms. Against the Timberwolves, Jokic sunk a fading, swerving dagger a step inside the 3-point line. Though he felt it was reductive to distill games down to individual matchups, the truth was that he'd bested Joel Embiid and Karl-Anthony Towns in the ongoing battle for big-man supremacy.

Asked which one he preferred, Jokic momentarily shed his cloaked media persona.

"Last one [versus Philadelphia]," he said grinning. "Less time on the clock."

Jokic's genius was firmly established among the NBA cognoscenti. He'd morphed in five quick seasons from obscure second-round pick to the face of a franchise. Within that rapid rise, he earned more money than he'd ever dreamed of. His perspective, on individual accolades, public criticism, and his own personal priorities, was astonishing given how much had changed.

He admitted that, at one time, numbers mattered to him.

"Yeah, of course, when you came here, it's in the back of your mind," he told the *Denver Post*. "I want to stay here. This is the league of the stats, the numbers. It's in the back of your head, but for me, not any-more."

Jokic had been paid handsomely. How many triple-doubles he accrued, or how many All-Star Games he made, didn't matter. Whatever records he broke were immaterial.

"It's over," he said. "I think the coach, the owner, the GM, the players want to win the game. That's the bottom line."

The criticism that came with his contract, or that dogged him during slumps, or that scrutinized his weight, didn't matter either.

"I don't read anything anymore," Jokic said. "I stopped."

In making that choice, Jokic seemed to simplify his relationship with the media. What was said about him barely registered.

"It doesn't bother me," he said. "People are . . . they assume things, and they cannot be right or wrong. They're just saying, if it's wrong [shrugs]. If it's good, if they are right, it's a good thing."

Despite his public indifference, few people realized how seriously Jokic took his responsibilities as the face of the franchise.

For a month and a half, Jokic's efficiency and production were both well below his career averages. And though there was an occasional burst—he registered three triple-doubles within the first month—the consistency wasn't there.

When he wasn't meeting the standard he set for himself, in perfor-mance or reliability, Jokic searched for a remedy. In conjunction with Fe-lipe, perhaps his most loyal confidant, they found one.

"He's always with me, he's always worked with me, he knows my body better than me, and he's my friend, so I trust him," Jokic said.

Felipe acknowledged his bloated size but tried to allay concerns over his production. Heavier, or potentially lighter, Jokic was still a force, he thought. Eichenberger's biggest concern wasn't his size; it was his availability.

"His durability, for us, is more important," Felipe reiterated to anyone who asked.

He explained to Jokic that some of his body pain would be alleviated if he played at a lighter weight. He told coaches and management to be patient, to give it time.

On one of their many car rides to the airport, Eichenberger ensured

Jokic's education continued. Endlessly curious, Jokic peppered him with questions for thirty minutes about strength and recovery.

During another road trip and another car ride, Jokic inundated Felipe with even more questions. The same thing happened a third time, as Felipe reinforced the commitment necessary to optimize Jokic's body.

Jokic took time to process information and metabolize it. After all, what they were discussing constituted work, and effort.

Felipe's argument was simple. Jokic's role within the team was more pronounced than it had ever been, and he needed to account for the increased workload.

"The only way to do this," Eichenberger told him, "is if we work out after the game, we can load you more and you can get a lot more done than just lifting the day after."

Felipe continued to push, though Jokic's resolve was tepid.

One day, Jokic sent Eichenberger a bodybuilding/motivational video he'd seen on YouTube. Eichenberger asked Jokic what he meant by it.

"It's work," Jokic replied.

There was nothing to sugarcoat. What Felipe was proposing was physically taxing and time-consuming.

"Okay, let's do it," Jokic said.

Eichenberger recalled the team was on a road trip in Sacramento when he walked into the coaches' meeting right before their pregame meeting. He explained to Malone how he was going to handle Jokic's extra workload and what the implications were. He might be more tired initially, he told him, but he'd drop the weight. More importantly, the added strength would equip him for the grind of a season.

"To understand Nikola's mind, he's the kind of guy if he tells you, 'I'm gonna do something,' and he looks in your eyes like, 'I'm gonna do this,' he will," said Felipe.

On a road trip in early December, Jokic maintained his rigorous regimen by tossing weights around in the bowels of arenas after games. It became such a dedicated routine that Jokic would sometimes take up to an hour after games before he'd fulfill his media obligations.

"I didn't change much, I just kinda changed my diet, my workouts," Jokic said, as if downplaying the consideration that went into it.

It had a marked effect. In February, Jokic averaged over 25 points per game on 64 percent shooting from the field, up 10 points from his no-shoot November.

"Nikola, he's been working really hard, before and after practice, I think he's been getting in great shape, and he looked fast out there," Malone said. "Five years now, and I've never said 'Nikola' and 'fast' in the same sentence."

When he was relayed Malone's verbiage, Jokic soared for the alley-oop.

"Yes!" Jokic said. "Finally, something athletic in the same sentence with me."

CHAPTER 50

CHICAGO

When Nikola arrived at his personalized dais for his All-Star Game press conference, he was overjoyed to see so many Serbian faces looking back at him.

Chicago has one of the biggest Serbian populations outside of the country itself, and numerous journalists huddled around Jokic's podium for the rare chance to query him in their native tongue.

What they discovered was a more relaxed, more assured version of their two-time All-Star.

Stalking the sidelines with faux outrage, Jokic was in his element coaching in a Special Olympics unified game that weekend. Kids and Special Olympians brought the best out of him—unbridled silliness that matched the energy of those around him.

"I have one question," he told a game official, stashing the punch line for later. "Are we up or down?"

He chided the referees for calls and pleaded for more points from the scorekeepers. When a graying Toni Kukoc subbed out of the game, Jokic levied serious criticism in his direction.

"Toni, we are minus 7 when [you are on the court]," he lobbed.

Whereas media obligations tended to drain the affable superstar, events like these rejuvenated him. And when a Nuggets staffer convinced him to wear a microphone for the event, fans got a rare glimpse at his preferred persona.

Jokic was an NBA All-Star, who *deserved* to be there. His distinct dominance was unlike any other star in Chicago that weekend.

"You've seen Larry Bird, he wasn't the fastest, but he dominated," said teammate Will Barton, Jokic's unofficial hype man. "Magic [Johnson] wasn't the most athletic, he dominated. Mike [Jordan] didn't really shoot threes, he dominated. Great players do it in their own different way."

That season, Jokic was on pace to join Wilt Chamberlain, Oscar Robertson, Larry Bird, Kevin Garnett, and Russell Westbrook as the only players ever to average 20-plus points, 10-plus rebounds, and 6-plus assists for a full campaign. Only Jokic had already achieved those benchmarks the season before.

There was a certain joy Barton derived from watching the process unfold.

"I would be laughing at the other big men because they're looking like, 'Man, what the fuck? This slow, fat motherfucker is killing us and we have no answer for him,'" Barton said laughing even though the shock factor had dissipated the longer Jokic was in the league.

The more basketball history Jokic carved, the less inclined he was to indulge his own accomplishments. But he did relish when an up-and-under, or a devious spin, left defenders grappling with nothing.

"Oh, yeah, that's the best thing just because it's kind of fun to see their faces, to see their reactions when you do something good," he said.

In many ways, Jokic's coming-out party was a referendum on how NBA fans consumed the league in general. A vicious jam got more play on highlight shows than did his no-look passes or gaudy numbers. Jokic's play unambiguously impacted winning. That that was harder to distill within social media clips was no fault of his. The last thing Jokic needed was validation from anyone on the internet.

"Everybody watches for highlights, high flying and shit like that, but if you know what you're watching . . ." Monte Morris said without having to finish the thought.

The All-Star Game was a perfect encapsulation of that dichotomy.

How Jokic could dominate an actual basketball game but be rendered useless in an All-Star exhibition seemed to undermine the integrity of the showcase.

Jokic was the default in-bounder, which often meant he never had to cross halfcourt. As his teammates leaked out for transition chances, Jokic ambled into the action at his own pace. Inevitably, his team would score quickly, initiating an about-face that left him scrambling back across half-court.

"I really enjoyed it," Jokic said. "Just enjoy the moment, just enjoy being around the guys. I scored two times, I was so happy. They snubbed me for [the] MVP award. It doesn't matter. Next year."

CHAPTER 51

PANDEMIC

When the Nuggets flew to Dallas in early March 2020, team trainers wore gloves and mopped seats with sanitizing wipes in an effort to protect Denver's traveling party.

At shootaround on March 11, Nuggets coach Michael Malone sat at a podium with an eight-foot barrier between himself and reporters. Rumors of the coronavirus swirled around NBA teams. The NBA and its Board of Governors floated the idea of games without fans present. Only essential team staffers were allowed close to the players.

"I was reading this morning, somebody threw out the potential idea of if a city has cases where there is the coronavirus, maybe they would cancel games in that city and hold it at a neutral site," Malone said.

Malone's comments reflected a universal ignorance of what the world, and less importantly, the NBA, was facing.

The lower bowl at American Airlines Center was crammed with fans eager to see Jokic face off against Luka Doncic that night. Both stars exchanged high fives, as did others on the court. One player traded an autograph for a squirt of hand sanitizer; another fan sitting in the first row stood out for his attire: a mask. The rest seemed unfazed.

"There was like little pieces of news that came out, and there was just this eerie feeling like there was going to be an avalanche of change to our sports world and just to our daily lives," said ESPN's Ryan Ruocco, who broadcast the game that night.

As the Nuggets jogged back onto the court for the third quarter, Nuggets president Tim Connelly told Malone that the Utah–Oklahoma City game had been suspended. Jazz center Rudy Gobert had tested positive, the first known case in the NBA.

Midway through the third quarter, the league made the unprecedented decision to suspend the season. News spread from press row, conveniently a few rows up from the court, to the crowd. Most players didn't know the scope of events, as the game trudged on with the world shifting around it.

It amounted to a landmark first step taken by the NBA, the loss to the Mavericks that night a footnote amid the historical events.

The Nuggets scrambled to adjust their travel plans in real time. A flight to San Antonio was scrapped in lieu of a return trip home to Denver.

After a surreal day, Malone was asked how he would spend the upcoming hiatus.

"I'm probably going to drive up to WeldWerks Brewery in Greeley, Colorado, get some Juicy Bits, get on my mountain bike, and figure out how we're going to move forward," he said.

As the team was swapping flight plans, Connelly asked whether two reporters, myself and Nick Kosmider of The Athletic, wanted to leave Dallas that night. There was a chance, we were told, that we could hop on the team plane.

We hustled to our respective hotel rooms, packed our bags, and scrambled back to where the Nuggets' team plane was waiting. There we provided IDs and had our luggage searched.

Amid the chaos of the evening, Malone began a text thread with myself and Kosmider. The unprecedented decision to let two reporters on the team plane came from Malone and Connelly.

"Nick was tested at the arena before boarding the bus," Malone wrote. "You will be tested at the airport. The exam is a rectal so hope you have proper hygiene."

A team trainer snapped his glove and walked to the back of the plane. To Malone's chagrin, it turned out that a temperature read was all that was necessary to secure a seat home.

As the two of us wrote, trying to describe a day when a global pandemic had upended the NBA season, a flight attendant walked by and asked whether I wanted anything. I quickly perused the menu.

"Steak, please."

CHAPTER 52

COUNTERSTRIKE

At 8:57, their phones would start to vibrate.

A group chat, featuring Jokic, Boban Marjanovic, Nikola Vucevic, Bogdan Bogdanovic, Milos Teodosic, and Luka Doncic, would light up as the nine o'clock hour approached.

The pandemic left NBA players grappling with the same problem as the rest of society: What were they supposed to do?

For weeks there was no sense whether the NBA would return to conclude the last month of the regular season. League officials pondered questions of safety, economics, equity, and time. It was a complicated set of factors, as even individual workouts were a chore to organize.

In the meantime, at 9 p.m. ET every night, the group chat would light up.

Who's available? Who's ready?

For at least two months, the group traded the camaraderie of the locker room for the next best thing: a headset and a controller.

"A lot of *CounterStrike*," Bogdanovic said. "That was the game we all grew up on."

For weeks on end, the group gathered, digitally, to defuse bombs and combat terrorists.

Doncic played on occasion but wasn't a regular.

"To be honest, [Nikola] and Luka are good at everything they touch," Boban said. "I don't know how. They play good video games, all the sports they love. They never played soccer, [but] both of them are gifted for soccer. That football, throwing the ball, it was like, 'Oh, the ball flew perfectly.' . . . [Nikola] has that gift. He can touch everything and make it gold."

Teodosic logged on from Europe. The group invited whoever was available, but the mainstays were Jokic, Marjanovic, and Vucevic.

And when the texts would pour in, a slight sense of guilt washed over Vucevic.

"My wife's looking at me like, 'Really'?" he said, responding in the name of friendship.

"Well, they're waiting for me."

Eventually, Vucevic said, their wives met up and complained about their husbands' habit.

Over headsets, they would strategize and tease, plot and joke. Boban said the group would argue as if they were about to play five-on-five pickup.

"You didn't have my back, you didn't have this," Marjanovic said. "It's not talking shit; we talk about tactics."

The nightly games provided some small semblance of normalcy amid the isolation. It was a welcome distraction as the Balkan players bided their time, like the rest of the world.

It was also a window into Jokic's relationship with a few of his countrymen. During *regular* regular seasons, dinners with Jokic's people were commonplace. In Atlanta, Jokic went to dinner at Hawks assistant and Serbian coach Igor Kokoskov's house, along with Bogdanovic and Vlatko Cancar.

"Whoever is speaking Serbian, he's more than welcome to come to the party," Bogdanovic said.

Cancar, a Slovenian, was a rookie during the 2019–20 season. Jokic looked out for him like he did other Europeans trying to get their bearings straight.

"Every time he had a holiday, basically, he would invite me over just because he knew I was here by myself," Cancar said.

Once, when Cancar arrived to Nikola's late, the punishment was steep. There was rakija, and Cancar had to play catch-up. He arrived around 7:30 and estimated he was asleep, in a guest room, by 9.

"I had the best sleep ever," Cancar said.

All-Star weekends tended to coincide with Nikola's birthday (February 19), which meant resident All-Stars Jokic and Doncic always found a reason to celebrate.

"He's a great guy," Doncic said. "Always joking around, he's just a simple and very amazing guy."

As is the case with most of Jokic's close friends, the two barely talk hoops when they're together. But to a league that has struggled to explain Jokic's inimitable brand of basketball, Doncic understood better than most. Neither Balkan star overwhelms with traditional athleticism, but it's their shared ability to shapeshift between positions that begins to define both of them. Playing at each of their preferred paces, both Jokic and Doncic have redefined what constitutes a generational player.

"All the players, all the coaches know how special he is," Doncic said. "He's right now probably the best basketball player in the world."

There's a certain indissoluble bond among the players who've made it to the NBA from that part of the world. Among Jonas Valanciunas (Lithuanian), Ivica Zubac and Dario Saric (Croatian), Vasa Micic or Nikola Jovic (Serbian), the respect level, for what Jokic has accomplished, runs deep.

"From the jump, he was doing big things," said Valanciunas, the Pelicans's former center who classified their relationship as more respectful than friendly. "He was learning, he was growing, but the talent was there."

There's a similar relationship with Zubac, the Clippers' center, who first guarded Jokic as a teenager during a tournament in Hungary.

"He puts you through so much [as a defender]," Zubac said.

Besides their regional origins, Zubac, Marjanovic, Cancar, and Jokic all played under the late coach Dejan Milojevic, whose Mega teams were known for grooming tough, physical NBA prospects.

Among all the talent that hailed from that part of the world, no one has as deep a history with Jokic as Boban, the beloved journeyman from Serbia.

"We're almost best buds," said Boban, estimating he's known Nikola for nearly fifteen years.

Boban, seven years Nikola's senior, played at Hemofarm with Jokic's older brother, Nemanja, which is where he got to know their family. Even then, Boban recalled Nikola doing the same things: dribble, score, assist, block. The moves were there, but his experience was not. Still, Boban saw enough to be convinced.

"You will see he will be the champion, to be honest," he said at the time.

A few seasons later, during the 2012–13 season at Mega, Nikola and Boban found themselves locked in big-man battles during training sessions. At Dejan's direction, they played a ton of one-on-one.

"Even after practice, we played a lot," said Boban, who had to reckon with Jokic's ballhandling and decided he was a point guard stuck inside a big man's body.

Their lone season as teammates was Jokic's first at Mega. He was a doughy prospect; Boban was an established big. They grew up together, blossoming into NBA players ahead of the 2015–16 season.

Now, when their paths cross, it's just like they're back in Belgrade.

"You hungry? Let's go to eat," Boban said, reenacting their conversations. "You're not? Let's go hang out. Let's go watch movie, let's go do this, let's go do that."

To see their goofy interactions is to see two people who'd be close regardless of profession. Despite their shared success, neither has ever grown too big for his seven-foot frame.

"He's for sure a Serbian hero," Boban said. "There's not even a doubt. I think every single kid wants to be like him. Every single person wants to meet him and shake his hand. To me, that shows everything."

CHAPTER 53

INSIDE THE BUBBLE

The NBA's return, in a sterilized Disney Bubble in Orlando, constituted a minor miracle.

Amid a global pandemic, and with racial tensions roiling, twenty-two teams descended on Florida intent on finishing the season.

The plan was ambitious and unprecedented. Making the Finals meant a stay of over three months inside the Bubble, where days were repetitive and boring. It was as much a test of mental endurance as one of physical capacity. Some players, unable to reconcile playing basketball as the news cycle fixated on police brutality, grappled with the decision to be there at all.

"It was extremely difficult for me, to be honest," said then–Nuggets forward Jerami Grant, who dedicated his press conferences to Breonna Taylor. "Debating whether or not I was going to go to the Bubble. Finally came to the conclusion that if I go, I don't want to bring attention away from what's important."

The ongoing racial reckoning from the murders of Taylor and George Floyd rendered the idea of playing basketball, in an isolated space, unappealing at best and unjust at worst.

"It was difficult to get me there, and then to be in there, for me, it was difficult," Grant said. "I definitely was close to leaving. A few guys felt the same way."

Gary Harris, according to Grant, was another who discussed leaving. Will Barton, who left due to injury, later referred to the circumstances as "jail."

There was a mental toll all players accepted just by setting foot on the campus.

The Nuggets arrived in spurts, owing to various COVID cases. Nikola Jokic arrived late after testing positive and serving his quarantine in Serbia. During the hiatus, photos circulated of a decidedly lean Jokic, which suggested he hadn't fallen off during the break.

"I didn't have a break at all in the weight room," Jokic said. "I basically worked out full-time."

There were more late arrivals (Harris, Michael Porter Jr., Monte Morris, and Torrey Craig) and other injuries to navigate, which, for one scrimmage, yielded a supersized starting lineup of Jokic, Mason Plumlee, Bol Bol, Jerami Grant, and Paul Millsap. The Nuggets, like the rest of the NBA, were flying blind, adhering to strict protocols and attempting to ramp up for the postseason.

The team had a dedicated meal room, practiced on two courts inside of an expansive ballroom, sought refuge at the pool, and played board games to entertain themselves. Aside from biking the short loop around the property, which players, coaches, and referees tended to do each morning, or grabbing a fishing pole at the centrally located lake, there wasn't much else to do.

(Jokic, an avid fisherman back home, occupied some of his time with the latter.)

Another account mentioned how effortlessly he dominated the team's cornhole games.

Assistant GM Tommy Balcetis recalled Jokic's first introduction to the sport.

After Balcetis explained the goal of sinking a beanbag into a hole, Jokic wanted to try.

"I give him the bag, and he sinks it on his first try," Balcetis said.

Jokic had shot it overhand.

On the court, the Nuggets were becoming whole.

During the eight seeding games that preceded the playoffs, Porter erupted for games of 37 points, 30, and 27, respectively. His 3-point shooting looked like an ideal fit next to Jokic.

"Jok obviously can be dominant scoring, but I think he is kind of like LeBron in the fact that he would rather facilitate," said Porter, who was still in the midst of an injury-marred and inconsistent rookie season.

Their *other* cornerstone, Jamal Murray, was hampered by a hamstring issue as the team reconvened in Orlando. When he did return for his first game in five months, his production—a near triple-double—hinted at the disciplined work he'd done leading into the Bubble.

"That kind of reminds us of the potential of our team," Malone said.

CHAPTER 54

PLAYOFF MURRAY

There was no hiding in the Orlando Bubble.

Two divisional rivals, stuck in the Gran Destino hotel for an indefinite period of time, couldn't get away from each other. Denver's meal room happened to be close to Utah's. They'd see each other when they ate, when they walked the campus, when they rode the elevator.

When they saw each other on the court, competing amid artificial fan noise, it was an extension of their odd proximity within a postseason battle. The playoff seeding for the No. 3 Nuggets versus No. 6 Jazz meant nothing. There was no such thing as home-court advantage on a neutral court.

The quicker that teams got comfortable with the circumstances, the more likely they were to last.

Murray was in his element from the jump. Sporting neon-green shoes that contrasted their dark uniforms, Murray seized on defenders Royce O'Neale and Joe Ingles en route to 36 points and a Game 1 win. In lieu of crowd noise, Murray talked his trash and issued a few icy glares at Utah's bench. He stalked the court as if there *was* a home-court advantage. Murray and Jokic outlasted Donovan Mitchell, whose 57 points were the third-highest playoff total in history.

"I am guarding him and he's hitting step-backs on me and he's guarding me and I'm hitting step-backs on him," Murray said. "I am smiling because those are the games you want to be in, those are games that are the most fun and most competitive."

The two devastating scorers had an individual battle brewing within the larger series. Yet after Game 1, with nowhere to retreat, Murray ran into Mitchell on the property and broadcast their interaction on his Instagram.

It got late, quickly, for the Nuggets, who dropped the next three games while Mitchell abused wings Jerami Grant and Torrey Craig. Denver's depth was reeling. As Gary Harris negotiated a hip strain that had kept him off the floor, veteran Will Barton left the Bubble entirely due to a knee issue.

In Game 4, Murray's 50-point eruption couldn't counter Mitchell's 51.

"No one wants to go home yet," Murray said convincingly despite facing a 3–1 deficit.

Facing the prospect of an early ouster, Nuggets GM Calvin Booth had begun thinking about what a first-round exit might mean.

Things aren't always linear, he told himself, trying to rationalize what looked like defeat.

The next morning, Booth happened upon a breakfast at the Three Bridges restaurant in the middle of the lake. He sat down with Jokic, the two barely broaching basketball.

"Just the energy he had, he was just calm," Booth said. "Nothing seemed stressed about him."

Booth couldn't wrap his head around it. It was *weird*. He expected a stiff, perhaps concerned disposition from Jokic and instead found a light one. As Booth left breakfast, he had a nagging thought.

"I was like, 'We might have a chance,'" Booth said.

With their season on the line, the Nuggets played calm, poised basketball in Game 5. Jokic sank five 3-pointers in the first quarter, fulfilling Booth's premonition and Murray's message after Game 4.

Even trailing by as much as 15 in the second half, the Nuggets refused to panic. Murray attacked Rudy Gobert with panache, including an electric 360 reverse layup that was as visually stunning as it was impactful. He saved 33 of his 42 points for the second half, where his emotions swayed from giddy to fierce. By the end of their Game 5 victory, Murray's torrid run had extended their stay for at least another game.

"When I play harder, everybody plays harder," Murray said.

Assistant Wes Unseld Jr. called the Bubble experience one of the most mentally taxing yet rewarding few months of his life. What Murray and Jokic were doing was astonishing.

"I'm sitting there like a fan, like, 'Are you shitting me right now?'" Unseld Jr. said.

The playoffs came to an abrupt halt after video circulated of the Jacob Blake shooting in Wisconsin. The paradox of playing, while insulated, was overwhelming. The NBA took a temporary pause to consider its options. Inside the Bubble, players and coaches gathered for an emotional meeting, where some were in favor of discontinuing the season.

The tense, unprecedented moment left players grappling for a purpose in Orlando. It was only after the league and its governors committed to increasing voting access (by converting team-owned arenas into polling places) and lobbying to end qualified immunity that players agreed to resume.

"Just because all the teams voted to stay, I have a feeling that when teams took an internal vote, that the vote to stay was probably 8–7, 9–6, 10–5," Nuggets coach Michael Malone said. "It wasn't unanimous."

CHAPTER 55

BALKAN BOYS

Following the emotional, impromptu meeting inside the Bubble where all relevant parties debated resuming the season or not, a group of Balkan players congregated at the Three Bridges, a restaurant at the heart of Walt Disney World's Coronado Springs Resort in Lake Buena Vista, Florida.

It was centrally located on Lago Dorado itself and had numerous access points that connected the various hotels.

The NBA season was in flux; players, some nearing nearly two months in the Bubble, needed a reprieve. The nature of their schedule—games were played every other day—inhibited big gatherings. But the hiatus created an opening.

A few of the teams left the larger meeting, including the Clippers, for smaller, more intimate discussions among themselves. That's where Clippers center Ivica Zubac found himself when the spur-of-the-moment gathering happened.

"I was a little sad I missed it," he conceded, settling for a dinner the following night.

The crew of six included Jokic and Boban Marjanovic (Serbian); Vlatko Cancar, Goran Dragic, and Luka Doncic (Slovenian); and Nikola Vucevic (Montenegrin). The group munched on sliders while grappling with their unprecedented predicament.

There was an age gap but an understanding among all of them. Dragic, Marjanovic, and Vucevic represented the old guard as Jokic, Doncic, and Cancar had helped usher in a new wave of unique Balkan talent.

Cancar was in the middle of rehabbing an injury and wasn't playing. He had a different attitude than the rest of them.

"I don't know what other people say, but I'm one hundred percent sure nobody wanted to drink alcohol that night," said Cancar.

The whole table started with waters, except Cancar.

"I want a double mojito," he said.

Before long, everyone had a drink in front of them.

Marc Gasol, then of the Toronto Raptors, was at a nearby table. So was former Jazz center Rudy Gobert. The Balkan boys tried to nudge their fellow Europeans to come and drink with them and were rebuffed.

Annoyed at their stubbornness, the group began hurling Serbian curse words across the outdoor patio. Gasol, who can speak Serbian, returned the favor.

"I feel like we were too intense for them," Cancar said.

The music in the restaurant provided the initial soundtrack, but it didn't suffice. Next they passed a phone around, as each player chose a song for the table. When the volume couldn't match their mounting energy, they sent Cancar to find a speaker.

As soon as he returned, "things escalated," according to Vucevic.

The emotions of the evening, spurred by COVID and the distance between themselves and their home countries, stirred into celebration. Despite their respective countries' recent turmoil, Vucevic emphasized that they all shared the same language.

"We don't ever talk about politics," Vucevic said, referencing the violent breakup of Yugoslavia in the early 1990s.

Instead, they rejoiced together.

"Our music is very emotional for us," Vucevic said.

Before long, the group was singing and standing, belting out songs they all knew by heart.

"We have one dance when we play music—Kolo," Marjanovic said. "Nobody knows anything . . . we know a couple steps and that's it. . . . Nikola's so gifted for everything, but not for Kolo."

Vucevic knew it looked funny to see a group of enormous basketball players partying in a restaurant, on a lake, in the middle of a pandemic, particularly with how sensitive a time it was in the Bubble. But they were all foreigners, far from their families, and in need of camaraderie.

They found it in the form of Club Three Bridges.

"We just made this great party out of nothing," Vucevic said.

The restaurant was so unprepared to stage an impromptu Balkan dance party that the bar started running out of alcohol. According to Cancar, they drank whatever was available.

The group partied late into the night, until the restaurant had to close.

"It was our music all over the place," Boban said with a grin.

But no one was ready to go back to their hotel rooms. The group headed to the pool, which was theoretically closed but alluring nonetheless. The same went for the slide.

"The slide didn't have water, so it was dry," Cancar said.

Vucevic and Dragic were there, but neither wanted to use the bone-dry slide. Marjanovic was there too, but "Boban was too big for the slide," according to Cancar, who was content watching the mischief.

That left Jokic and Doncic. Jokic jumped in off the slide without a problem. Doncic, however, was insistent on a belly slide.

Cancar reenacted the screech of skin from his fellow Slovenian.

Skrrt.

Doncic's attempt left a "bruise from the fucking slide," Cancar said.

It was a seminal night in the Bubble for all of them.

CHAPTER 56

3–1

When the games resumed, Jamal Murray was tuned up. The twenty-three-year-old tended to meet the moment. Ever since Game 4, Murray had worn customized Adidas shoes adorned with the faces of Breonna Taylor and George Floyd.

By Game 6, another must-win for the Nuggets, the paint was cracking on the portraits. The more emotional Murray was, the more vigor he pumped into his team. Murray, as he would say later, "found something worth fighting for."

With composed, decisive moves, Murray carved up Utah's defensive schemes. He danced through the lane, keeping his dribble alive, only to seize on improbable angles when their defense relaxed. He burned the nets from the 3-point line on nine separate occasions as part of his 50-point assault on the Jazz.

Jokic hadn't played poorly, but this was Murray's moment. His *second* 50-point game of the series became secondary after he broke down in tears during an emotional postgame interview on TNT.

"Even though these people are gone, they give me life," he said.

When he returned to the locker room, he had a text message waiting for him. It was a screenshot from moments earlier, when Murray had knelt on the rampart to compose himself.

"Can't tell you how proud I am of you," Kentucky's John Calipari, Murray's college coach, told him.

Until Game 7, Murray's incomprehensible run had overshadowed Jokic's steady play. Not that anyone cared; Jokic played to win, not to shine.

The Nuggets had already landed two gut punches to Utah's chances of advancing, staving off elimination twice. A Game 7 was in their wheel-house, especially Jokic's.

Despite a gritty, grimy defensive affair, Jokic found space to soften up Utah's resistance. He lumbered across the lane into open jumpers. He rolled off screens as if he were a guard and not a hulking 280-pound big man. He toyed with Rudy Gobert, deking and spinning and pumping un-til the three-time Defensive Player of the Year was thoroughly perplexed. Tied at 78 with less than thirty seconds left, Jokic sunk a spinning, fading floater over Gobert's outstretched hand to notch a 30-point effort.

When Gary Harris, back from his injured hip, poked the ball free with ten seconds remaining to initiate a fast break, the Nuggets could see the second round. But Torrey Craig botched the layup, yielding one final last-ditch effort for the Jazz. Mike Conley's 3-point prayer swirled around the rim, a fingernail from dropping.

Nuggets players were so stunned they couldn't even rejoice. They'd be-come only the twelfth team in NBA history to survive a 3–1 deficit.

"When it was 3–1, I just played free," Jokic said. "We don't have noth-ing to lose."

CHAPTER 57

3–1 (2)

Clippers center Ivica Zubac knew what awaited him as soon as the Nuggets survived the Jazz.

The burly Croatian center knew that guarding Jokic wasn't like guarding other centers. Jokic, Zubac conceded, did it all. More devastating, his conditioning was off the charts. The Jokic assignment was all-encompassing.

"Everything's different [about guarding him]," Zubac said. "He's involved in every action. There's not one possession you can take off. . . . He just plays super, super hard. That's an underrated part of his game."

The Clippers presented a different front than Utah with a primary center (Zubac) and physical forwards JaMychal Green and Montrezl Harrell at their disposal. Jokic plowed, or pirouetted, through them all. His *counters* had counters.

Late in Game 2—the only game Denver won of the first four—Jokic had an undersized Harrell at the elbow. He briefly entertained a pass to a cutting Michael Porter Jr. before spinning to his left and leaving Harrell to play catch-up. When he did, Harrell launched himself toward where he presumed Jokic would shoot. But Jokic slow-played the sequence, using the rim to protect his reverse layup. His defenders were *landing* just as he was taking off.

After the game, Jokic was asked about the strategy behind his offensive cadence.

"I'm patient because I cannot really run fast," he said. "That's my only option."

There was always a kernel of truth within his jokes. Jokic had mastered *his* strengths, which entailed an inability to be sped up.

After Game 4, Michael Porter Jr. raised concerns about being included in the offense alongside Denver's two pillars. It wasn't the time (down 3–1) nor place (in a press conference) to voice those issues, and *still* the Nuggets were confident in their ability to rally.

In Game 5, buoyed by a scuffle between veteran Paul Millsap and instigator Marcus Morris, the Nuggets erased a 15-point second-half margin to stave off elimination yet again. Porter's lone basket—a 3-pointer from the wing with barely a minute remaining—was only a good shot because it dropped.

"I think the locker room is a little bit, kind of, looser, funnier, if I can say that, when we are in elimination games," Jokic said. "We don't have that much pressure."

It seemed impossible to corner him. He was elusive, which made him dangerous.

In Game 6, as if ratcheting up the difficulty on one of Jokic's video games, the Nuggets trailed by 19 points in the third quarter, again, facing elimination. With suffocating defense and a steely resolve, they chipped away. In the fourth quarter, Jokic connected on three rainbow 3-pointers that broke the Clippers' spirit. During timeouts, the Clippers looked downtrodden and lost, as if the series was already over.

True to Jokic's word, the Nuggets smiled easily and whipped their towels, an underdog seizing an opening. It was the fifth time they'd faced elimination, and the fifth time they'd prevailed.

Jokic's 34-point, 14-rebound, 7-assist performance was unassailable.

"They tried everything to stop that guy," said backup center Mason Plumlee. "And he had emergency shots, floaters, threes, got it on the block."

By Game 7, most of the drama had already seeped out of the Bubble. Jokic and Murray stared elimination in the face so many times over the prior two postseasons that they forgot to blink. The Clippers, having failed to oust the Nuggets in their two previous chances, were a shell of themselves.

Tired of Jokic abusing their frontcourt, the Clippers sent consistent double teams whenever he touched the ball. But his genius was in his processing; he *preferred* to pass his way to victory.

An assist, he was fond of saying, made two people happy.

As soon as a defender vacated his man, Jokic looked for a cutter. With another triple-double—16 points, 22 rebounds, and 13 assists—Jokic controlled the game with a surgeon's precision. The Larry Bird comparison he elicited on the ESPN broadcast was apt.

It was the first time in NBA history that any team had recovered from two 3–1 deficits in the playoffs.

In the postgame locker room, Jokic got sentimental about what they'd accomplished, calling for his team's attention.

"Hey, I want to thank you guys," Jokic said, according to Plumlee. "I'll always remember this team."

That evening turned into one of the most memorable nights in the Bubble for the Nuggets. The entire team, front office included, headed to the Three Bridges to celebrate their *second* stunning comeback. Nobody could believe that they'd survived.

The soundtrack bounced between rap and Serbian music, a fitting tapestry for their group. Sensing the moment, Connelly seized on the opportunity to distribute shots to anyone within arm's range.

Then their shirts started coming off.

"Tim wanted to take [executive] Ben [Tenzer's] shirt off," Vlatko Cancar said. "Everybody was pretty much shirtless."

After the initial party, a handful of staffers headed for the pool and went swimming until 3 a.m.

"I didn't make it to the pool party, but I was there for the shirtless Serbian dancing," said assistant coach Jordi Fernandez.

In one infamous video saved for posterity's sake, Jokic danced, shirtless, as Dr. Dre's "Forgot About Dre" bumped in the background. A Nuggets staffer far more familiar with the lyrics rapped the chorus behind him.

CHAPTER 58

GROUNDHOG DAY

LeBron James paid the Nuggets nothing but respect as he kicked his feet up during their *second* 3–1 comeback.

James knew the exertion required for a 3–1 comeback himself. He had authored a mesmerizing response to the Golden State Warriors during the 2016 NBA Finals, clinching a title for Cleveland. He lauded Denver's toughness and raved about head coach Michael Malone, who was an assistant with James in Cleveland earlier in his career.

When asked about Jokic, James revealed a deep admiration for his approach. Few, if any other players in the NBA, dissected the game—or were capable of playing it—like the fellow savants.

"Being able to get your teammates involved, putting the ball on time, on target, being able to see things happen before they happen and seeing the reward go to your teammates, it's the best part of the game," James said of their shared proclivities.

Unlike Denver's first two opponents, the Lakers had waves of big bodies to throw at Jokic. JaVale McGee was an impediment, as was Dwight Howard. When cross-matched, Anthony Davis's long limbs were effective at deterring too. Game 1 revealed how Los Angeles was uniquely built to obstruct Jokic and defeat Denver.

The series swung, irreversibly, two nights later. Trailing by eight with 3:03 left in the game, Jokic scored nine straight points to grant the Nuggets a late lead. He and Davis traded one more clutch bucket each before Davis drained the shot of the series, and perhaps the playoffs.

Down by one with two seconds remaining, Davis curled to the perimeter where Mason Plumlee was expecting Jerami Grant to pick up his coverage. When it didn't happen, the lapse was devastating. Despite a strong contest from Jokic, who'd been guarding the in-bounder, Davis buried a dagger 3-pointer not two feet in front of Denver's bench.

"I kind of felt that it was going in," said Jokic, who admitted there was a miscommunication on the play.

The Nuggets were two seconds away from changing the complexion of the series. Instead, down 2–0, they were left to grapple with what if.

"I always tell people this story," said then–Lakers guard Kentavious Caldwell-Pope, who was traded to the Nuggets two years later. "If AD didn't hit that three, I figure we would've lost that series."

Murray and Jokic were unrelenting in Game 3, which should have been expected by that point. Jokic nailed several improbable, falling fadeaways and Murray, insistent that they should've won Game 2, ensured they didn't fall into a 3-0 hole. His 28-point, 12-assist, 8-rebound night reinforced his steely gamesmanship. The dejection of Game 2 hadn't defeated them.

"He is built for the big shots," said Nikola Jokic. "I really, truly believe that he's a superstar."

Murray was again spectacular in Game 4, flashing an array of shifty drives and fearless jumpers, but Jokic's foul trouble limited Denver's ceiling. The Lakers' size was overwhelming. It came in droves and left bruises. Facing another 3–1 deficit, the only comforting aspect was that they'd been there before.

"I feel like Bill Murray, I wake up and it's Groundhog Day," Nuggets coach Michael Malone said, alluding to the mental toll of the Bubble and not their repeated dalliance with 3–1 deficits.

After eighty-two days in the Bubble, the Nuggets succumbed to LeBron James and Anthony Davis in Game 5. Jokic and Murray clawed, but they were spent. A riveting, historic run ended, prompting the Lakers to party deep into the night at the Three Bridges.

The Nuggets finally left the next day, following breakfast at the same establishment. The gains they'd made, in terms of perception and mettle, were invaluable.

"We didn't quit," Jokic said. "And that's something that is going to be our mentality and our focus in the next years."

When they returned home, their families met them at the airport carrying congratulatory signs and overwhelming relief. The circumstances of resuming the NBA season were exhausting for all involved.

"There wasn't a dry eye in the place," said Nuggets president Tim Connelly.

CHAPTER 59

MIND GAMES

Less than three months separated the Nuggets' magical postseason ride from another season's start.

The COVID crunch forced teams to reassemble faster than anyone wanted.

During the abridged offseason, Jokic married his longtime girlfriend, Natalija, in a low-key ceremony surrounded by their closest friends.

Dejan Milojevic, then closer to a brother than a former coach, was there. He'd had to endure Nikola's sensitive moments, when Natalija was in the States and Jokic, a vulnerable teenager, was trying to establish his career.

"I always tried to give [my players] advice, not just about basketball but about life," Dejan said. "I'm super happy for them because she is a lovely person, and I love her also."

With Natalija, Nikola ensured he'd stay grounded. His loyalty to her, even across continents, never wavered. She was his rock.

Rather than return to basketball fatigued, Jokic was energized. If there ever was a season to make a statement about his fitness levels or his mental toughness, this was it. Owing to the pandemic, the Nuggets were scheduled to play seventy-two games from December to May. Testing was rigorous and just one more obstacle in a season full of them.

A monster start to Jokic's year fueled his teammates' reverence.

"At this point, what more can I say about him?" Will Barton said. "I tell him before every game, 'Just go out there and win MVP. You could be the best player in the world if you want to.'"

Jerami Grant unexpectedly bolted Denver in favor of Detroit as a free agent. His frontcourt replacement, JaMychal Green, saw how Jokic could dissect a defense (as he'd done to Green's Clippers in the Bubble) and immediately recognized how special his gifts were.

"Never seen a big with that touch," Green said.

And he'd played with Zach Randolph and Marc Gasol.

His touch, Green said, extended from the paint to the perimeter.

"He's so special," Green said. "He's a different type of talent. . . . He's the best passer in the league right now."

Early that season, Jokic heaved a one-handed bounce pass, on a fast break, that hit Green in stride. It was Green's indoctrination to the Jokic Rules.

"If you run, Jok gonna find you," Green said.

Jokic was on a rampage to start the year and racked up triple-doubles on a near-nightly basis. In the third game of the season, he dished a career-high 18 assists against Houston.

Several weeks later, with Jokic having secured a handful more triple-doubles, the Nuggets hosted Utah in a Bubble rematch of the two elite big men.

"I remember one day he gave Rudy Gobert 47 on a Sunday at like three p.m. just on some like, Defensive Player of the Year Rudy Gobert too," Gary Harris said. "It's so simple to him."

But the beauty of his game was that it never became one-dimensional or predictable. Jokic kept Gobert off-balance and guessing the entire afternoon.

Nuggets GM Calvin Booth had a catalog of Jokic-Gobert games to sift through and noticed a striking trend about most of them. What he saw began to unpack the complex layers to Jokic's brilliance.

Booth relished, as he called them, "the games he plays within the games."

It wasn't enough to dismantle a player; Jokic liked to prove a point.

"I just think it's really intriguing how the best strategy against Gobert would probably be to stretch him out, and he's very capable of doing that, but oftentimes he wants to make a point of showing him that he can score on him in the post," Booth said.

"He'll just play out of the post the whole time and show like, 'I know you're supposed to be good at this. I'm gonna beat you at what you're supposed to be best at.' I feel like, that's a different kind of mind-screwing so to speak. . . . If you're supposed to be really good at something, and I engage that and beat you at that, how can you beat me?"

Booth's observation indicated a concerted effort on Jokic's part to demoralize opponents rather than just beat them. The games, in other words, didn't unfold by accident as Jokic sometimes liked to imply. Occasionally there was an agenda, and one that Jokic would never, ever admit.

"I never talk trash to anybody, I'm just playing the game," he said. "I'm really into the bad karma. You know, karma's gonna get you back if you're cocky or whatever."

CHAPTER 60

MISSING PIECE

The Nuggets had always coveted Jrue Holiday, viewing him as a defensive lynchpin that could bolster their perimeter defense.

At the 2020 trade deadline, he was closer to becoming a Nugget than anyone ever knew.

About a day before the deadline, discussions picked up between Denver and New Orleans, a source said.

The deal would have included a combination of Gary Harris, Monte Morris, and two first-round picks, sources said. The hang-up came when New Orleans insisted on a late pick-swap that thwarted negotiations.

"If there was more time, it would've been done. An extra ninety minutes," according to a source with knowledge of the deal.

When it didn't happen, and the Nuggets watched enviously as Holiday got traded to Milwaukee months later for a bounty of first-round picks, Denver was left sitting on its assets—picks and prospects.

But Jerami Grant's abrupt free agent departure left a rangy, 6'9" hole in Denver's frontcourt.

Team president Tim Connelly knew they needed to act. So did general manager Calvin Booth.

Nikola Jokic was in the midst of an MVP-caliber season. His surge provided ample incentive.

"It's hard not to be inspired by his level of play, and while we never want to feel like we have to rush anything or skip steps, when you see a guy playing at that level, it's extra motivation to try to even be that much more aggressive," Connelly said.

In order to compete in the West, against LeBron James and Kawhi

Leonard, Denver needed size and versatility. They needed someone capable of shrouding wings.

"That's how you cap off championship-level teams," Booth said, citing the Pistons' 2004 acquisition of Rasheed Wallace as the piece that vaulted Detroit to a title.

Aaron Gordon was the No. 4 overall pick in 2014 and had wallowed in Orlando ever since he'd been drafted. He'd had as many head coaches (five) as playoff games. It was hardly the environment to develop. When he requested a trade, he was searching—begging—for consistency in his career.

He'd also been tasked with facilitating and scoring on offense while simultaneously checking opponents' best offensive players. It was a lot to ask of Gordon, who also challenged himself to remedy the environment in Orlando.

"I felt like it was time," he told the *Denver Post*. "I spent a good seven years in Orlando doing my best to change the culture, uplift the culture, turn the culture into a basketball mecca. . . . It was difficult."

The Nuggets did extensive background research on him. What they discovered was a player eager to change his circumstances and even more willing to sacrifice if it meant being optimized.

In Orlando, he was the team's second or third offensive option. In Denver, he'd be their fourth or fifth option. In theory, they could simplify Gordon's game and allow him to focus on what they most needed: rugged defending.

The Nuggets envisioned him protecting Jokic in the paint, bombarding the boards, and roaming the baseline as a perpetual lob threat.

As the team rolled to the airport that day, with talks of trades in the air, Nuggets players were anxious about the impending deadline.

"We were on the bus, and the bus was like stopped for like thirty, forty-five minutes in front of the plane," then–Nuggets guard R. J. Hampton told the *Denver Post*. "We all knew it was trade deadline. We knew someone was getting traded. Me, Will [Barton], Monte [Morris], Gary, we were all yelling up to the front of the bus, like, 'Yo, Tim, who's getting traded? Tell us!'"

The Nuggets sent locker-room pillar Gary Harris, Hampton, and a future first-round pick to Orlando in exchange for Gordon. As news filtered out, Harris and Hampton said their emotional goodbyes.

"Last time we were all on the same team together, last time we rode the bus together," Harris said. "It was definitely a lot of emotions. You look back on it, man, you can't do nothing but smile."

It was the end of one chapter and the beginning of another. The foundation that Denver had carefully cultivated was being displaced in place of a championship chase.

"I'm just happy that I found a new home," Gordon said.

CHAPTER 61

DEVASTATION

Upon Aaron Gordon's arrival, the Nuggets unleashed basketball nirvana.

Three games into his tenure, he was already roaming in space as defenses revolved around Jokic. His on-ball creation wasn't necessary. The opportunities, as long as he moved, were going to be there. In early April, Gordon was Denver's answer to the Clippers' Kawhi Leonard.

When he was able to mitigate Leonard's impact, better than anyone on the Nuggets could before his arrival, team officials were giddy. The convincing 101–94 win over the Clippers suggested a team capable of defending at an elite level. Los Angeles had won 8 of its previous 11 games, with an average of over 115 points per game.

If the Nuggets could limit such a potent offense, officials believed, Denver might have the best team in the NBA.

The next game, coincidentally against the Magic, Gordon scored Denver's first 12 points of the night. He battered his former team inside, a rejuvenated player in a winning environment. The broad smile on his face after Jokic found him for a give-and-go suggested he'd realized how much simpler the game could become playing alongside a generational passer.

"He's in the locker room, like, 'Man, these are the easiest passes I've got my whole career,'" Monte Morris said.

Gordon's new basketball reality transformed the Nuggets into a budding juggernaut. In the seven games (7-0) they played since he joined the team, Denver averaged nearly 116 points per game. Conversely, their defense ranked 11th in the NBA.

"The main thing and the best thing that he did is that he accepted the role," Jokic said. "He knows why he came here. . . . He came to win something."

The Nuggets were steamrolling opponents, and Gordon was essential to their formula. He learned to lurk around the baseline, where lobs were plentiful and virtually unguardable. Denver's shooting threats—Jamal Murray, Michael Porter Jr., and Will Barton—ensured Gordon could fly under the radar.

In the first six games of their shared partnership, Jokic assisted Gordon 16 times, which was *already* one more assist than he'd gotten from a Magic teammate throughout the first 25 games of the season.

"It just makes the game so easy," Gordon said. "His ability to see the play before it even develops is amazing."

The Nuggets had reason to be jubilant. Their gambit, in projecting Gordon into a different and more optimal system, looked seamless. Teammates felt they had the most complete starting five in basketball, with the postseason barely a month away.

Everything they wanted was in front of them until April 12, inside the Chase Center in San Francisco, when Jamal Murray's left knee buckled.

Late in a game that was all but decided, Murray drove toward the basket and planted hard on his left leg. He collapsed, writhing in pain near the basket stanchion, gripping his left knee in agony. After several minutes he was offered a wheelchair but refused. He hobbled off with his arms draped around two staffers.

In the raw, sensitive moments after Murray's injury, he had a visitor who could commiserate. Klay Thompson, who'd torn both his ACL and later his Achilles, was with Murray in the visiting locker room. The show of solidarity transcended their competitiveness.

"I told him that I felt for him, first off," Thompson told the *Denver Post*. "If he channels that competitiveness into his daily tasks he has to do for his knee, he's going to be an All-Star level player again."

Murray's ACL tear brought back wrenching memories of Thompson's own traumas.

"I hated seeing it," he said. "He's so important to their team, him and [Nikola] Jokic. I really felt for him in that instance, because I've been there, and it's kind of uncharted territory. He's in the prime of his career. It just sucks, not just for the Nuggets but for the whole NBA."

On the bus ride to the airport the following morning, Murray was so distraught he asked his coach whether they were going to trade the injured star.

"That was his first thought," Malone said, consoling Murray like a parent. Malone reassured him that that wasn't going to happen, then vowed they would support him as he returned a stronger player.

Murray's ACL tear compromised the mission, yet the Nuggets had a choice: they could either concede a lost season or compete knowing that their championship odds had taken a significant hit. As was the case when they were down 3–1 in the Bubble multiple times, the Nuggets showed their character.

"We're going to miss [Jamal] as a team, he's a big part of our team, but that doesn't mean that we're going to quit," Jokic said.

Driving what appeared to be an MVP campaign, it was his job to lead them.

CHAPTER 62

MVP

A red Lamborghini SUV adorned with the license plate JOKER pulled into the players' parking lot on April 19, exactly a week after Murray's devastating injury.

It was a loud car for someone whose attire amounted to a rotating cast of Nike tracksuits. The scene didn't quite make sense considering Jokic's distaste for attention.

"That's actually my car," Strahinja Jokic, Nikola's older brother, told the *Denver Post*. "He's just driving it. He's not that guy."

That season, Jokic *was* that guy.

Perhaps to his chagrin, Jokic was charging toward the league's Most Valuable Player award. Heading into that night, his scoring (26.4 points) hovered around top ten in the league, as did his rebounding (11.1). His assists (8.8) were fourth in the league, ranking him among the game's best point guards. Most importantly, the Nuggets were still in contention for home-court advantage in the playoffs, an indication of the team's prowess.

A few months earlier, amid a litany of MVP inquiries, Jokic stammered through a question he didn't know how to answer.

How would you define MVP? he was asked.

He said something about being the "best player," and the "top scorer," neither of which was convincing or satisfying.

"That's a really good question," Jokic said. "I really don't know, for real."

To his teammates, the answer lay in the example he set.

"Last year, and the year before, if he didn't really want to play that day, he'd kind of just chill," Michael Porter Jr. said. "This year, it's like he knows this is his team, and he's going to go out every single night and be the MVP."

MVP | 253 |

Behind the scenes, in the weight room or in the team's second-floor practice gym, there were eyes on him.

"Definitely learned a lot from him, even if he didn't know it," said Bol Bol, then a second-year center who'd yet to gain traction in his career.

Bol watched as he went through drills at game speed, never short-changing the workouts.

"Honestly, he's one of the hardest workers I've ever seen," Bol said.

Jokic had assumed responsibility for the Nuggets' fortunes and all those who fell under his purview. His rise was their rise, his journey was theirs too. Nothing Jokic did was ever a singular endeavor.

When his brother's Lamborghini rolled into the players' parking lot that evening, Jokic felt the weight of a team reeling after losing Murray. The MVP campaign couldn't have been further from his mind when he mauled Memphis that night. He scored 47 points in a resounding double-overtime win, capping off the masterpiece with a rainmaking 3-pointer. Denver needed all of his 15 rebounds and 8 assists too, a reminder that he was a multifaceted force.

Will Barton replaced Murray as Jokic's preferred pick-and-roll partner, the two carving up the Grizzlies on their shared institutional knowledge. Jokic hadn't missed a beat. And if the Nuggets were going to be competitive without their fiery point guard, he was going to have to be other-worldly.

"That's why you're the MVP of the league," Barton told him on the bench that night.

Jokic effectively shrugged when asked about his signature moment that stamped his MVP credentials.

"There's a lot of players in this league that are playing at a really high level," Jokic said. "That's my answer."

"I think he loves that adversity," Nuggets coach Michael Malone said. "Some guys run from it. He cherishes that opportunity."

CHAPTER 63

UNDERDOGS

The Nuggets' rash of injuries hadn't stunted their optimism as they charged into the postseason.

They'd sustained Murray's season-ending injury, a significant hamstring injury to Will Barton, another hamstring injury to backup-turned-starting-point-guard Monte Morris, and an adductor strain to wing P. J. Dozier. The injuries, according to Michael Malone, were a product of the condensed, COVID-crunched schedule.

Their depth had been decimated, but the Nuggets still closed the season with a 13-5 spurt, the third-best record in the NBA over the final month.

That was a testament to Jokic's willpower, and Denver's resiliency as a whole.

Almost irrationally, the Nuggets still believed.

A starting lineup of Jokic, Porter, Aaron Gordon, Facu Campazzo, and Austin Rivers symbolized how far-fetched that notion was. Campazzo, who spent his formative years playing for Real Madrid, was technically a rookie getting a crash course on NBA survival. Rivers had been out of the NBA for two months in search of his next job when the Nuggets called late in the regular season.

Their first-round opponent—a rematch against Portland—provided a stark contrast in positional talent. Damian Lillard and C. J. McCollum were still among the most lethal backcourt combinations in the NBA. Campazzo, a feisty 5'11" Argentinian, played like he had Red Bull coursing through his veins. His energy was tenacious.

"Do you think they were frustrated?" Campazzo asked, reflecting on defensive assignments like Lillard and Steph Curry throughout the year. "If they were frustrated just for a couple minutes, it's a goal for me."

Around Jokic, Denver could compete. Two-way guard Markus How-ard was a 5'10" flamethrower in college who'd only played out of necessity.

"I don't remember the last time I was able to have open shots," Howard said. "In college, I never got them. . . . Playing with Joker these past couple games, I've been open a couple times and I was almost a little surprised by that."

Jokic's malleable nature gave the Nuggets a chance. Whether it was a two-way player, a rookie, someone on a ten-day contract, or a veteran, Jokic erased his teammates' blemishes and amplified their strengths.

"Whoever's on the floor, we can find what he's doing good," Jokic said. "To be honest, I think I could play with anybody in the lineup."

Given Denver's depleted ranks, any outcome was plausible. But for Portland, the series was a referendum. If they couldn't beat *these* Nuggets, who could they beat?

In Game 1, Lillard came as advertised. He rained down 3-pointers, exposing a disconnected and undersized defense. The Trail Blazers seized home-court advantage by turning Jokic into a scorer (34 points) and lim-iting his help (1 assist). Accustomed to postseason deficits, the Nuggets weren't dismayed.

In Game 2, Lillard doused Denver for eight 3-pointers in the first half despite a new defensive coverage (Rivers). When he pulled up a few feet in front of the Nuggets' halfcourt logo, it foreshadowed a long night and po-tentially quick series. At halftime, newcomer Aaron Gordon volunteered for the assignment.

The Nuggets' patchwork of players hadn't tamed him; perhaps a bigger body like Gordon's could navigate screens and impede his vision.

"In the second half, they came out and said I was going to start on him for the first possession," Gordon said.

The Gordon wrinkle worked. Defensively, they had *something* to con-tain Lillard's blistering shooting. On offense, it was inevitable that Jokic would solve Portland's defense. Jokic softened up the stout defense Jusuf Nurkic had offered in Game 1 with a bevy of jumpers and methodical post moves. After Nurkic, Portland's reserve big Enes Kanter had nothing for Jokic.

It was the latest iteration of Jokic's attack.

Nuggets GM Calvin Booth's career had overlapped with Dirk Nowitzki's in Dallas, playing under innovative coach Don Nelson. The way that Nelson had utilized Dirk resonated with Booth.

"Dirk was always close to the nail," Booth said in reference to the middle of the free-throw line.

There, with the ball in his hand, he could inflict the most damage. Since it was such an exposed piece of real estate, opponents were hesitant to send double teams, and furthermore, everyone was one pass away. And for Dirk and Jokic, that shot was the equivalent of a "layup," Booth said.

When Booth arrived, he implored offensive expert and assistant coach David Adelman to explore that space with Jokic. He felt it was underutilized for a player of Jokic's caliber.

For years it has been quietly emphasized and become a staple of Jokic's arsenal. The Trail Blazers felt the pain of that addition.

Jokic bludgeoned the Blazers for an efficient 38 points (and 5 assists) as the Nuggets rolled to a Game 2 victory.

In Portland for Game 3, Jokic was again magnificent but he had help from an unlikely source. Austin Rivers, who only months earlier was on a couch wondering whether he'd ever play in the NBA again, drained four fourth-quarter 3-pointers to silence the below-capacity crowd in Portland and stun the Blazers.

"We are really a team, it's just a true team," Rivers said. "I've never been somewhere where I've just fit . . . not just basketball-wise, but culture-wise, I fit."

As reserve forward JaMychal Green said: "We got Jok, we knew we can still beat that team."

That was the level of confidence Jokic instilled in his teammates. He turned two-way players into reliable scorers and journeymen into postseason heroes. He had a habit of lifting those around him.

The Blazers throttled Denver in Game 4 due to an uncharacteristically cold shooting night from Jokic. It may not have mattered if anyone else was impactful since a superb Jokic game was all but a prerequisite to win.

Regardless, the Nuggets came to Portland and swung the series back in their favor. The Nuggets were headed home tied 2-2, a best-of-three to decide who'd advance.

Describing Lillard as unconscious in their Game 5 first-round series would've undersold his rhythm. Irrepressible was more apt. He sank one step-back 3-pointer to send the game to a first overtime, then hit another to send the affair to a second OT. He scored 55 points that night on an NBA-playoff-record twelve 3-pointers.

The waves of defenders Denver tried couldn't withstand his tsunami.

Yet Jokic's near-triple-double (38 points, 11 rebounds, 9 assists) was also remarkable, and he had help. When Michael Porter Jr. floated to the corner with 1:35 left in the second overtime, Jokic waited patiently until a double team arrived near the far elbow. As Aaron Gordon's sacrificial cut drew Porter's defender a half-step toward the basket, Jokic lobbed a pass into Porter's waiting hands. The ensuing triple was the dagger.

The Nuggets withstood an outrageous display of clutch shooting to assume control of the series.

"It's a shame we wasted one of the all-time best performances by not being more supportive of him," said his sidekick, C. J. McCollum.

Buoyed by the confidence he'd shown in Game 5, Porter came to Portland to close out the series. He sank six 3-pointers in the first quarter, some off designed screens and others off his own activity.

Content to let Porter cook in the first half, Jokic saved 27 of his 36 points for the second half. He twirled Nurkic into knots.

On the bench, Murray, Will Barton, and P. J. Dozier—the Nuggets' all-infirmary squad—danced and bounced at each subsequent bucket. Their beleaguered squad was there in engagement if not production.

While the Nuggets celebrated, the Blazers could do nothing but reflect. They'd lost, in six, on their home floor, against a team that was decimated.

Years later, McCollum was wistful at the result. Now in New Orleans, it marked the last playoff series McCollum ever played alongside Lillard.

"We should've won the series, but they outplayed us," he said. "That was the end of us, basically."

CHAPTER 64

BREAKING POINT

By virtue of their first-round upset, the Nuggets had already over-achieved.

"I don't know how many playoff teams in NBA history have won a series with their starting backcourt out," said Nuggets coach Michael Malone. "We're gonna be the underdogs again this series [versus Phoenix]. We don't mind that. I think we're really comfortable with that."

The Suns had significantly more firepower than Portland in Chris Paul, Devin Booker, Mikal Bridges, and Deandre Ayton. Paul, the future Hall of Fame point guard, was the straw that stirred the drink.

The Suns made a concerted effort to exhaust Jokic on defense. Paul ran incessant pick-and-rolls that impeded Facu Campazzo's path and called for Jokic to meet the action at its zenith. That either left Paul on an island with Jokic, left a small guarding Ayton, or induced help coverage, which left a Suns sniper open. Paul seized on Denver's vulnerabilities.

Neither of the first two games was close. Paul diced Denver for 26 assists, an indication of his profound control of the series.

In the middle of the second round, the NBA made official what had almost been a foregone conclusion: Nikola Jokic was the NBA's MVP. He was the Nuggets' first-ever winner and made history in doing so. Prior to Jokic, the lowest draft picks to ever win the award were Giannis Antetokounmpo and Steve Nash, both of whom had been selected at No. 15 overall. Jokic had lasted until the second round, at No. 41, the most improbable MVP in NBA history.

Not that he was impressed with himself. When he was asked about the impending award late in the season, he downplayed the accomplishment. When he was invited on national podcasts to discuss his rise, he politely declined. Jokic wasn't interested in taking credit despite a superlative season amid unprecedented circumstances.

"It's not just my award," Jokic said during his MVP press conference, which came over Zoom. "It's an award for everybody who works for me and with me."

According to one team spokesman, team staffers had been more excited for the announcement than Jokic ever was.

Baked inside his eighteen-minute press conference, he revealed something illuminating. Jokic always struggled to put his legacy in perspective. If his story inspired others, then that was good enough for Jokic.

"What I really want is that kids are going out and playing basketball," Jokic said. "They don't need to play basketball, they can play whatever sport they want to play, just to go outside and play sports. If I do that for the kids back home, I think that's going to be my biggest accomplishment."

With his brothers at midcourt to present him the trophy, Jokic accepted the award ahead of Game 3 in Denver. He was sheepish and almost embarrassed at the attention, as "MVP" chants delayed his brief remarks. Jokic was more eager to get on with the series than he was to bask in adulation.

That night, Jokic played like the runaway MVP. He registered 32 points, 20 rebounds, and 10 assists in an awe-inspiring line that still couldn't overcome the talent gap against Phoenix. Jokic was so hell-bent on winning, he apologized to his teammates after the game. If it wasn't so genuine, it would've been laughable. Jokic joined Kareem Abdul-Jabbar and Wilt Chamberlain as the only three players in playoff history with those numbers, yet the result, a 3–0 deficit, lingered.

The Nuggets were severely compromised, their deficiencies in size and talent too glaring to mask.

By Game 4, the only remaining question was how hard the Nuggets intended to fight for their season. They were within three possessions late in the third quarter when Jokic, mentally and physically exhausted from the season, swung down on the ball and caught Cam Payne in the face with part of his right arm. Payne fell in a heap, and Suns star Devin Booker started jawing with Jokic before teammates arrived.

Jokic seemed to have reached his breaking point and was ejected from the game. His season, and the Nuggets' campaign, were over.

Jokic again apologized to his teammates and took responsibility for his impulsive swipe.

"He pushed himself to the limit," assistant coach David Adelman said of his historic, season-long romp.

Before Jokic spoke to the media that night, he told the coaching and front-office staff to stay put.

"Nobody leave," assistant Wes Unseld Jr. recalled him saying.

When he returned from his postgame press conference, he came armed with a couple of cases of beer. Sitting among coaches, executives, and owners Stan and Josh Kroenke, the group processed their season. Also among the group was head coach Sean McVay of the Kroenke-owned Los Angeles Rams. Eight months later McVay's team would go on to win the Super Bowl.

As abruptly as the season ended, the reality was that the group won a playoff series without Murray, their second-best player. There was the sting of a sweep and the stench of Nikola's ejection, but there was also a sense of achievement relative to their circumstances.

For better or for worse, Jokic knew it was worth savoring.

"He's an experiential guy," Nuggets president Tim Connelly said. "He's more about the input than the output."

Unseld was struck by Jokic's poise and his insistence on examining the season that was.

"Who does that?" said Unseld, still grappling with his decision to convene.

Some three hours after the game ended and Jokic's gathering dispersed, two reporters walked out of the building and found Jokic at a stop sign adjacent to the players' parking lot, signing autographs for a couple of fans. It was his last official act of the season. When I told Nikola I was planning a trip to Eastern Europe that summer, he laughed.

"I'll tell you where I am," he said, "but you will not find me."

CHAPTER 65

@JOKICBROTHERS

When the Nuggets convened for training camp in San Diego the following October, their leader, Nikola Jokic, wasn't with them.

He was tending to more important matters.

"Probably the highlight is we have a baby coming," Jokic said. "That's probably the highlight of my season, [of] my life. Other than that, it was really short [offseason]. The second good thing is my horses won fifteen to twenty races this year. They're doing a good job."

His priorities intact, Jokic finally had a full offseason to physically recover. In the meantime, the Nuggets returned their entire core in free agency and reached key extensions with Aaron Gordon and Michael Porter Jr. Denver's moves signaled a vote of confidence for their direction, even without a healthy Jamal Murray.

Collectively, because of Jokic, the Nuggets felt they could still contend for a championship that season. There was immense pressure on him just weeks into it.

"I feel for Nikola because reigning MVP, and so much is being asked of him every night," Nuggets coach Michael Malone said. "I'm worried that he almost feels he has to play perfect. Not for us to win, for us just to have a chance. We all know that when I take Nikola out sometimes, it's kind of like, 'All right, what's about to happen?' . . . He's not Atlas, he's Nikola."

That weight got heavier only nine games into the season, when Michael Porter Jr. tweaked his back on a breakaway opportunity. Porter already had two back surgeries, before the Nuggets entrusted him with a max contract that offseason. The Nuggets could ill-afford to lose their *other* max player for an extended period.

Nikola's burden was becoming outlandish, yet he continued to level up.

In November, he averaged almost 28 points, 13 rebounds, and 7 assists. There was seeming no amount of weight under which he'd crumble.

The only way to make him crack was to physically challenge him.

Miami forward Markieff Morris didn't know the chaos he'd spark when he threw his shoulder into Jokic late in the fourth quarter of a matchup in early November. Jokic took exception to Morris's jab and retaliated with a violent, blindside shoulder to his back.

Morris suffered an apparent neck injury in what Heat coach Erik Spoelstra deemed a "dangerous, dirty play."

Jokic admitted some level of remorse but defended his response.

"I thought it was going to be a take foul, [but] I think it was a dirty play," he said. "And I just needed to protect myself. I felt bad, I am not supposed to react that way, but I need to protect myself."

Jokic had a hair-trigger temper that could be unleashed if he felt tested.

In the back hallway, Heat players peered menacingly outside their locker room toward Denver's.

Between the two teams, nothing else escalated. But both sets of brothers weren't finished with the matter.

"Waited till bro turned his back smh. NOTED," Clippers forward Marcus Morris tweeted late that night.

The Jokic brothers, like Nikola himself, didn't have social media accounts. Strahinja and Nemanja started a Twitter account to defend their brother.

The only problem was that "@JokicBrothers" was an unverified account, with an empty avatar. The only account they followed was Jamal Murray. Their threats, directed back at Marcus Morris, had yet to be noticed.

I had a working relationship with the Jokic brothers but was stunned to see a text from Strahinja Jokic, depicting a screenshot of their account. He confirmed it was really he and Nemanja who'd started the account. And then he asked me to share it.

"You should leave this the way it is instead of publicly threatening our brother! Your brother made a dirty play first. If you want to make a step further be sure we will be waiting for you !! Jokic Brothers," read their response, which quickly went viral once fans realized it was truly them behind the account.

Their account opened the morning after the fracas, before Nikola was suspended one game and Morris fined $50,000 for his role.

"We opened that account to respond," Strahinja told me, ". . . to that stupid idiot."

Jokic's brothers had taken on almost mythical status within NBA circles, both for their role in rearing Nikola and for their unwavering, sometimes unhinged defense of their youngest brother. Their Twitter rebuttal led the NBA news cycle that day.

Three weeks later, when the Nuggets traveled to Miami, the Jokic brothers were there too, sitting directly behind the visiting bench. A hostile crowd showered Jokic with boos every chance they got, but the Nuggets prevailed.

After the game, Jokic was asked whether he was intimidated by the noise.

"I played in Serbia, brother," he said, his tone betrayed only by the floral blue button-down shirt he was wearing. "I wish you guys could feel that."

Injuries once again decimated Denver's depth that season. Jamal Murray (ACL), Michael Porter Jr. (back surgery), and versatile wing P. J. Dozier (ACL) were all facing long-term recoveries. That magnified little injuries, like nagging wrist issues or lingering ankle woes. The Nuggets were trying to outfit their rotations on a piecemeal basis, with an occasional positive COVID test to thwart even the best-laid plans.

The Nuggets were just trying to survive.

In early December, Jokic slow-rolled his way to a 39-point triple-double in an overtime win in New Orleans. The night was highlighted by a twirling, bruising pirouette around brawny big man Jonas Valanciunas.

"I just did a lot of spins," Jokic explained.

And of his aggressive mindset, the one the Nuggets desperately needed to remain a .500 team?

"To be honest, I don't want to do it, but they made me do it," Jokic said. "I'm joking."

His teammates—at least the ones who were available—learned to read him. Just because he was swarmed on one end of the court didn't mean he wasn't aware of an open teammate on the other. Guys like Aaron Gordon and Monte Morris learned to see his process and adjust. While Jokic waited patiently for the defense to sag and orbit around him, Gordon would screen Morris's defender to open up a 3-point window.

They could trust that their efforts would be rewarded.

"He's telling guys where our shots really gonna be at *before* the game," said Morris, the team's starting point guard that season.

Teammates were in awe of how he processed the game in real time.

That season, Nikola far and away led the NBA with 100 touches per game. But unlike the other ball-dominant players, which almost exclusively meant point guards, Jokic's decisions were rarely prolonged. He averaged just 2.6 seconds per touch, according to NBA.com's tracking data. The league leaders in that category, guys like Luka Doncic, Trae Young, and James Harden, all hovered at more than six seconds per touch. Jokic's processing was unparalleled.

"[The game's] moving even slower for him [compared to last season's MVP campaign]," said Will Barton. "He's just in control of everything."

This was a level of dominance no one had ever seen before in NBA history. To wit, his averages (26.5 points, 13.8 rebounds, 7.3 assists) had never been reached.

During a January trip to Dallas, Jokic gave Nuggets fans a late Christmas gift. When he was asked about Nowitzki, he unwittingly reinforced his commitment to what he'd started in Denver.

"[Dirk was] one of the few guys that was playing for one team their whole life, their whole career," Jokic said. "He won the title, he won a ring. I really, really admire him. Just because of that. Because he didn't quit, he didn't abandon the team."

In a season of tumult, it was a welcome (albeit unnecessary) pick-me-up from the greatest player in the franchise's history. Jokic refused to crack under the burden of three condensed seasons, the hopes of a franchise, or the newfound responsibilities of fatherhood. He insisted on playing—his availability a testament to his mental toughness.

"It's never one guy for me," Jokic said, rebuffing the idea that Denver's depleted roster didn't have enough to compete.

When he threw an absurd, crosscourt game-winning assist to Aaron Gordon two weeks later, it was tangible evidence of the trust he had in his teammates. It was the only way the Nuggets were going to endure waves of double- and triple-team coverages. The assist set Gordon up for a dramatic overtime 3-pointer, capping Jokic's 49-point, 14-rebound, 10-assist night. Only Larry Bird and Russell Westbrook had ever amassed lines so overwhelming.

To Nuggets GM Calvin Booth, there was something familiar in the way Jokic drew the best out of his teammates. It wasn't a coincidence that Booth enjoyed the best year of his career playing alongside Steve Nash in Dallas.

"The energy with the passing, the confidence he gives to his teammates," Booth said. "That's what Nash did."

Point guard Monte Morris wasn't Jamal Murray, and Nikola never expected him to be. What Morris couldn't replicate in terms of Murray's scoring production, he made up for in steady guard play. He was a savvy, intuitive point guard who'd had to scrap his way into the NBA by virtue of the second round of the draft. There was more than enough basketball acumen to forge a bond with Jokic.

"The IQ," Morris said of their common denominator. "We would communicate with just our eyes."

As Nash had done with Booth, Jokic imbued a level of confidence in Morris.

"He wanted me to take big shots," Morris said.

Coming from a player of his stature, Morris said, his confidence skyrocketed.

The Nuggets trailed by two with only 5.9 seconds left in a game at Golden State, their final test before the All-Star break. Morris in-bounded the ball to Jokic, who pummeled his way inside the paint. Jokic intended to take the last shot, but when Steph Curry rotated into a double-team, the reigning MVP sought an outlet. He found Morris waiting on the perimeter, waiting to bury the dagger 3-pointer.

Teammates mobbed Morris, who was at the center of the roving pile, and not Jokic, who'd registered 35 points, 17 rebounds, and 8 assists.

"My mom, she's a coach," Morris said. "She always will text me, like, 'Y'all need to help Nikola.' . . . I kinda knew it was good once I let it go."

Malone gushed at the varied ways Nikola continued to win games. He reminded himself not to take Jokic's greatness for granted.

"I try to do the same thing with my wife," he said.

CHAPTER 66

BILL WALTON

Nikola was knee-deep in a video game when TNT announced he was named to his fourth consecutive All-Star Game.

"I was playing the game, like, ughhh," Jokic said. "I was kinda watching on the phone with Natalija, and I was playing the video game. And then after they select me, I was like, 'Oh, bye-bye.'"

Around mid-February, it had become routine that Jokic be included at the league's annual showcase. His play always warranted it. Furthermore, it was no longer a novelty for him to be there alongside LeBron James, Giannis Antetokounmpo, and Luka Doncic.

He was one of them.

"I think they just accept me," Jokic told the *Denver Post*. "I think that kind of shows the respect."

The All-Star Game was in Cleveland that season and coincided with the league's 75th anniversary. To celebrate, the NBA trotted out its 75th anniversary team. Before the ceremony, the NBA assembled its greatest living luminaries within a practice gym inside the Cavs' arena itself.

Michael Jordan and Magic Johnson. Hakeem Olajuwon and Kareem Abdul-Jabbar. Charles Barkley and Shaquille O'Neal. All were there to celebrate the game.

Bill Walton, a two-time champion and league MVP, was in attendance too. Inside the practice facility, with NBA legends swapping stories and reliving rivalries, Walton took a seat. He didn't want to be hurried when he shared what he told Nikola Jokic.

"I just said how proud I am of him and how happy I am for him and what he's been able to do to create the life, to create the world, and to move our universe to a better place," Walton told the *Denver Post*. "And the style, the grace, the elegance, the dignity, the class that he brings each and every day, and it's just a fresh ray of sunshine."

Walton was a pioneering big man and one of the forebears at Jokic's position. His creativity on the court reflected the way he lived off it. His appreciation for Jokic's style, and perhaps more so, his joy, was radiant.

"I'm so grateful for the way he plays because it represents the best of the human spirit in terms of inclusion, in terms of opportunity, team, sacrifice, discipline," Walton said. "He's just really, really great. He is brilliant."

Walton called Jokic a "creative genius," then went full Walton.

"It's a privilege for me to watch him play basketball," Walton said. "He is Colorado. He's a pioneer. He's an innovator. He's a creator of a new and better path to tomorrow."

Their interaction might have been the highlight of Jokic's weekend. It certainly wasn't the All-Star Game itself, which tended to showcase windmill dunks that Jokic could never dream of. Asked after the game whether All-Star Games were actually "hard" for him, Jokic offered an all-time response.

"For me it is, actually," he said. "I don't know what to do."

CHAPTER 67

HORSEPOWER

The 1967 Ford Bronco stammered and stalled up Colorado Boulevard as if the operator hadn't yet been granted his learner's permit.

The driver was, in this case, Nuggets forward Aaron Gordon.

"It was a stick shift, unbeknownst to me," Gordon said.

Before then, Gordon had only driven stick once or twice in his life. It was the first practice after the All-Star break, and Gordon started to panic.

"I was basically racing the clock, trying to get this Ford Bronco to practice, before practice started, while I'm stalling it out in the middle of Colorado Boulevard."

Gordon pleaded with cars to go around him. He beckoned for them to pass.

"I'm grinding it till I find it," he said, a smile broadening across his face.

While Nikola Jokic was in Cleveland for his fourth All-Star appearance, Gordon went to a vintage auto shop and settled on the 1967 Ford Bronco. He bought it as a thank-you to Nikola for his friendship, for the example he set, and for the assists he'd already steered in Gordon's direction.

But first he had to get it to him. With about ten minutes to spare before the team's practice started, Gordon sputtered into the players' parking lot.

"It finally clutched up," he said.

Jokic couldn't believe the gift.

"He was like, 'Bro, for real?'" Gordon said.

Gordon's motives weren't complicated. He'd arrived at the trade deadline the previous season and immediately benefited from Jokic's unselfishness and his court sense. The ease with which buckets fell into his lap was unlike anything he'd ever experienced in Orlando.

"Just gratitude," he said. "Just grateful for all the assists he throws me, how much easier he makes my job. . . . I wasn't going to give him an actual horse, so I feel like I could give him some horsepower."

But that wasn't the only thing he gifted his teammate.

Gordon had an old massage therapist who made horse saddles in her free time. Gordon commissioned one for Nikola, with a "Jokic" insignia and a Serbian flag on it.

"I love Joker, man," Gordon said. "I'd run through a wall for him."

O

The assists greased their relationship, but Jokic was funny.

"Joker's hilarious," said Aaron Gordon. "He's hysterical. To the media he kind of comes off as . . . He's funny, man. He has a really dry, dark sense of humor. . . . It's awesome. . . . Dry humor tests your intelligence, and dark humor, I love dark humor."

Gordon joked that only a select few ever got to see Jokic with his guard down.

"[His is] the humor that wouldn't probably go over well in the media."

With Porter and Murray injured, Jokic's relationship with Gordon flourished.

They soon discovered a shared competitiveness for . . . *anything*.

"Could be darts, could be bowling," Gordon said. Might be betting, might be jacks.

"It doesn't matter," he said. "We're both gamers."

There was a genuine fondness between the two. Jokic was a humble, unassuming European who approached the game cerebrally. Gordon, a self-described "Renaissance man," had innumerable hobbies and was endlessly curious. In describing Jokic, Gordon settled on a word few had ever used to describe him: *congruent*.

"What you see is what you get," Gordon said. "You know the inside is the same as the outside for him. His values, his personal life, everything is just so . . . *good*."

What management couldn't have known when they traded for Gordon was just how flawlessly the two laid-back personalities would mesh.

On the court, the fit was perfect. Gordon had been the multidimensional forward the Nuggets identified to complement a roster around Jokic. Defensively, he could protect him. Offensively, he was the roaming, bruising lob threat that mandated that teams not cheat toward Jokic.

Gordon's awakening in Denver was profound.

"I would make reads that other centers would not be able to see," Gordon said. "It was just frustrating for me because . . . I'm beating my man without the ball, and it just goes unnoticed. Okay, I face-cut him here, I back-cut him here, I have him sealed here, and it's just not happening. The Joker, he sees it every . . . single . . . time."

In fairness, *no one* had a center that could distribute like Nikola. But in Denver, Gordon's game became simpler and, therefore, optimized.

Gordon vividly remembered Murray setting a back screen on his defender, which opened up an uncontested dunk.

"It was like the first time I'd had a wide-open anything in the NBA," Gordon said. "Everything was so tough in Orlando."

Nothing validated their friendship like the efforts Gordon made to visit Jokic. In the offseason, Gordon always had an itch to travel and explore the world. In the summer of 2022, Gordon arrived, unannounced, at the O2 Arena in Prague as Jokic was suiting up for the Serbian national team at EuroBasket. Without any need for special accommodations, Gordon sat in the stands and watched his teammate.

"He was so excited to see me when I pulled up," Gordon said.

But the biggest stamp of approval came when Jokic hosted Gordon in Sombor. He took him to the racetracks, where Gordon began to understand the pull of Jokic's beloved horses. Together they drank beer and sweated out a few victories from his horses.

"It was dope," Gordon said.

Jokic, according to Gordon, has become an extension of his family. He said Jokic's brothers look out for him, just as Gordon's siblings have Nikola's back. Their relationship transcended the court. Basketball, Gordon said, would never define Jokic.

"As good of a player as he is," Gordon said, "he's an even better person."

CHAPTER 68

POINT OF PRIDE

The Warriors picked their poison.

Golden State, Denver's first-round opponent in the 2022 postseason, respected Jokic's ability to find weaknesses within their defense, so they opted not to present them.

Sacramento Kings coach Mike Brown was then the defensive coordinator for the Warriors. Brown, with Michael Malone on staff, had also coached LeBron James during his formative years in Cleveland. He believed the key to inhibiting such multifaceted forces was to limit their ability to help others.

"Our whole thing was, back then, we're okay with Jokic scoring 50, but if he gets more than seven assists, that's when we're in trouble," Brown said.

Out of respect for his passing, they didn't want to double-team him. They wanted him to believe that he needed to score every time down, while simultaneously running him ragged in Steph Curry pick-and-rolls. If he outscored them throughout a series, so be it. It was the gamble the Warriors were willing to make.

The Warriors' Kevon Looney was a stout, physical center who worked directly with assistant coach Dejan Milojevic, Jokic's mentor and coach at Mega. If not Looney, it was future Hall of Famer Draymond Green hounding Jokic.

"Most guys who are that dominant, you want to send a double team," Green said. "He's one of the best passers we have in the league, so he picks double teams apart, and you can't give him the same look. . . . I think the nimbleness, and most importantly, it's his touch. He gets the ball on the rim, it's going in."

Green knew what he was facing.

In Games 1 and 2, Golden State's design worked flawlessly. They stayed home on Jokic and dared him to beat their single coverage. Both games he was inefficient, and both games yielded a Warriors rout. Jokic was so frustrated with the scheme, he got ejected midway through the fourth quarter of Game 2.

At home and facing essentially a must-win situation, Jokic was far more efficient and far more productive. He reeled off 37 points and snatched 18 rebounds, Herculean numbers that under normal circumstances would have amounted to a win. But Denver's margin for error was nonexistent. They just didn't have the potency to compete with Klay Thompson, Jordan Poole, and Curry from the 3-point line, nor did they have the wings to defend them. Gordon, with way more responsibility than typically accustomed to, also wasn't himself in the series.

"When it comes to this kind of thing, the first person I look at is in the mirror, every single time," Gordon said.

Facing another 3–0 deficit, Game 4 became a point of pride.

Another 37-point effort from Jokic catapulted the Nuggets to their first win of the series. He was inimitable. Jokic was ruthless in transition chances and from the 3-point line. He dropped in floaters and fade-aways. Facing elimination, Jokic was, as always, calm. He wicked away pressure like raindrops off a jacket. As if to illustrate how dire Denver's circumstances were, they needed rookie Bones Hyland to play supporting actor to Jokic's lead. Hyland sank three 3-pointers, each from about thirty feet out.

They were in no position to legislate where their help came from.

Back in San Francisco, the Nuggets scrapped to avoid elimination. They were tied at 90 with 2:26 remaining on the strength of Jokic's rosy shoulders. With clutch jumpers and soft hook shots, Jokic bulldozed for 30 points and 19 rebounds. But the Warriors prevailed to oust the Nuggets en route to their latest championship.

After the game, Draymond Green found Jokic on the court.

"I just told him thank you for making me better," Green said. "It's an honor and a pleasure to play against someone so talented and so skilled."

CHAPTER 69

SURPRISE

The plan was hatched in secrecy and with urgency.

Nikola's brothers approved of it, while his wife, Natalija, helped coordinate.

The Nuggets knew Nikola Jokic had won a second consecutive MVP a few days before the news leaked publicly. Given that Jokic had become the first player in NBA history to reach 2,000 points, 1,000 rebounds, and 500 assists in a single season, his coronation as a two-time MVP wasn't a shock.

But as soon as the Nuggets learned the news, those closest to Jokic devised a covert, international surprise party that would leave tears streaming down the incomparable superstar's face.

Michael Malone fired off a text to Nuggets president Tim Connelly.

"I said, 'Listen, man, no one other than you and me should be giving him this award over there,'" Malone said.

Connelly, who was always up for an impromptu overseas mission, concluded, "We gotta be at the [horse] stables. How are we going to do this?"

The official team included Malone, Connelly, assistant coach Ogi Stojakovic, strength coach Felipe Eichenberger, PR director Nick O'Hayre, and cameraman Bob Nicolai. Perhaps in jest or possibly out of genuine concern, there was at least some discussion about being discreet. Translation: avoid Nuggets paraphernalia at Denver International Airport.

O'Hayre had another issue. The forty-pound crystal MVP trophy he toted in his carry-on was flagged at security. He insisted on having it searched in a private room, far from prying eyes and curious cameras. With that, the Nuggets were on their way to Sombor, Serbia, by way of Munich and then Belgrade.

Nikola was generally protective of his hometown, but in this instance, he had no say in the matter.

When the group landed, they hopped in a Sprinter van to accommodate their numbers and camera equipment. Stojakovic, more than familiar with the route, was the obvious choice to drive.

Nuggets governor Josh Kroenke flew separately but made it to Sombor around the same time as the team's traveling party. They convened at a gas station near Nikola's horse stables, passing out customized MVP shirts.

"Some people want to see you fail," the shirts read. "Disappoint them."

Enthused by the nature of the trip, Connelly encouraged the cameraman to start filming.

"This is awesome," Connelly said. "We're at a gas station in Serbia right now, man!"

With barely ten minutes to spare, the group hustled to Jokic's stables, where musicians—friends of the Jokic family—began playing traditional Serbian music. They were playing a song about a long journey on horseback when Jokic, riding behind his horse, turned the corner and spotted them.

"I get emotional thinking about this," Malone said. "When you see him realize what's about to happen . . ."

Upon seeing his friends, Jokic was overwhelmed. Between the setting and his attire—a black tank top, with shorts and black socks—it could've been the most unassuming MVP celebration in NBA history.

There were as many hugs as there were tears.

"I'm gonna remember that—I don't want to sound poetic—but probably forever," said Nebojsa Vagic, Jokic's godfather. "It was sunny, it was nice music, his horse and the coach were coming into the stable and everything was so close to perfect. . . . They just didn't come around the corner. They came from the other part of the planet."

The group began drinking a bit before heading to a farmhouse where Jokic's parents had prepared a spread. The plan was to head back to the stables for his TNT interview after some revelry.

"The hardest-working guys there were the three musicians," Malone said. "They never stopped playing. . . . As we're partying and we're singing and we're dancing and we're drinking, it's beer—which they call pivo—

and it's rakija. Next thing you know, Nick goes, 'Hey Joker, we gotta go back to the stables for your interview.' And Nikola's face, it was classic. He goes, 'Brother, I'm drunk. I cannot do interview right now.'"

Jokic asked to postpone. Not an option.

"Ernie Johnson's waiting for us," Malone said.

The group headed back to the stables, where the backdrop, of his favorite horse, Dream Catcher, would be broadcast on national television. It was picturesque until the Wi-Fi at Jokic's remote stable conked out. For twenty minutes, Malone, Connelly, and Kroenke cackled at the chaos.

Finally, mercifully, they could hear Ernie, who conducted an emotional and revealing interview at one of Jokic's most tender moments. His appreciation for the organization's investment was palpable. For a second, he seemed to pinch himself at his origin story. Asked by Johnson whether he considered himself a long shot, Jokic smiled.

"If it's not me, who is it?" Jokic said.

The group returned to the farmhouse, where the rakija and the music flowed liberally. For those closest to Nikola, the night was an unforgettable touchstone of how far he'd come from his humble beginnings.

Even Kroenke, reveling in the celebration, danced to the Kolo, Serbia's national folk dance.

"I was just smiling all the time," his godfather said, "like I had a cramp in my face."

The rakija got the best of Malone. After a night of reveling, he found himself alone in the back seat of a sports car. He had no idea where he was, who he was with, or where Tim Connelly was.

"I'm right behind the driver," Malone said. "I can't tell who the driver is."

The plan was to go back to Belgrade that night. When Malone came to, he didn't know the answer to any of those questions.

"I thought I was in the movie *Taken*," Malone said.

As he drove along a dark road, thoughts raced through Malone's head. He finally breathed a sigh of relief when the car pulled into a gas station and the light flicked on.

"Coach, you need anything?" Misko Raznatovic asked.

"Oh, fuck, okay," Malone said. "I'm not being kidnapped."

The next day, Kroenke, Connelly, and Malone left for London to watch Kroenke's Arsenal take on Tottenham. There was a wistfulness to the entire trip, something almost romantic about how the three had helped change the course of the Nuggets' franchise. But more change was possibly afoot. Connelly had received overtures from the Minnesota Timberwolves, potentially threatening the house they'd collectively built. To those on the trip, those overtures were well-known.

Back in Sombor, Jokic proudly took those who remained to his favorite ice cream shop. He was well-known there long before he was a two-time MVP and one of the greatest basketball players in the world.

"He's the same person," Stojakovic said.

The trip was never meant to be invasive, as the Nuggets tried to respect his space in the offseason. But the occasion was too sweet not to commemorate.

"I like when he feels those emotions," Vagic said. "It's good to let them go sometimes. I think it purifies him."

CHAPTER 70

RARE AIR

Nuggets GM Calvin Booth had at least one advantage over his predecessor, former president Tim Connelly.

Booth spent ten years in the NBA as a reserve big man. He considered his actions through a player's perspective.

When Connelly left for Minnesota that summer—a wrenching decision that was influenced in part by a bigger salary—there was never any consideration to the job going to someone else. It was Booth's responsibility to replace him.

Unassuming and not as gregarious as Connelly, Booth was savvy and, as one source at the time remarked, "a killer."

His relationship with Nikola Jokic was strong, but his new position afforded him a different vantage point.

For any decisions he made, or was considering making, Booth thought how it would affect Jokic.

"I try to put myself in his shoes," Booth said.

Furthermore, Booth thought about his time as a player and considered how much traffic Jokic had to sift through on a daily basis: people texting him, trying to engage him, attempting to get his attention. Booth felt his best approach, in general, was to give him space. Jokic had all the support he needed, from his family and from the organization.

When he needed to, he'd engage him. But Jokic was so low-maintenance, it's a safe bet that he appreciated that approach.

"What can I tell this guy?" Booth joked, meaning insight that Jokic didn't already know. He was underselling himself. Booth's experience, understanding of locker room dynamics, intelligence, and conviction made him a valuable resource to Jokic, if he wanted to use it.

But there was one decision, at least early, that Booth had to bring to the Jokic family's attention: it pertained to the five-year, $270 million contract the Nuggets intended to offer Jokic that summer, which at the time would be the largest deal in NBA history.

Booth and assistant GM Tommy Balcetis had lunch with Nikola's brothers, where the team allayed any concerns about Connelly's departure.

When free agency officially opened, Booth was on his way to Sombor to get Jokic's commitment and ensure Denver's title window would be open for years.

"We were joking, like, 'Man, I can't go wrong with my first signing,'" Booth said.

Booth hadn't been part of the team's covert MVP surprise; in fact, though he'd been to Belgrade, this was his first trip to Nikola's hometown.

His round-trip flights took him twenty-four hours combined, while he was within the country for only forty hours. But the time spent was invaluable. It afforded Booth time with Jokic in *his* element.

Booth spent the first night in Belgrade, dining with assistant coach Ogi Stojakovic and Jokic's European agent, Misko Raznatovic. Stojakovic, as he'd done just two months earlier, drove to Sombor the next day with Booth. Raznatovic drove separately and convened at Jokic's parents house for the formalities.

The next stop was Moj Salas, a remote restaurant in a field about five miles outside the city. Those who were there recalled it being one of the hottest days of the year. There, a spread of traditional Serbian food awaited them. Unlike the MVP surprise party, this celebration was more intimate.

"MVP party was like a party-party, crazy, emotional, exciting, surprise," Stojakovic said. "This was kind of like a family reunion."

The only people there were Booth, Raznatovic, Stojakovic and his wife, along with Nikola, Natalija, Nemanja, and his parents. Strahinja was "there in spirit," according to Booth, FaceTiming from the States.

There were also two guitar players—naturally, friends of the family—who provided a jovial soundtrack for the event. Swept up in the excitement, Jokic and his wife couldn't help but dance. It was a triumphant moment for the family.

Booth relished seeing Jokic at ease, among the people he cared about most.

"He makes you feel a part of it," said Booth, who noticed another curiosity about the Jokic ethos.

"None of their kids ever cry," he said. "They all just smile and are happy because the energy's so chill."

Jokic regaled Booth about Sombor, while little of the conversation broached basketball. The aspects that did, Booth recalled, were some of his most transparent moments. Booth was captivated.

"He has an all-time great mind," Booth said.

Booth sat listening as Jokic unwrapped his thinking. Individual accomplishments did little for him, and he'd already won two MVPs. He wondered aloud what it took to achieve team success.

"I don't know how hard I need to work," Booth recalled Jokic saying.

That morning, he'd worked out in a hot gym, conditioning, dripping sweat until he was about to pass out.

"Is that enough?" Jokic said, according to Booth. "I'm not sure, we haven't won anything yet. I don't know what it takes to win."

Booth found himself spellbound by the conversation. This was a two-time MVP, who already had an elite work ethic by NBA standards. And he was gauging whether he needed to work *harder*?

"And he's trying to figure out, what did the Kobes do, what did the Michael Jordans do, how hard do you need to go to be Tim Duncan and win the championship?"

CHAPTER 71

SECRET SAUCE

The Nuggets were in West Hollywood, at Cecconi's, an upscale Italian restaurant, laying the foundation for a season with endless intrigue.

It was the offseason, and Michael Porter Jr., GM Calvin Booth, and owner Josh Kroenke were there. So were recent acquisitions Kentavious Caldwell-Pope and DeAndre Jordan, the former arriving via trade with Washington and the latter a free-agent signing.

"Mike had blond hair," Jordan recalled at the time.

In the weeks since assuming the top decision-making duties, Booth had plugged several glaring holes. In the draft, he'd seized Christian Braun fresh off a national championship at Kansas and snatched Peyton Watson, a long, rangy prospect that Booth envisioned developing into an elite defender. He'd also signed Bruce Brown, who'd been miscast in Brooklyn as a forward, and projected him as a lynchpin of Denver's second unit.

There was a clear and obvious intention: The Nuggets sought wing defenders to outfit a roster around Jokic. If they could shoot, even better.

The Nuggets had targeted Caldwell-Pope dating back to the prior trade deadline. They viewed him as an elite two-way guard, whose simple game would supplement Jokic's passing. They also liked his recent history; Caldwell-Pope had helped contain Jamal Murray in the Bubble, when the Lakers went on to win a championship after dispatching Denver.

At the restaurant, as the group was analyzing the season to come, Booth asked Caldwell-Pope two pointed questions.

What distinguished those 2020 Lakers? Why had they raised a banner?

Caldwell-Pope pointed to the table.

"This right here," DeAndre Jordan remembered Caldwell-Pope saying.

Their camaraderie—even finding ways to get together throughout the COVID hiatus—had made those Lakers impenetrable.

"I do remember that conversation," Caldwell-Pope said.

With Caldwell-Pope's insight, the Nuggets had a blueprint to the intangibles of a championship roster. The offseason outings, including movie nights, bowling, and dinners, were necessary ingredients to the secret sauce, he said.

When adversity inevitably struck, it was those moments that offered an avenue forward. If a teammate had a bad game, or was mired in some prolonged struggle, Caldwell-Pope had seen the formula work.

"I know how to approach him," he said. "I can level with him."

Jordan, though he hadn't won a title, was a huge proponent of Caldwell-Pope's approach. The off-court relationships made the on-court interactions seamless.

"Then you're listening to what somebody says," Jordan said of the dinners.

The 2022–23 Nuggets season was different in that regard, both Caldwell-Pope and Jordan said. The former couldn't even hazard a guess how many team dinners they had throughout the year. The biggest culprits were two of the newcomers: Caldwell-Pope and Jordan, the self-proclaimed liaison. They were consistently organizing outings on the road.

"Everybody came," Caldwell-Pope said.

Free-agent signee Bruce Brown played with Jeff Green and DeAndre Jordan in Brooklyn, as well as Ish Smith in Detroit. Brown had no trouble acclimating to his new team.

"We were always together," Brown said.

If it wasn't dinners with his aforementioned teammates, then it was hanging at Aaron Gordon's lounge, or doing something with Caldwell-Pope.

"We knew what we were trying to do," Brown said.

They were invested in each other as people rather than content to know each other simply as teammates.

"It's not always just about basketball," Caldwell-Pope said.

Nikola Jokic was their North Star. For years he'd poured himself into the team. When the Nuggets hit the road and had an off night, Jokic was there. Often he wore a comfortable tracksuit, but he was still present.

"He showed up," Caldwell-Pope said. "He understood what was the goal."

CHAPTER 72

THE COMEBACK

Jamal Murray mentally prepared for a return from his torn ACL the prior postseason.

In his mind, the target date would be about a year removed from his operation.

But reality didn't meet expectations. In pickup games against reserves, Murray was tentative. He paused navigating contact and screens. He was reluctant to leap for rebounds.

"I'm like, 'Man, I gotta think, and obviously I can't go guard Steph like that,'" Murray said.

The last thing Murray wanted was to return, prematurely, and cost his team in the postseason.

Nikola Jokic was more than patient with his favorite pick-and-roll partner. He'd never pressured Murray to return before he was ready. At training camp in San Diego, it was apparent their institutional knowledge hadn't eroded over Murray's eighteen-month absence.

"It feels really natural, it feels easy," Jokic said. "I think we're gonna be back really soon."

When Murray finally did return, Jokic, diplomatically, turned down the temperature.

"I love to play with him, of course," Jokic said. "I know he's gonna be really bad for the next twenty games, but we're gonna survive."

Jokic's shrewd jab was both funny and a public message to Murray: *you're not going to get it back all at once.*

An underwhelming Murray was still better than not having him at all. Having him back was an unequivocal relief.

Three games into the season, in a win over Oklahoma City, the story wasn't that Jokic tied Wilt Chamberlain for the most triple-doubles by a center in NBA history (78). It was that Denver's revamped roster, under Booth's watch and around Jokic, was titillating. Michael Porter Jr. buried five 3-pointers, while Kentavious Caldwell-Pope drained six. Murray was only in the nascent stages of his return yet Denver's offense was *already* ruthless.

Defenses were helpless. They either stuck to Denver's cadre of shooters or sent help against the reigning back-to-back MVP. Jokic's mere *presence* created shooting pockets for his teammates.

"I'm gonna eat a lot," Caldwell-Pope said, in what amounted to roughly the same realization Aaron Gordon had when he got traded to Denver.

A few weeks into the season, Jokic was already bored.

"We travel, you go to dinner, wake up, weight room, shootaround, nap, game, travel, wake up, shootaround," Jokic said. "That's it."

His fulfillment came via his family and seeing his daughter develop. The relentless nature of the schedule was at odds with what brought him the most joy.

The pandemic interrupted what had become one of the best traditions on the Nuggets' schedule: a basketball clinic with Colorado's Special Olympians. By late 2022, the event was back on.

Jokic spent an afternoon tossing bounce passes to wide-eyed hoopers or rolling the ball to willing partners. He was exuberant around them, professing astonishment at how adept their ball skills were. The Special Olympians hovered around him, as did their appreciative parents.

"I love to be around them," Jokic said. "They have a special energy."

Of course, they sensed it in him too.

The next night, Jokic surpassed Chamberlain with yet another triple-double and was presented a game ball autographed by his teammates.

"It's nice," Jokic said. "It's not just my success. I cannot do it without my teammates. I just wanted to remember one day, when I find that ball in a closet, just to see who I played with."

CHAPTER 73

OLD HEAD

Jeff Green could assemble a team of first-ballot Hall of Famers among the more than 250 teammates he's had in his career.

Kevin Durant and Russell Westbrook in Oklahoma City. Kevin Garnett in Boston. LeBron James in Cleveland.

Green's superpower resided within his staying power; not only the way he took care of his body but in the relationships he forged.

Naturally, he found something worth cultivating in Nikola Jokic. When Jokic's "international" crew, as he deemed it, went out for dinner, Green secured an invite too.

Eager to learn about his background, Green relished those dinners with Jokic. During the offseason, when Green's daughters took to horseback riding, it was an easy way to engage Jokic from afar.

In San Diego for training camp, Green and DeAndre Jordan organized an outing to a Padres game, making sure Jokic came with them.

"Actually, I thought [baseball] was boring before, but we were in the first row," Jokic said. "It was a little bit different."

The two had a ton in common. As girl dads, Jokic could pick Green's brain. As old souls, they shared a dry, biting sense of humor.

Green was smart enough to know not to compare Durant to LeBron to Jokic. The comparisons, he thought, were reductive.

"He's his own entity," Green said.

Green appreciated how Jokic never sought the spotlight.

Green saw how genuine he was, that his unselfishness and thoughtfulness were real. His mood wasn't predicated on how he was playing. Jokic was content when his teammates were happy, he said. And as for the expectations of a superstar persona, of what a player of that caliber *should* be like, Jokic undermined them all.

"He kills that stereotype, that perception," Green said.

Just as stats wouldn't define Jokic's legacy, his stature wouldn't either.

"He treats the game as if he's the fifteenth guy on the bench, meaning he works hard every day," Green said.

Green knew the NBA like few ever have. He knew Jokic was an anomaly among NBA giants.

CHAPTER 74

HUMILITY

Jamal Murray had recaptured a few of his athletic gifts, and he'd even had a couple of scoring outbursts.

But he'd yet to summon a moment, since returning from his ACL tear, like he had in Portland in December 2022.

His dagger, step-back 3-pointer on former teammate Jerami Grant was evidence of the fourth-quarter assassin that laid dormant for a year and a half. The corner triple left just 0.9 seconds on the clock and elicited an icy sneer from Murray. Nikola Jokic had flipped the ball to Murray in the game's defining sequence. Not only did Jokic trust Murray in those moments, but the reigning two-time MVP had another capable closer.

In the cramped visiting locker room in Portland, Murray held court with a throng of reporters who peppered him for close to ten minutes. He revealed a vulnerability he'd never shared before.

"There were so many doubts of, 'Am I gonna be different? Am I gonna play the same? Am I gonna be worth it?'" Murray said.

The trust between the two stars never dissipated. Jokic knew what he had in Murray.

A week later, Jokic was presented the inaugural Michael Jordan Trophy, the NBA's new name for the MVP award. Instead of parading it alongside him at a press conference, Jokic hid it. The locker next to Jokic's was vacated by a G League player on assignment. He took two foam rollers, roughly 23.6 inches tall (for Jordan's number and titles won), and hid the hardware behind them.

Asked about the award, Jokic deflected.

"It's cool," he said, noting that the novelty would be over as soon as there was a second award winner.

The award itself was a physical piece that could sit in a display case as easily as it could serve as a doorstop. Jokic allowed that the best part of his unprecedented success in Denver was the relationships it fostered among people he cared about.

There were a handful of people Jokic interacted with on a daily basis who made him comfortable. They were people in the organization who made the team function, and not necessarily devised offensive schemes. All of them approached their roles with a level of humility. Always observant, Jokic noticed.

Jokic had a tendency to gravitate toward those people because, as he said, "I think I see good guys in them."

Equipment manager Sparky Gonzales had been with the team for decades. Since Jokic's arrival, he served as something close to a father figure for him within the organization. On game days, their routine always involved Ping-Pong matches. On one of the rare occasions Sparky won, Jokic had a horrible game that night. Arturas Karnisovas popped his head into Sparky's office and told him, "You can't beat him on game days!"

Sparky fired back, "We only play on game days!"

Once, when Jokic needed some deodorant after a game, Gonzales tossed him a spray that Jokic found disgusting. He thought it was better used for "killing spiders." When he complained about it during a live TV interview, Gonzales went to the store and outfitted his locker with five high-end female deodorants.

Only Jokic wasn't fazed.

"They smell nice, so I'm good," Jokic said.

It's because of Sparky that, to this day, Jokic prefers women's deodorant.

Every year, Gonzales hosted a backyard barbecue for the team's ballboys. When Jokic learned of it several years ago, he decided to show up, unannounced.

"He ate all the goddamn wings," Gonzales said.

On road trips, they'd occasionally have dinner together, and during the offseason, it wasn't uncommon for them to trade texts with pictures of their latest fishing exploits. Jokic found something in Gonzales's humble approach to his work. He was among his most trusted confidants.

One of Sparky's understudies, Sam Fruitman, diligently hustled towels to and from the locker room during games. Postgame, he was on laundry duty. Whenever Jokic won a Player of the Month award, Jokic tapped Sam to take his car keys and leave the trophy inside. Sam's official title had no bearing on the way Jokic treated him.

Once, when Jokic overheard that Fruitman had an upcoming date, he gave him a hundred dollars.

"Take her somewhere nice," Jokic told him.

Then he did it again a second time.

He viewed Taylor Vincek, the team's videographer, the same way. Tasked with documenting behind-the-scenes moments for fans, Vincek would occasionally keep private moments between Jokic's family private. Jokic recognized her thoughtfulness and appreciated her discretion.

He also valued the team's PR director, Nick O'Hayre, whose job it was to insulate Jokic from the flood of media inquiries he had no interest in doing.

"I can sense or feel a good person," Jokic said. "I love Sam, Sparky, Taylor, Nick, there's a couple others. [Strength coach] Claus (Souza), I love Claus. Felipe, of course . . . Those people are important. Okay, coach, GM, owner, whatever, but those people are holding something too."

CHAPTER 75

TETRICK

Nikola Jokic's head hit the pillow at 4:30 a.m. on Thursday, January 26. Two hours later, he was knocking on his friend's door, eager to get their day started.

The Nuggets had flown to Philadelphia that night, after playing a back-to-back in New Orleans and Milwaukee.

"Let's go, Timmy," Jokic said after arriving, via Uber, to Hall of Fame harness racer Tim Tetrick's house.

Tetrick has won more than 13,000 races in his career, which includes earnings of more than $250 million. The two formed a friendship several years earlier, when Jokic wanted to connect with fellow horsemen in the U.S.

"Hey Timmy, I'm Nikola," began an innocuous text message conversation with his soon-to-be friend.

In the car, Jokic was giddy with excitement.

"He said, 'This is great,'" Tetrick recalled to the *Denver Post*. "This is all I want to do is go track to track and race horses."

First the duo drove an hour and a half north, to a farm where they could jog horses for the morning. Then they drove two and a half hours south to Dover Downs, a harness-racing track in Delaware.

Tetrick was eager to talk hoops. Jokic was eager to talk horses.

"He's like, 'Why'd you drive that horse that way?' I'm like, 'Blah, blah blah,' and I'm like, 'Joker, how come you didn't pass it to KCP there?'" Tetrick said. "You can tell he doesn't even want to talk basketball. He's asking all the other drivers, guys that he would know, that are the Michael Jordan and stuff of [harness racing]. He wants to talk about us, and all we want to do is ask him questions about, 'Well, how'd you meet Michael Jordan?' or, 'What'd you think about LeBron?'"

That night at the racetrack, Jokic's worlds collided.

On one TV, there were the ongoing harness races. On the other, across the ESPN ticker, came the All-Star Game starters.

"I'm in!" said Jokic in mock relief at being named a starter for a third consecutive year.

"People were kind of looking at me funny," Jokic said. "I think they didn't expect me there."

Jokic has returned the favor, hosting Tetrick at numerous basketball games along the East Coast or in Denver.

"He loves horses more than he does basketball," Tetrick said. "It's kinda like when I go to a game, or get to go down to the locker room with him, I've got stars in my eyes, and he's like, 'You're an idiot, this is boring. Let's go back to the track.'"

Once Tetrick understood Jokic's passion, he made it easier for him to follow his first love. Tetrick gave Jokic the password to his Racetrack Network account, which allowed him to watch harness races from North America to Australia.

"It's like ten dollars a month to watch any race you want to," Tetrick said.

When he wasn't leading fast breaks, Jokic was usually buried in his phone watching horse races.

Tetrick was initially astounded at the person Jokic was. It was tough to conceive that all the reigning two-time MVP wanted to do was discuss racing strategy. Now they banter over texts like brothers.

"'You've got my dream job,' he always tells me," Tetrick said.

The next day, following a practice at Temple University, Jokic's equestrian bubble was shattered. There were pressing questions about his All-Star selection—"It was good"—and the looming matchup against Philadelphia's Joel Embiid.

"People try to create the bad blood," Jokic said. "There isn't any. I respect the guy. The guy's the most dominant player right now, probably, in the league."

CHAPTER 76

NOISE AND NONSENSE

At All-Star weekend, Nikola Jokic admitted his least favorite part about being a professional athlete.

"Media," he said, without hesitation.

Then he amended his answer.

"Media and celebrity, out, everything else, good," he said, though fully capable of speaking in complete sentences.

Jokic lamented the number of interviews he was required to do, and the repetitive nature of all the questions he fielded. He wasn't interested in sharing strategy, and he preferred keeping his family out of the spotlight. He hated discussing things like his legacy, or what a certain statistical achievement meant to him. He always tried to be respectful, but sometimes he didn't know what to say.

"A lot of the media, it's not something that I ask for it, it's not something that I wanted, people give it to me," Jokic told the *Denver Post*. "You can just see, not the hate, just all the bad things. . . . I don't know why people are saying something like that in my direction or whatever."

Jokic's teams won—the Nuggets had been in first place in their conference since late December. He was unselfish, probably to a fault; his assists that season hovered at a career-high 9.8 per game. His teammates became better versions of themselves playing alongside him. What was there to criticize?

Earlier in his career, the only time Mason Plumlee could recall Jokic getting mad at the media was when ESPN displayed his name but showed highlights of Jusuf Nurkic.

"He was pretty mad at that," Plumlee said, laughing.

Which brought Plumlee, unsolicited, to Kendrick Perkins's claim that Jokic was "stat-padding" during the 2022–23 season. It was a laughable argument against someone who didn't get remotely excited about statistics—other than their correlation to winning. It was also quite a charge to make.

"His numbers are so pure," Plumlee said.

Besides, it didn't make any sense.

"Joker's just as happy to get a couple extra minutes of rest," he said.

When he reached his 100th career triple-double in Houston in early March, Jokic acknowledged Perkins's claim.

What does reaching 100 triple-doubles mean to you? he was asked.

"When you're stat-padding, it's easy, you know?" Jokic deadpanned.

It was the first time he ever confirmed he was aware of what was being said about him. Moreover, it was the first time he publicly responded.

When Perkins then said, incorrectly, that 80 percent of the MVP voters were white, and therefore inclined to vote for Jokic, it was enough to make Jokic repulsed at the whole charade.

"I just find it interesting to say something just to . . . give those guys something to talk about," Jokic said.

Perkins's opinion, in other words, was nothing more than bloviating. Jokic was effectively done discussing the MVP race. If opinions could be shared without merit but devoid of consequence, then what was the point of Jokic engaging?

"I think that's not really healthy," he said.

Jokic got an unwelcome taste of what could come if he were to win three consecutive MVPs, something only Bill Russell, Wilt Chamberlain, and Larry Bird had done. It was easy to see how a fixation on a secondary goal could derail the ultimate one. Late in the year, a national reporter asked him about it.

"I don't think about it anymore," he said, graduating from the vitriol. "It's past."

CHAPTER 77

MICHAEL MALONE

Nuggets coach Michael Malone nestled into his office chair and dug deep into the well of memories he and Jokic shared together.

There were quiet moments, like during an early trip to Golden State when Malone invited Jokic into his hotel room to check on him.

"Forget the basketball," he told him. "How are you doing?"

Malone was sensitive to the fact that Jokic preferred to be a homebody. Malone was concerned enough about Jokic's well-being that he reached out to his brother, Nemanja, just to get another opinion.

"There was a lot going on," Malone said.

There was the visit to Serbia, in the summer of 2017, where the Jokics opened up their doors and welcomed Malone like extended family. They wanted him to experience Serbia, not just Sombor.

The excursion began on a boat, alongside Nikola and all of his immediate family. They dined, they drank, and they swam while a friend of the Jokic's played music throughout. When they got off the boat, a horse and carriage strolled through a gorgeous field of sunflowers before settling into an authentic Serbian meal under a traditional thatched-roof home. The feast, and his host's hospitality, sat with Malone for years.

"Some of my visits with Nikola and his family . . ." Malone began before his voice trailed off.

One summer later, Malone learned just how seriously Jokic took the business of horse training.

When Jokic invited Malone to the horse track for a training session, he afforded him the rare opportunity to ride in the carriage.

"Coach, your turn," he told him.

Channeling Billy Crystal in *City Slickers*, Malone felt he could handle the horse after a quick tutorial. On his first lap around the downtrodden track, Malone neglected the braking portion of the lesson.

"Coach, slow down, slow down, you're going too fast," they told him.

The next lap, Malone ignored their pleas again. When he returned, Jokic and his trainer were apoplectic. They kicked him out of the carriage and Jokic told him, "Coach, you will never ride my horse again. You ruined practice!"

Later that day, Nemanja and Strahinja were angrier with Nikola than with Malone. Neither one of them had ever been given the chance to train the horses.

Their relationship was what allowed them to endure the tense moments incumbent of their partnership.

"There were definitely moments where Nikola and I butted heads," Malone said. "Me being emotional, stubborn. Him being emotional, stubborn."

Early in his tenure, during an exit interview with Gary Harris, Malone asked his shooting guard what he needed to do to improve.

"Coach, from day to day, we don't know which Coach Mo is going to show up," Harris told his tempestuous coach.

Malone knew he needed to be more consistent and less mercurial. Furthermore, he couldn't in good faith ask Nikola to ease his temperament with officials when his mood swung, drastically, depending on a game's result.

Again, Malone heard his dad.

"Be with your players," he told him via text countless times. They had to know he cared about them.

As Jokic matured, so did Malone. He tried to improve on his body language and overall demeanor. Doing so insulated his relationships throughout the entire locker room.

"Fuck Xs and Os," he said. "That, to me, is the easy part of the game. The managing of the personalities, the egos, having a vision, getting guys to buy in and commit to that."

Jokic represented the pinnacle of that challenge. He was a player so gifted, and so cerebral, that every day Malone knew he needed to be accountable. When the team hit the court for a practice or a walk-through,

Malone insisted his coaches were prepared. The consequences were dire. Malone knew how quickly Jokic would lose respect for him if he wasn't prepared.

"When you're coaching a guy with the IQ of Nikola Jokic, you better be on your game," he said.

The "why," as Malone described it, was essential. The best coaches were teachers. Game plans had to make sense, and Malone needed to justify why they were teaching a certain coverage. Lessons from his dad rang daily in his head.

Malone also heeded advice he received from Gregg Popovich: empower your players.

Jokic was so smart it would have been foolish not to use him as a resource. Not to mention that his perspective on the floor was different than the one Malone had roaming the sidelines.

"He deserves that," Malone said.

Their relationship, while sometimes turbulent, was unequivocally fruitful. Both evolved, improved, and matured as they each grew more comfortable in their own skin. When Jokic became a dad, his responsibilities, to his family and his team, crystallized. In giving Jokic some semblance of ownership while simultaneously holding him accountable, Malone remained true to his job and himself.

"It's a great relationship, nine years in the making, every relationship, like my wife and I have been twenty-five years married," Malone said. "It's not fucking twenty-five years of wedding bliss. What lets you get to twenty-five years is getting through the tough times."

CHAPTER 78

OBSESSION

Point guard Reggie Jackson was a late-season addition brought in as backcourt insurance ahead of the 2023 playoffs.

He was taken aback by how different the outside perception of Nikola Jokic was from the teammate he saw on a daily basis. Upon arrival, Jackson observed Jokic's work ethic, from the way he attacked practices to the way he honed his body.

Before he knew better, Jackson admitted he was "envious" that Jokic lacked an "Adonis body" but still dominated. He made assumptions because he wasn't chiseled.

"The most impressive thing is how locked in he is, especially the narrative is, 'He just wants to go home, and people may not think he views it with the same passion as other players,'" Jackson said.

He, and they, couldn't have been more wrong. Once he was around it, Jackson said, Jokic's commitment to excellence was obvious.

His approach in discussing the game, dissecting the game, spoke volumes. During timeouts, Jackson listened intently when Jokic offered his insights. During his rest minutes, the way Jokic remained engaged served as evidence for how invested he was.

"The guy's one of the most cerebral players I've been around," he said. "It's mind-blowing."

Despite the pressure, and the opportunity facing the Nuggets to enter the postseason healthy, teammates sensed a poise from Jokic. There was a composure from their leader.

"Nothing really rattles him and that's very rare, especially in our game and how emotional and up and down it is," veteran DeAndre Jordan said. "But you need a guy like that who can kind of settle the waters and kind of make everybody feel calm in the sense of he's not panicking, almost like a Tim Duncan effect."

Jokic won two consecutive MVP awards but had just one playoff series victory to show for it. Critics eager to castigate Jokic for underwhelming in the postseason—which wasn't true—conveniently ignored injuries that killed Denver's depth.

None of it mattered.

Jokic insulated himself, which reverberated throughout the locker room. He was asked whether it was important for him to leave basketball, and all its accompanying pressures, at the gym.

"I mean, it is and it's not because I think if you want to be successful, you need to be obsessed with it," Jokic said. "But it helps sometimes when you don't think about it. It's a line between to be obsessed and still have time to relax."

Jokic wouldn't concede whether he was "obsessed" with basketball or not. His balance, in prioritizing his family, suggested he would never allow his profession to supersede his obligations as a husband, father, or brother.

"Yeah, I mean it depends," Jokic said. "If you love the game and you want to be obsessed, and you want to be the best ever, probably, it's not [hard], probably, it's fun. Depends, I mean, depends with the player. Depends on the personality, character. . . . . I'm just playing the game."

Jokic was deeply committed to winning, which was why he did something he'd never done before.

During the play-in games, which would determine who Denver was going to face in the first round, Jokic hosted the team at his sprawling house.

He told them to arrive at six thirty.

"I was excited as hell," then-rookie Peyton Watson said. "I was there at six twenty-nine."

Watson, whom Jokic looked out for that season, was among the first to arrive. He was treated to a quick tour, including the display cases that housed Jokic's various awards.

Once the rest of the team arrived, Jokic's personal chef prepared food for the night. His teammates—his extended family—were there with his wife and daughter.

"We were at his crib, vibin'," said Bruce Brown, who still has a picture on his phone of the whole group gathered inside Nikola's "big-ass" living room.

"When your best player and the best player in the world is that welcoming and that open to letting the whole team come over, hang out, lay on the couch, have a good time, that's pretty cool to see," said then-rookie Christian Braun.

It wasn't that simple.

Throughout the regular season, there were times when Jokic asked Jordan to organize group outings for the team. But Jordan didn't oblige. He, Jeff Green, Ish Smith, and Bruce Brown had been on Jokic's case about taking ownership of the team.

It was his team, they told him.

"Brother," he'd respond, trying to shirk responsibility.

"I'm like, 'You speak English, motherfucker,'" Jordan told him. "You can do this."

Jordan felt he "got away with it" for years as others took the responsibility out of convenience or comfort. The language barrier was a weak excuse.

Besides, when he commanded attention, everyone listened.

"It's rare," Jordan said, acknowledging his volume increased the deeper they got into the season.

For him to host the team signified a comfort in being the team's leader, an assumption of responsibility.

The mood at Jokic's house was lighthearted but focused.

"You could tell everyone was on a mission," said Nuggets newcomer Reggie Jackson.

As everyone settled in for the game, Jokic circled back to Watson, who had no idea what rakija was.

"Dude, he was giving me shots back-to-back-to-back," Watson said. "By the end of the night, I was like, boy, that Serbian liquor is *completely* different."

Jokic gave Braun a little too, but he was careful not to overindulge.

"Not that time," Braun joked.

It was all new to Watson, who was still just a rookie embarking on his first postseason run. But it was odd that Jokic had never done anything like that before.

There was a first time for everything.

"[Jamal's] like, 'So now we gotta go win a championship,'" Watson said.

CHAPTER 79

OLD FRIENDS

Timberwolves executive Tim Connelly admitted it was weird that the first postseason series with his new team would come against his old one.

Connelly held an impromptu press conference the morning before the No. 1–seeded Nuggets hosted his No. 8–seed Timberwolves in Game 1. In it, the man responsible for drafting Nikola Jokic made an odd concession ahead of the series.

"There's not really any matchup for Nikola," Connelly said.

The Rudy Gobert trade hadn't been executed with Jokic in mind, he said. But the trade had made the Wolves more formidable in the paint, more versatile on defense, and longer. That, in theory, could help.

In Game 1, Jokic was pedestrian by his standards. The Wolves, primarily, deployed Karl-Anthony Towns on him so that Gobert could roam the baseline. He finished with a modest 13 points, though the Nuggets played such suffocating defense, it didn't matter. Jamal Murray returned to his playoff form, seizing on gaps in Minnesota's pick-and-roll defense and playing with his fiery panache.

"I'm best when I'm feeling myself," he said after the rout.

Murray was, again, feeling himself a few nights later. He ripped off 40 points in carving up Minnesota's backcourt. As if back in the Bubble, dueling Donovan Mitchell, Murray ratcheted his play up in response to Anthony Edwards's 41 points. As Jokic navigated a new coverage—Gobert this time—Denver's two-headed monster emerged.

"It's like watching Stockton and Malone," Nuggets assistant David Adelman said earlier in the season.

To which Murray spat back, "I don't think Stockton could score like me."

Up 2–0 in their first-round series, the Nuggets were in the driver's seat headed back to Minnesota.

Rudy Gobert drew the Jokic assignment, and again it didn't go well for the three-time Defensive Player of the Year. Jokic played through Gobert's chest en route to a 20-point, 12-assist, 11-rebound triple-double. On pivots and dips, he kept Gobert spinning. In other instances, he leveraged his strength. There was little Gobert could do to mitigate his scoring. The assists only amplified the damage.

After the game, Jokic scoffed at the idea that there was any playoff game they could afford to lose.

"We needed to win," said Jokic, now up 3–0. "We didn't want to give them life."

Jokic's 43-point effort, against every defensive iteration Minnesota could unfurl in Game 4, wasn't enough for Denver to seize its first playoff sweep in franchise history. Down 12 with less than three minutes to go in regulation, Jokic and Michael Porter Jr. authored a feverish rally to force overtime. But Edwards's steely 3-point rebuttal late in overtime ensured at least one more game of their first-round series.

"We were supposed to make someone else beat us," said Jokic, lamenting their missed opportunity.

Back at home with a chance to end it, Jokic, perhaps overzealous, slogged through a miserable shooting night. Towns's physicality coupled with Gobert's length forced him to recalibrate on a possession-by-possession basis. It was uncharacteristic for him to force it, yet 29 shots to reach 28 points was a glaring incongruity. With 17 rebounds and 12 assists, it wasn't as if Minnesota had solved him.

However, in either of the prior two postseasons, that inefficiency might've been enough to catch the Nuggets for a game. But Minnesota couldn't account for Murray's marksmanship. He rained 3-pointers and flipped in circus shots, preening and stalking after each big bucket. The Nuggets ousted the Timberwolves in five games. Jokic and Murray's show of strength was clinical and unambiguous.

"[Jamal] was our best player this series," Jokic said.

The Nuggets' irascible guard was back in the postseason, where his reputation was first stoked. After two exhausting years, Jokic had a worthy dance partner.

CHAPTER 80

KD

Suns superstar Kevin Durant rolled his eyes so hard they tumbled into the adjacent locker room stall.

As I tried to explain Nikola Jokic's apparent indifference to individual honors, like the MVP award, Durant got more suspect the more I shared.

It didn't compute.

Jokic *really* didn't care about racking up MVPs, which could validate him as an all-time great, Durant asked.

He was more than skeptical.

If he doesn't care about awards, then what does he care about, Durant asked.

"Horses," I told him.

Another eye roll.

"And winning."

After a lengthy and vigorous debate, we settled on a happy medium: stats—and therefore accolades, mattered to Jokic in so far as they correlated to winning. Durant accepted that.

But before we even engaged in the discussion, Durant was dubious of the premise.

"You know that nobody can stop him," Durant said. "You just want to hear it more and more."

Content with my defense, that I was more interested in substance than flash, Durant professed a profound respect for Jokic's game.

He saw Jokic's nuances up close when the Suns collided with Denver in the Western Conference Semifinals.

"Joker has come a long way," Durant began. "He's a simple ball player. . . . He's not into the glitz and glamour, not into the showmanship of the game, it's just all about getting it done. Taking efficient shots, playing off his teammates. I just love how he plays games sometimes where he'll be 5-for-5, 10 points, 15 rebounds, 16 assists, and they win.

"I love that about him because that's the type of games that I like about myself because you've got to find the beauty in those games. It's harder to find the beauty in those games as opposed to the big scoring nights, the 35, 15, and 15. That's so obvious. But when you have games when you're 7-for-8, 16, 18 points, and you're doing everything to control the game, a real basketball mind has gotta really focus in on that game and pull out the beauties of that game. He brings a lot of that to the table. I think that's what separates him. . . . That just makes him the all-time great that he is."

In other words, Durant appreciated Jokic for his ability to shapeshift. Whatever a game called for, Jokic could accommodate. It was within Jokic's (or, for that matter, his own) less-heralded games that Durant distilled the beauty of their respective dominance.

"The game's about efficiency," he said. "That's how all the great players played, in my opinion. I know I can shoot every time I want, I know I can dominate the ball all game, but can my teammates still shine, and I still be me? That's the game when you're at this level of a Jokic."

It was interesting, then, I responded, how Jokic's form of dominance was so unique yet similarly impactful as the rest of the NBA's standard-bearers.

"There's different ways to do it," Durant said. "Mike did it his way, Kobe did it his way, Joker does it his way, and I do it my way."

CHAPTER 81

INTERPRETATION

Back in Belgrade, Nikola's former Mega teammate Nenad Miljenovic stewed on a text message.

They had communicated off and on throughout the years since they'd been teammates, but Nenad, respecting Jokic's space, was hesitant to engage. It was almost like meeting a girl and developing a relationship.

What was the right amount of communication, especially for a player of Nikola's stature?

Nenad was careful never to ask anything of Nikola. He couldn't imagine how many favors people had tried to call in with his friend.

There would be a couple of conversations throughout the year, and when Nikola came to Belgrade, the two would meet for lunch or dinner.

But once the 2022–23 postseason arrived, their communication changed. It became daily, sometimes multiple times a day. Back and forth, across the eight-hour time difference.

Not only are the two of them friends, but Jokic deeply respected Nenad's basketball acumen. He felt he was supposed to be an analyst or an NBA scout, some position where he could impart his insights.

To some degree, Jokic sought his opinion. He might have also been seeking an outlet.

The funniest comedians, Nenad believed, were the ones who refrained from laughing at their own jokes. Their dry, slow stories seeped over the audience, landing with only those smart enough to follow.

At Mega in Belgrade, humor was the basis for Nikola and Nenad's friendship. They lived off sarcasm, eager to tease one another or communicate over someone's head. Nenad relished their shared language.

"He never knows with me if I'm joking or not," Nenad said.

It was even harder to interpret intent over text messages. That made the game more fun.

"He's an asshole," Nenad said.

When Nenad woke up in the morning, eight hours ahead of Nikola, there was a message waiting on his phone from him. The Nuggets had already dispatched the Timberwolves and were awaiting the start of their Suns series.

"Yeah, this is 4–1, Phoenix," Jokic wrote to Nenad.

"Nah, I don't think so," Nenad responded. "I said, '4–1, Phoenix?' Is he fucking with me? What is he doing?"

It was against everything they held dear to seek clarification, but Nenad had a sneaking suspicion that Jokic, behind whatever joke he was trying to play, wasn't that confident. He hadn't won anything yet, not in the NBA nor with the Serbian national team.

At EuroBasket in 2022, the Serbian national team had been unceremoniously bounced from the tournament in the Round of 16, to Italy. It was a tournament some believed Serbia was favored to win.

When they didn't come close to the medal stand, it was an unsettling result for Jokic. How could a team with the NBA MVP get ousted so early? Nenad thought that disappointment lingered.

Still, something gnawed at Nenad.

Four to one, Phoenix. Is he fucking with me?

CHAPTER 82

ECLIPSED

Kevin Durant knew the roiling offense he and his Suns teammates were set to encounter.

Jamal Murray was scintillating in the first round, Michael Porter Jr. was an "X-factor," according to Durant, and Nikola Jokic wasn't to be categorized.

"You can't just call him a great passer or a great big man," Durant said. "He's just a great basketball player. You put labels on guys you take away from them a little bit."

In Game 1, the roles were reversed: Jokic played sidekick to Murray, his baskets coming in transition or off feeds from Denver's pugnacious point guard. As it had been against Minnesota, it was Murray's stage to seize. He ripped six 3-pointers, launching bombs with abandon. Instead of having to watch his team get pummeled by Phoenix, as had happened two seasons before, he savored the havoc he wrought.

"I've been waiting for a while to be healthy," Murray said after the Nuggets cruised to an 18-point win to open the series.

Game 2 was Jokic's turn.

It was a master class in finesse from an alleged plodder. He leveraged his strength like a sumo wrestler, twisting and weaving Suns center Deandre Ayton into helpless positions. Jokic's 39 points also spotlighted an area that often went underappreciated: his conditioning. In more than 41 minutes on the court, Jokic consistently beat Ayton up and down the floor. If his effort didn't yield a transition basket, then it dictated who owned valuable real estate near the basket. His teammates were uncharacteristically cold, so Jokic made a concerted effort to carry them.

"My team needed me to be aggressive," he said.

While Devin Booker paced Phoenix with 35 points, Jokic assaulted the paint, the perimeter, and wherever else he roamed. Despite the Suns' excess of snipers, Jokic appeared to be an unsolvable riddle.

Up 2–0 on Phoenix and riding a 6-1 postseason record to that point, the MVP announcement mercifully came the following day.

"Zero interest," Jokic said of the result.

Would he watch the TNT ceremony?

Jokic offered a resounding no.

"Hopefully, it's going to be a sunny day, so I can be in the swimming pool," he said sincerely.

Jokic officially finished second to Philadelphia's Joel Embiid, relieving him of an unnecessary distraction. The discourse around the award turned into an ugly referendum on basketball commentary. He decided he didn't need it. The only prize that mattered to Jokic was still in front of him.

Nuggets coach Michael Malone was insistent; all a 2–0 lead meant was that his team held serve.

Suns sniper Devin Booker proved that theory correct when he erupted for 47 points in Game 3. His and Durant's scoring ability could be just as overwhelming as the Jokic and Murray two-man tandem. Had Booker and Durant not burned the nets, it likely would've meant an insurmountable 3–0 deficit; Jokic orchestrated a 30-point, 17-rebound, 17-assist masterpiece that amounted to nothing. His level of dominance was incomparable, but Phoenix was a talented challenger.

They filmed the same movie in Game 4. Jokic boasted a career-high 53 points in defeat. He played a surly, burly bear in the post, exposing Deandre Ayton's interior defense. The decision to guard Jokic one-on-one forced his hand. Yet the Suns wrested a 2–2 tie from their home stand on the twenty-five combined buckets between Durant and Booker.

By Game 5, it was apparent the Suns had no answers for Jokic. He was an offensive machine almost metronomic in his approach. He sought cutters, and he fed mismatches. When he had single coverage, he obliterated it. With 29 points, 13 rebounds, and 12 assists, Jokic surpassed Wilt Chamberlain with his tenth postseason triple-double.

"I think sometimes we maybe take Nikola Jokic for granted because what he is doing is simply incredible," Malone said. "Every single night."

In supporting roles, Michael Porter Jr. and Bruce Brown were magnificent, thrusting the Nuggets to the verge of the conference finals. The Nuggets held serve, remaining undefeated in Denver.

In Game 6, Kentavious Caldwell-Pope seemed intent on validating his prediction.

"We're making it out of this series," he vowed.

Caldwell-Pope dropped 17 points in the first quarter of Game 6 and the rout was, spectacularly, on.

As Jokic bludgeoned Phoenix's front line, and Murray stretched its defense to the perimeter, the Nuggets mounted a 32-point lead *before* halftime. Their dominance was so thorough that disgusted Suns fans lavished their own team with boos. The Nuggets were a rollicking, frothing offensive juggernaut that dismantled a supposed favorite, on their floor.

"We looked like a championship team," Jokic said. "We were so focused. . . . Well, I guess I don't know how a championship team looks. But I think that was how it's supposed to look."

Jokic was right. The Nuggets booked a conference finals appearance for only the fifth time in their franchise history.

CHAPTER 83

UNDER PRESSURE

Nenad Miljenovic, Nikola's Serbian confidant, laughed as Jokic did the opposite of what he'd predicted.

Four to one, Suns.

No matter what his friend said, Nenad always had to allow for the possibility of a joke. Even if he was at the center of it.

"You can assume," Nenad said.

Naturally, Nenad assumed there was a strategy to Jokic's curious texts.

"He's toying with everything," Nenad said. "He's taking some pressure off him a little bit."

That was the beauty of Jokic's riddle.

If he suggested a confidence that the Nuggets would roll through a given opponent, that would only disrespect an opponent and add pressure. Unnecessary, at that. Jokic was, admittedly, a big believer in karma.

The objective was twofold: lower expectations while messing with his friend.

"Of course, the message before the Lakers series, it was like, '4–2, Lakers,'" Nenad said.

"I'm like, 'There's no way they're beating you.'"

CHAPTER 84

UNCHARTED TERRITORY

The previous seven times Denver faced Los Angeles in a playoff series, the Lakers had prevailed.

They were an ignominious foe, with a vaunted history.

The most recent, a conference finals collision in the Bubble in 2020, marked the furthest the Nuggets had marched in the Jokic era. This time the Nuggets were the No. 1 seed. And so far, they'd played like it.

"They're a really, really, really, really good team," LeBron James said.

James knew they were good in the Bubble, but conceded they were even better now.

"To be honest," a dishonest Jokic said of what he'd gleaned from their prior series, "I don't remember."

The Nuggets were a well-constructed roster of complementary pieces that endured their share of postseason scars; the Lakers, though they had franchise pillars James and Anthony Davis, underwent a significant roster overhaul at the trade deadline and survived the play-in tournament.

The Nuggets were favored. This was uncharted territory.

In Game 1, Jokic worked Davis from all three levels. He was a magnet on the glass, a sniper in the midrange, and a magician from outside. Late in the third quarter, Jokic heaved a falling, flailing 3-pointer from two steps beyond the 3-point arc. When it improbably fell, Davis turned to him in disbelief.

"I just looked at him and just smiled," said Davis, who scored 40 of his own. "Nothing else I could have done."

Jokic's 34-point triple-double staked Denver to a 1–0 lead, though a quiet fourth quarter gave the Lakers hope. Los Angeles deployed reserve big man Rui Hachimura on Jokic with some semblance of success.

Nuggets coach Michael Malone, always quick to burnish the overlooked narrative, responded ahead of the next game.

"It's the first time I've ever been in a series up 1–0, and the series is over in everybody's eyes because they put Rui on Nikola Jokic for six possessions," Malone said.

In Game 2, against a platoon of Davis, Hachimura, James, and former teammate Jarred Vanderbilt, Jokic was less efficient than he had been. He *still* recorded his fourth consecutive postseason triple-double.

The difference, however, was Murray, the flamethrower who looked like he was shooting into the Pacific Ocean. The symbiotic relationship of Jokic and Murray meant that an overcorrection on Jokic could alleviate pressure on Murray. Both players were capable conductors, lightning rods of production.

The Nuggets entered the fourth quarter trailing before Murray morphed into an assassin. He dropped 23 of his 37 points in the final frame on outrageous step-back 3-pointers and shrewd swerves through the lane. The attention that Jokic garnered was diverted; Murray was now Denver's magnet.

"He was special," Jokic said, up 2–0 on Los Angeles. "He won us the game."

Murray's torrential downpour extended to the start of Game 3; his 30 first-half points put the Lakers on notice. Their LA jaunt was a business trip of epic proportions. A-list celebrities like Denzel, Jack, and Adele sat stone-faced as Murray painted the court.

Role players like Kentavious Caldwell-Pope and Bruce Brown kept the game close while Jokic battled foul trouble, before a feverish fourth quarter revealed Denver's championship mettle. The Nuggets rode their most reliable action: Jokic and Murray, over and over again, to ice the game.

"That was Nikola's call," Nuggets coach Michael Malone said.

Jokic and Murray's 22 combined fourth-quarter points ushered a stunned, silent crowd out of the arena before the game was over. They were ruthlessly efficient in the clutch and had their sights on something bigger.

"You need sixteen wins to win a championship," Murray said. "We've got five more to go."

CHAPTER 85

NONSENSE

Nenad had come to expect Nikola's nonsense.

The Nuggets were a game away from reaching their first-ever NBA Finals. They had a chance to oust the Lakers, on their floor, into a humbling offseason exit. Never, in any round, had the Nuggets swept a playoff series.

Nenad woke up to a text that had become all too predictable.

"Before Game 4 with the Lakers, at LA, Nikola said, if they win tonight, they're gonna win the series, 4–3."

BROOMS

By halftime of Game 4, the Lakers had a commanding 73–58 lead.

LeBron James authored one of *those* halves. He knew the juggernaut he was up against and took matters into his own hands. He bulldozed through Aaron Gordon and shirked Michael Porter Jr. He rained threes as if it was actually a strength of his game. His 31 points built the Lakers a sizable cushion, momentarily breathing life into the moribund series.

In the third quarter, Denver's defense engaged. It swarmed, swiped, and pilfered. It busted through screens and scrambled on closeouts. The Nuggets refused to reenact the Minnesota series, where they'd dropped Game 4 only to end it at home. In Los Angeles, there was a statement to make.

The urgency on defense translated to execution on offense. There was no set defense to navigate, which yielded transition opportunities and glaring mismatches. Jokic, Murray, Porter, and Gordon seized on the opening. The 36–16 quarter was jarring in its disparity; Denver had a slight lead heading into, potentially, the last quarter of the Lakers' season.

Ugly and physical, the Nuggets plodded along. When Gordon slipped a screen and Jokic unearthed him for an and-1 dunk, Jokic unleashed a primal scream near halfcourt. With a 5-point lead and only 3:34 left, Jokic sensed it.

As the Lakers threatened, Jokic delivered his signature moment. The possession was all but extinguished when Jokic ambled outside the 3-point line, rocked back on one leg, and catapulted a prayer just inches from Anthony Davis's outstretched hand. Murray stood on the far side of the court, beckoning for the ball. When it plunged through the net, both James and Davis dropped their shoulders. Murray stared at the Lakers' bench, savoring their disgust. Jokic, unamused, galloped back on defense.

Asked later about his propensity for sinking off-balance shots, Jokic delivered again.

"I'm off-balance my whole life, so that's kind of normal for me," he deadpanned.

Two minutes later, Jokic bludgeoned Davis for one more bucket to give Denver a 113–111 lead with less than a minute left. When James took the final possession, driving the left side of the lane to tie it, Murray met him followed by Gordon. Together they smothered the slim window James had.

The sweep was complete.

On the strength of Jokic's 30-point triple-double, the Nuggets secured the franchise's first trip to the NBA Finals.

"He's real," coach Malone said. "What he's doing is real."

At center court for the trophy celebration, Jokic, who was named Conference Finals MVP, did what he always did: deflected. The MVP trophy was a reflection of his teammates, he said. The team's success was a nod to their entire organization, beginning with the team's equipment managers. When the team posed for a picture, Jokic took his place in the back row. While Bruce Brown held his MVP trophy, Jokic planted a kiss on DeAndre Jordan's cheek.

Once the ceremony subsided, the team retreated to the locker room for more revelry. But Jokic was only there a few minutes. He turned left out of the locker room, where his wife and daughter were waiting. After a few tender, quiet moments, Jokic slipped behind a black curtain where the strength coaches had assembled a makeshift weight room.

The historic night wouldn't curb his routine.

Before his two brothers came dashing behind the curtain, the music started playing.

"Some people call me the space cowboy . . . Some call me the gangster of love . . ."

The soundtrack for Jokic's postgame workout?

"The Joker," by the Steve Miller Band.

CHAPTER 87

TAO OF JOKER

As the Nuggets awaited word on their Finals opponent, Jokic was at ease.

He parried questions on well-trod topics in front of the media, then used the break to spend time with his family.

Did he pay attention to the results of the Eastern Conference Finals between Boston and Miami? Nah, he claimed. He was on a walk with his daughter.

"I'm lying, I watched the first quarter," he said.

Even during the postseason, Jokic's priorities were intact.

"Basketball is not main thing in my life and probably never gonna be," Jokic said. "To be honest, I like it."

How could his competitive spirit reconcile with that approach? And what if it was *because* of that balance that he achieved his success?

Pelicans star C. J. McCollum has grappled with Jokic in the playoffs and has been privy to a few lighter moments too. As part of the same agency, Excel Sports, there's a relationship with Jokic grounded in mutual respect.

When Jokic celebrated his birthday over the All-Star break in Salt Lake City with Luka Doncic, McCollum happened to be in the same place and sent drinks to the group.

"He loves basketball, he just loves other things too," McCollum said. "I think it's great to have a balance, that gets misconstrued a lot. I love basketball, I love other things too. You have to have a balance in this life, or it'll drive you crazy."

For McCollum, like Jokic, it's the people around him.

"I'm nothing without my family," he said.

What does this game mean if you go home to nothing? he pondered.

McCollum would only concede that the NBA was a *part* of his life and not what defined him.

Then he circled back to Jokic, who he acknowledged had the requisite work ethic, preparation, and skill to be great. It wasn't one-size-fits-all, he said.

"Some people can kill you with kindness," McCollum said. "He's an assassin, he's a killer, but he's smiling while he's doing it. Does that mean he's not a killer?"

McCollum offered the description in contrast to Kobe Bryant, whose maniacal approach depicted one route to success.

Former Nuggets teammate Mason Plumlee spent time in the offseason working out at Lower Merion High School in Pennsylvania, which Bryant attended. He's built relationships with some of Kobe's former teammates and coaches. When he brought up a comparison of the two, he spoke from a place of familiarity.

"Kobe was the face of the league, and there's like this pure, intense, this model for success," Plumlee said. "To me, Joker, one of his qualities on the court that's just unbelievable, he's never hurried, never rushed, never doing anything he doesn't want to do. There are different things to admire and look at from any competitive perspective where it's like, this guy was amazing in his own way."

CHAPTER 88

PREDICTION

Once Game 7 of the Eastern Conference Finals was over between Boston and Miami, Nenad waited to hear from Jokic.

"He was like, '[Miami] beat everybody,'" Nenad said.

Jokic held deep admiration for how hard Jimmy Butler and Bam Adebayo played the game. But by that point, having teased his way through the Suns and Lakers' series, Nenad had his suspicions.

After Game 7, the text Nenad was expecting arrived.

"Heat in five," Jokic wrote.

CHAPTER 89

PINNACLE

Nikola Jokic's circuitous path was enough to warrant genuine respect from Heat center Bam Adebayo.

"Second-rounder, nobody knew his name," Adebayo said. "To be one of the perennial superstars in this league, you love to hear stories like that."

Adebayo appreciated how far Jokic had come.

"It's always been respect," said Adebayo, whose job it was to corral the untamable.

In Game 1 of the Finals, Jokic wielded control despite only taking 12 shots. The 14 assists he served, including 10 in the first half, empowered his teammates. He preferred they ate before he did. His dissection was surgical; windows needed only be slightly ajar for him to exploit them.

He seized on mismatches, communication lapses, and hot hands. Jamal Murray, who scored 26, was happy to indulge. Denver's lead ballooned to 24, and the result was never in question. Staunch defense and a peerless Jokic set the tone.

"I don't force it," Jokic said after the Game 1 win and yet another triple-double. "I never force it. . . . That's how I learned to play basketball."

By Game 2, Heat coach Erik Spoelstra succeeded in minimizing Jokic's damage, which constituted a funny way of describing his 41-point outburst. But with just 4 assists, it was true.

"Yeah, that's a ridiculous—that's the untrained eye that says something like that," Spoelstra said when asked about turning Jokic into a scorer *or* a passer.

"You know, twice in two seasons he's been the best player on this planet. You can't just say, 'Oh, make him a scorer.' That's not how they play. They have so many different actions that just get you compromised."

Nothing compromised the Nuggets like Miami's blistering 3-point shooting. The Heat shot 17-of-35 from outside. Amid the parade of triples, Denver's defense was disconnected at best, complacent at worst.

"Let's talk about effort," seethed Nuggets coach Michael Malone after the Heat snatched Game 2. "This is the NBA Finals, we are talking about effort."

When Murray's 3-pointer at the buzzer rimmed out, sealing Miami's 111–108 win, it was Denver's first home loss of the postseason. The Nuggets had been 9-0, but the Heat's indomitable will ruined that streak.

Tied 1–1 in the NBA Finals, there was plenty to reckon with having lost home-court advantage. What followed was a "very honest" film session, according to Malone, where he forced the Nuggets to take ownership of their faults.

There were seventeen clips in total. Instead of dictating their lapses, Malone wanted his team to acknowledge them.

"I gave each player a clip, and I said, 'You tell me what you see and what should have happened,'" he said. "And all the players took ownership."

Michael Porter Jr. had been the culprit on a few of those breakdowns.

"It was a very vocal film session," he said. "You can't be sensitive. Me personally, I know I gotta play better."

Later, down in Miami, they flushed their Game 2 disgust at Jeff Green's South Florida home. Steak, chicken, risotto, and kale salad were on the menu.

Green had planned to host the team before their demoralizing defeat. The impact, given the circumstances, was therapeutic.

"The kale salad was fire," Jordan said.

By Game 3, the Nuggets had reset. All they needed to do was steal one on the road and wrest home-court advantage back in their favor.

As if attached by some invisible mind meld, Jokic and Murray were intertwined in Game 3. Their elasticity, in operating as a two-man unit and not just teammates who understood each other, was shocking.

If Murray was sizzling, he probed just a bit deeper to drag Jokic's defender a step out of position. If Jokic had an advantage, Murray's defender inevitably bit, which left Denver's precocious point guard open. The two *shared* a hot streak like a perpetual flame in *NBA Jam*.

Jokic dominated inside. His line of 32 points, 21 rebounds, and 10 assists had never been done before in NBA Finals history. His rebounding in particular underscored the size advantage Denver held.

"We're running out of things to say," Murray said.

One leak portended another. Murray slithered for 34 points, whipped 10 assists, and snatched 10 rebounds.

No two teammates had ever assembled dueling 30-point triple-doubles, ever, including the regular season and the playoffs.

"By far, their greatest performance as a duo in their seven years together," said Malone after his team's Game 3 win.

But a funny thing happened in the cramped but proud postgame locker room. Jokic approached rookie Christian Braun and told him he'd won them the game. Jokic said it aloud to the team too.

Braun erupted for 15 points off the bench. It was almost as if the Heat hadn't accounted for what he could do, especially in the face of two historic performances. Braun was a defensive sparkplug and an offensive roamer. His fearlessness was one of the traits that first attracted GM Calvin Booth's attention.

"Even when he makes a mistake, it's an aggressive mistake, so you cannot be mad at him," Jokic said of Braun. "He won us the game."

Of all the moments that resonated from Denver's stirring playoff run, for Braun, that was it. To this day, he tells his friends about it.

"I had 15 points," he said for emphasis. "*It was 15 points.*"

Then Jokic went before hundreds of cameras broadcasting to millions across the world and claimed the rookie won them the game.

"The MVP just said I won him a Finals game when I had 15 points and he had 32/21/10," Braun said, astonished at Jokic's unselfishness.

CHAPTER 90

JAMAL MURRAY

Jamal Murray couldn't remember who called who, and the details of the conversations were hazy.

But Nikola Jokic was definitely shirtless.

When the Nuggets surprised Jokic in Sombor with his MVP trophy, the contingent partied into all hours of the night. Somewhere amid the revelry, Jokic appeared on Murray's phone.

"I think the FaceTime in Serbia, we were drunk," Murray said. "His shirt was off."

The call was light and funny, the duo laughing and giggling "about everything," Murray said, still mired in his ACL rehab at the time.

Jokic rarely divulged much about their off-court relationship but remembered Murray telling him to be patient. That he'd eventually be back to his old self to help shoulder the burden.

"I talked to him a couple times under the influence of something," Jokic said.

A Canadian and a Serbian, from two disparate parts of the world, remained close despite their physical separation. No celebration would have been complete without Murray. A similar call happened later that summer, when Jokic signed a five-year, $270 million contract to remain in Denver. For two seminal moments in Jokic's journey, Murray was there.

"Yeah, sometimes we have fun," Jokic said.

It's not that the two of them have spent ample time together off the court, but it's a bond that is there whenever necessary.

"Like, [Aaron Gordon] goes to see him in Serbia, right? But [Nikola] doesn't do anything here," Murray said. "He kinda keeps to himself."

That, in no way, was a referendum on their relationship.

Jokic and Murray have an inside joke that reflects the depth of their rapport. Their secret "handshake" isn't actually a handshake at all. It's what they call the pocket pass one throws to the other coming off a chase action—their term for Denver's patented dribble handoff.

Baked into their two-man game was a shared understanding that what made them so devastating was their selflessness. Their willingness to get off the ball made them even more problematic to stop.

"Okay, I have 40 points, I have a mismatch on me, but so does he, and I'm giving it to him willingly," Murray said.

However, there was another ingredient to the formula. There were hundreds of occasions, Murray said, where they'd be in a huddle discussing how to attack a defense. Murray might have a suggestion, Jokic might offer his opinion, but the conversation always ended with a simple arrangement: it was best to improvise.

Nothing, they'd say, needed to be predetermined.

"Everything that we've ever done is on the fly," Murray said.

When Jokic and Murray tortured Miami's defense in their historic Game 3 Finals performance, it was because neither cared who got the credit. Their mutual trust, built on years of handoffs and pick-and-rolls, was corporate knowledge.

"He knows what I'm capable of, and he lets me just be me and doesn't have any animosity towards anything I do on the court, which is lovely," Murray said. "I think a lot of the guys in the league, nowadays, so many stars on the team, you can feel like you don't know who's going to get the ball, or if it matters, or 'He should've taken the shot,' or, 'It should've been him.' . . . With us, it's like, man, we're just reading, playing the game."

What differentiated—and elevated—the 2022–23 Nuggets, Murray said, was that everyone understood their roles. He knew Jokic could go off at a moment's notice, which meant Murray didn't need to concern himself with his center's production. He knew his offense was readily available too. If it meant feeding Michael Porter Jr. on the wing, or hunting for Kentavious Caldwell-Pope in the corner, Murray didn't care.

"The game is so pure here," Murray said.

Murray knew that despite his prodigious shooting, he was never going to be the anchor of Denver's offense. It was never a sticking point.

"He's gonna be a top-two center of all time," Murray said. "I think I should be okay."

CHAPTER 91

CLOSING TIME

The posters tacked to the wall inside the visiting locker room were a nod to equipment manager Sparky Gonzales.

"Knowing is not enough, we must apply," the one inside Murray's stall read, referencing Bruce Lee's mantra.

"Willing is not enough. We must do."

On the way to the shower was a Jokic quote that summed up his unique irreverence toward the situation.

"We have a chance to do something nice."

In the moment, that meant getting greedy. They had already seized home-court advantage back, but to make quick work of Miami, Game 4 was essential. Twice throughout the postseason when asked about the psychology of needing another road win, Jokic scoffed. It was the playoffs, he groused. Every game was a must-win.

That mindset prohibited complacency.

In Game 4, Jokic was great, not superb. Murray was impactful but inefficient. All season, Denver's depth was under the microscope. Could it endure stretches without Jokic? was a constant refrain. Was Aaron Gordon capable of stretching outside his comfort zone? Would supersub Bruce Brown continue his run as the steal of free agency?

Embracing the moment, Gordon played the game of his life. With an efficient 27 points, he bulldozed through Miami's frontcourt and imposed his unique combination of size and strength. When he drained three 3-pointers, flashing a layer to his game that had proven elusive, the Heat had no answers.

Brown's bullish drives underscored Miami's math problem. His 21 points were a source of even more unexpected production.

When Jokic went to the bench early in the fourth quarter with his fifth foul and the Nuggets sitting on a 10-point lead, it was gut-check time. All the questions that percolated were unavoidable.

Murray sank a 3-pointer, then unsung hero Jeff Green drained one too. A transition break found Brown open beneath the hoop. The Nuggets held water while Jokic watched. When he checked back in at the 4:09 mark, the lead was still 9. Miami had its chance and squandered it.

The outcome of the series may not have changed, but the sequence was as emblematic as any throughout the entire postseason, or really, Jokic's time in Denver.

"The only way is together," Jokic said of his team's 108–95 win, "and that's how we won the games."

When he was asked about his individual rise, Jokic responded about his team's growth and his teammates' buy-in. Up 3–1 in the NBA Finals, Jokic wasn't interested in talking about himself.

"I mean, my journey is—I don't think it's that interesting," he said.

At home, with a chance to seize the franchise's first title in forty-seven years, the Nuggets talked themselves into some mental gymnastics. *They* were down 3–1, they told themselves. That was the urgency required to oust Miami.

It was the culmination of a poise GM Calvin Booth noticed in the wake of the Lakers' sweep.

"There was a composure about [Nikola] that suggested that he knew we had more to do," Booth said.

The deeper the Nuggets marched, the less that needed to be said among the group.

"The predator hunting the prey," Booth said.

Game 5 was a tight, tense affair. The game trickled rather than flowed. Both defenses were stifling.

The Heat entered the fourth quarter up a single point, without any margin for error against a team that was 9-1 in its last 10 games. Jokic played the hub in the center of the paint. From there he was unassailable, a queen on a chessboard.

He and Murray's partnership, the bedrock of Denver's success, shined with a title in reach. For the first eight minutes of the quarter, only Jokic and Murray found the basket. Having garnered so much attention, Kentavious Caldwell-Pope was open from the perimeter with 4:09 left. His triple gave the Nuggets a 7-point lead before a string of 8 consecutive points from Jimmy Butler froze Ball Arena.

Miami led 89–88 when Brown snuck in for a baseline put-back attempt that gave the Nuggets a one-point edge. Denver's defense was so connected it conceded just five Heat buckets the entire quarter. The final minute, the Nuggets snuffed out one pass from Butler, then offered a strong contest on another 3-point try.

The Heat was resigned. When Caldwell-Pope snatched the final defensive board with nine seconds left, Miami let the clock dwindle. There was nothing left to contest.

The Nuggets were NBA champions, concluding a journey that was decades in the making.

Jokic didn't celebrate. He beelined toward the Heat's bench to congratulate every opponent he could find, including Miami's deep reserves. There was a glazed look of awe, without a hint of glee, on his face.

Save for a hug with an overzealous security guard, Jokic barely rejoiced.

His postgame on-air interview yielded one of the seminal lines of his career.

Asked what it meant to be a champion, Jokic couldn't mask his relief.

"It's good, it's good," he said. "The job is done, we can go home now."

In Jokic's case, the job meant becoming the first player to lead the NBA in points (600), rebounds (269), and assists (190) in a single postseason.

It was only when his oldest brother, Strahinja, lifted Nikola's seven-foot frame off the ground that he finally cracked a broad, gleaming smile across his face. Nikola's biggest pleasure always derived from others' happiness.

Onstage, Nikola tried to cede the spotlight to the rest of the organization. He only moved to the front to receive his Finals MVP trophy, while clutching his daughter in his arms. As soon as he could, he receded, again, to the back with his wife by his side.

In the locker room, he wasn't in the throes of the champagne showers like the rest of his teammates. He was content with a tallboy of Michelob Ultra. When Aaron Gordon, Michael Porter Jr., DeAndre Jordan, Jeff

Green, and Christian Braun belted out Queen's "We Are the Champions" in the locker room, Jokic wasn't among them.

As they reveled in a dominant postseason romp, Jokic offered this reflection on how his team got here.

"If you want to be a success, you need a couple years," he said. "You need to be bad, then you need to be good, then when you're good you need to fail, and then when you fail, you're going to figure it out."

It was sage advice from someone who had remained patient.

The championship parade, Jokic learned, wasn't until Thursday—three long days away.

"No," he said. "I need to go home."

Jokic's perspective was unmatched.

"Nobody likes his job, or maybe they do," he continued. "They're lying."

As good as he was, Jokic wouldn't allow himself to be defined by basketball. He cared way more about the relationships his job forged.

It was nearly 1 a.m. when Jokic huddled in front of his locker, championship trophy in hand, with his unofficial team surrounding him: strength coaches Felipe Eichenberger and Claus Souza, assistant coach Ogi Stojakovic, and athletic trainer Jason Miller.

It was Miller who knew Jokic's body better than almost anyone. He had helped him navigate the spate of injuries that were inevitable throughout an NBA season. Miller was alongside Jokic at every All-Star Game and was with him during national team appearances in China, the Czech Republic, and Germany. But his most cherished memories of Jokic were the interactions he had with his two young sons.

When Miller's boys practiced jiu jitsu, Jokic inevitably challenged them.

"I can take you," he told them.

The fact that they knew who Jokic was as a person, and not just a basketball player, meant the world to Miller. Still, there was some surprise when Jokic showed up at his son's birthday party toting a bag of presents for *both* boys. The picture captured of his son, with Batman face paint standing next to Joker, was one he savored.

The one taken on championship night was almost as meaningful.

While the group posed, his brother Strahinja scrambled over to be part of the moment. It was one to cherish; those were a handful of people most responsible for Jokic's success.

Once the cigar smoke lifted and the locker room began to clear, Jokic's brothers, both wearing Serbia jerseys of their youngest brother, helped commandeer the speakers. As soon as he heard his native Serbian music, Nikola finally started dancing. Before long, Strahinja and Michael Malone were in the middle of the locker room, twirling each other around with drinks in hand.

By 1:30 a.m., with around a dozen people left in the locker room, a Serbian dance party broke out. Outfitted in all black dress clothes, Jokic stood in front of his stall, waving his arms and dancing.

The party was on.

CHAPTER 92

P-WAT

The Nuggets were on a road trip in March when then-rookie Peyton Watson saw what it meant to be Nikola Jokic's teammate.

Denver had a back-to-back—against the Knicks and Nets—which afforded a rare night out in New York.

DeAndre Jordan hosted a handful of Nuggets at an exclusive spot in lower Manhattan. Numerous teammates came, including Jokic, Michael Porter Jr., Aaron Gordon, and Watson. Wine flowed generously as the team hung out, keeping tabs on the ongoing NCAA Tournament games.

Watson was green, by NBA standards and certainly by any normal measure. The rangy forward was only twenty at the time. His rookie salary for that season was just $2.1 million.

Watson spent most of the season with Denver's G League team but occasionally got called up. Though his opportunities on the court were limited, Jokic had an affinity for him. He was oozing with potential, and beyond their shared representation, Jokic liked who he was as a person.

So, he looked out for him.

"He was on me a lot about spending as a rookie," Watson said.

That night in New York, Watson arrived with his favorite accessory: his silver chain around his neck.

Jokic approached Watson, calling Jordan over for reinforcement. And a witness.

"He's like, 'If you get another chain, I'm going to punch you,'" Jordan said Jokic told the rookie.

Jokic knew how precious NBA contracts were; he encouraged Watson to wait until he'd gotten a second contract before spending lavishly.

Watson didn't feel like waiting, quoting Colorado coach Deion Sanders.

"When you look good, you feel good," Watson said with a grin.

By the end of the season, he purchased a second chain. He vividly remembered walking into a room with both on when Jokic spotted him.

"He was like, 'Brother, I'm gonna punch you right now,'" Jokic told him.

Three days after the Nuggets hoisted the Larry O'Brien Trophy, Watson had his trademark chains at the team's parade through downtown Denver.

"We're celebrating the parade, obviously lit, out-of-body experience," Watson said. "He's like, 'Brother, let me wear the chains.'"

CHAPTER 93

STAY ON PARADE

Nikola Jokic and Jamal Murray floated by Union Station in Denver on a No. 15 fire truck.

Streets overflowed with Nuggets fans eager to celebrate their unprecedented title and eager to bask in the glory years of Denver basketball.

Jokic had his daughter in his lap; Murray wore a New Balance shirt that read "~~Playoff, Finals,~~ Champion Murray."

The Larry O'Brien Trophy and the Finals MVP trophy stood beside them, as Nuggets owners Stan and Josh Kroenke sat in the row behind. Both superstars were flanked by their families: Murray with his dad, Roger; Jokic with his two brothers and his wife. Misko Raznatovic, Jokic's agent and the founder of Mega Basket in Belgrade, was on the day's final float as well. He wore a jersey that precious few people have—a baby blue and pink Jokic jersey from his days at Mega.

As Murray flung his signature celebratory arrows into the crowd and caught beers from adoring fans, Jokic basked in the hundreds of thousands of fans chanting "MVP" in his honor. Some moments he indulged the adulation, blowing kisses to the crowd. Other moments, it was overwhelming.

"Okay, okay, okay, *okay!*" he stammered from the podium in front of an estimated 750,000 people, all craning to give Jokic his due.

"You know that I told that I don't want to stay on parade, but I fucking want to stay on parade," Jokic said. "This is the best day."

Few had ever seen Jokic drop his guard, publicly, like he did. Dry and sarcastic were his favorite languages, but the occasion called for something more sincere. Jokic indulged.

As the team gathered for a picture on the stage of the Civic Center, hundreds of thousands of fans draped behind them, Jokic fell into his comfort zone: the backdrop. He was stashed between Jeff Green and Aaron Gordon, happily among his peers.

While the team started to disperse, there were whispers of one final hurrah that evening: Vegas.

After the parade, the team flew to Sin City, where one more dinner and a night of partying awaited them.

Bruce Brown sat next to Jokic at dinner. He had an angle he was trying to exploit.

"So, we drinking tonight?" Brown asked him.

"Yeah, we're drinking," Jokic told him.

As they sipped on Jameson, Brown told Jokic the plan: "All right, I'm gonna get you drunk."

Jokic scoffed.

"He's like, 'We'll see,'" Brown said.

When the team, including Josh Kroenke and at least one member of the front office, hit the club, Brown said they brought out a bottle of something he'd never seen before. He didn't know what it was. He later deemed it some type of Serbian whiskey, which in all likelihood meant rakija.

"I'm like, 'Nikola, just get me another one, keep filling me up,'" Brown said.

Brown only remembered bits and pieces from the club—unfortunate because videos from that night showed Jokic "swag-surfing" with members of the organization.

"I was just in and out blackout the whole night," Brown said. "In and out, in and out."

As was protocol, team security escorted Brown to his room.

"Lights-out," he said.

The next morning, Brown missed the team's private flight home and had to figure out his own transportation back to Denver.

"It was worth it, though," he said.

CHAPTER 94

HOME

Nikola Jokic's favorite bungalow sat on the quiet bank of the Danube, the biggest river in Serbia.

He had one of his own too, but that one was always bustling, with parents and kids, wives and friends. There's too much commotion for his liking and no place to be himself, to be quiet surrounded by nature.

That's why he cherished the place his best friend, Nemanja Pribic, has.

"His lake house doesn't have electricity, it's a little bit off the grid," Jokic said. "The river is *right* there."

At Jokic's lake house there's fishing, but it doesn't compare.

At Nemanja's, Jokic can "just get away from everybody else."

The summer after their championship run, Jokic sent his godfather, Nebojsa Vagic, a text at 3:30 in the morning from the bungalow. It was a picture of a small fire, too small to be a bonfire but big enough to feel its warmth. Amid the glowing red embers, Vagic knew what the picture meant. His godson was happy and content.

In Sombor, he was always that way.

"When we can be just us, with our closest friends, I saw in his face that he's enjoying the moments like that," Pribic said.

Once every offseason, Jokic and his old teammates gathered for a reunion to celebrate their 2012 Vojvodina regional championship. The tradition, called "Pepiada," in a nod to the Olympics, began around 2015. They hung out in the woods, played soccer, listened to music, and drank. The all-day event always turned into a barbecue, according to Pribic. Their old coach, Isidor, came too. When he brought out photos of a young Nikola or a young Nemanja, it was hard not to smile, to consider where they started.

Ever since that 2012 regional title, there was a running joke at Nikola's expense.

"Okay, you can win those individual awards, but you cannot win any team title without us," they told him.

It was those friends who began to explain how Jokic remained so humble.

In the wake of the championship, the fame that Jokic achieved was almost unconscionable. Now, he admitted, it had become a burden.

The best part of his celebrity?

"You can get restaurant [reservation] even if it's full," he said wryly.

His fame also granted him opportunities to interact with interesting people throughout his career, though that's only worthwhile assuming he wanted that.

"I don't know if it's worth it or not because I have some great people that nobody knows about," he said. "I really don't know, is it worth it all that fame."

Pribic needed only to look across the fire to consider his friend's plight.

"I was thinking about what I would be like if I was that famous," Pribic said. "I would change for sure. . . . What keeps him the same, I don't know."

Almost miraculously, their dynamic hasn't changed. Pribic enjoyed asking Jokic what he remembered about their friends' eighteenth birthday parties.

"I do that because I know he missed almost every one of them," Pribic said.

Now, when Jokic is back home, the "only difference is that he's picking me up in front of my apartment in a better car," Pribic said.

It's not that Jokic doesn't recognize how fortunate he and his family are, but there were unintended consequences of his meteoric rise.

"It's one way to sacrifice yourself, basically," he said.

Which explains why he was so fiercely protective of his space, both mentally and physically.

Nebojsa used to tell Nikola how nature helped reset him. Hiking, kayaking, fishing, or swimming, all were invaluable hobbies. Within those activities, Jokic could decompress, which wasn't possible while lifting a franchise.

"I think he has great, great sense of responsibility for him and his family and for his club," Nebojsa said. "He said to me fifty times, 'I have to be best as I can tonight.' . . . Of course, I told him, 'You don't have to be best, just relax a little bit. You're gonna be good enough.' . . .

"He's carrying a big burden. . . . He doesn't want to disappoint anybody. There is a lot of that."

The weight Jokic felt revealed itself in the way he dealt with postseason exits. He was often emotional and reflective. When asked specifically about that pressure, he said there was growth within those painful moments.

"I think every season you can learn from it, even if you don't win," he said.

He tried to gather his thoughts and settled on one cogent declaration.

"I just love to win," he said in stark, simple terms.

He loved to disconnect just as much.

Among the highlights of every summer were the rafting trips Nebojsa organized on the Tara River, coasting through parts of Montenegro and Bosnia and Herzegovina.

"He's planning right now," Jokic said some six months ahead of when their group would go. "He's obsessed with that."

"We go there and we are alone," Jokic said.

The adventures tended to take on a life of their own, the jokes bleeding from one trip into the next. The three brothers relished making fun of Nebojsa for how meticulous he was in planning the excursions, but the easiest target was Strahinja, who could never drop his rigid demeanor.

"We laugh when we mention Strahi because he always acts seriously regardless," Nebojsa said.

The inside jokes, among the brothers and Nebojsa, flowed as fast as the rapids themselves.

Before Nikola became an All-Star and won multiple MVP awards, Nebojsa prepared a cake upon his arrival back home in Serbia one offseason.

The cake read: "I don't want to practice anymore."

"Every time he said that, he took some life out of Strahinja," Nebojsa said. "Strahi never [took] that as funny. Not a single time. He was so stressed hearing that from Nikola."

Nebojsa didn't like Jokic's aversion to work either, but it was a joke funny enough to revisit.

"Just wanted to tell him how we appreciate him saying that bullshit," Nebojsa said.

CHAPTER 95

QUIET ON SET

The 6 a.m. call time was unapologetic and abrupt.

Nikola Jokic and second-year forward Peyton Watson were in Los Angeles for consecutive preseason games when off-court obligations commandeered their attention.

Both players were exhausted heading into the day. They got into a car en route to the set, and neither said a word.

One was the reigning Finals MVP, the other a bright-eyed budding prospect from Southern California. Both were represented by Excel Sports, which was how the pairing came to fruition.

Upon arrival, both players—but especially Nikola—were out of their element sitting for hair and makeup. The Hotels.com spot was the biggest ad campaign Jokic had ever been a part of.

Even though both were unaccustomed to the pampering, Watson said everything was comfortable on set. The chemistry between the two was palpable.

"We weren't biting our tongues or anything like that, they just allowed us to vibe, display our chemistry, improvise a little bit," Watson said.

The day began early in the morning and didn't conclude until around four-thirty or five. Within that time, Jokic and Watson starred in four commercials that roughly mirrored their actual relationship. Jokic played the self-assured superstar with an affinity for ponies; Watson played his innocent sidekick.

Naturally, Jokic kept it light. When he forgot a line, he hurled Serbian curse words at himself.

"Nobody necessarily understands what he means, but they understand the energy he gives off," Watson said. "It's just his demeanor that's funny."

In the wake of their championship, at least one campaign recognized Jokic's disposition for what it was: hilarious. He'd been willing to do sponsorships before but wanted to be paid what he deserved.

There was a similar story regarding Nikola's shoes. He'd worn Nike his entire NBA career, but if there was a better opportunity, he was open to it.

Aaron Gordon, who'd been with 361, a Chinese shoe company, for four years, used to joke about landing Nikola. Yes, it was far-fetched that the best player in the world would sign with a Chinese shoe company, or that they'd be willing to pay what it took, but everything about Nikola was unconventional.

Gordon had spent part of the offseason visiting Nikola in Sombor. Next, he headed to China to promote his own shoe, along with his agent Calvin Andrews, his brother, Drew, and his sister, Elise.

While there, the group shared an impromptu toast to Nikola. Gordon took a video and sent it to Jokic.

Perhaps Gordon's comfort with 361 transferred to Jokic, or perhaps it was simply the "great respect," as Jokic later described, that they showed from the beginning. But during the Nuggets' marquee Christmas game that season, Jokic was wearing his new signature high-tops.

Jokic, it seemed, was open for business. What he wasn't, however, was interested in divulging the process. When a representative from Tom Brady's new podcast asked about Jokic's interest in appearing, Nikola politely declined. The same thing happened when Peyton and Eli Manning sought a Jokic appearance on the Manningcast. He just wasn't interested in talking about himself.

Around the All-Star break, Universal approached Jokic's representation about another ad campaign. Knowing how rarely he agreed to appear in commercials, they were confident in their pitch yet skeptical that he'd actually approve. It didn't hurt, they thought, that the spot could appeal to his daughter.

Despicable Me.

While storyboarding the script, a writing team from ESPN stumbled on a video of Jokic dressed like Gru from *Despicable Me*. In conjunction with Universal and Illumination, they had their concept. Jokic was game.

"I love the guy," he said.

The spot was filmed in Denver in late March. Jokic drove himself to the shoot.

On set, he was just as he'd been for the Hotels.com ad: humble, polite, and maybe a bit nervous. He didn't like to be pampered. He also didn't take himself too seriously; when he botched a line, he cursed himself in Serbian.

They filmed the whole commercial in an hour. At the end of the shoot, he graciously signed a few basketballs.

When Universal gave Jokic a customed zip jacket and accompanying black and gray scarf, à la Gru, it served as a gift. But when Jokic's stylist suggested he wear the outfit ahead of Denver's opening game of the play-offs, the reigning Finals MVP thought it would be funny.

It was never in his contract to dress like Gru. It was simply Nikola all along.

EPILOGUE

Tragedy struck in January.

Nikola's longtime mentor, Dejan Milojevic, suffered a heart attack and later died during a road trip in Salt Lake City. Milojevic, a Warriors assistant coach, was at a private team dinner at an upscale Italian restaurant when he suffered the medical emergency.

Warriors coach Steve Kerr kept Nuggets coach Michael Malone informed while Milojevic was in the hospital. When the news of his death ultimately got to Nikola, he was numb. The Nuggets were on an extended road trip, then in Boston. Whereas the Warriors' game against the Jazz was postponed, Jokic and the Nuggets had little time to grieve.

The loss was shocking. Milojevic was only forty-six. Even though he'd only been an assistant in Golden State for three seasons, Dejan's imprint across the NBA was profound.

Nikola chose not to speak in Boston that night despite helping snap the Celtics' twenty-game home winning streak. With a heavy heart, Jokic had led the Nuggets to their signature win of the season. Two nights later, he registered a season-high 42 points in another win. The road crowd in Washington, which included his wife and daughter that night, applauded Jokic's superlative effort. Again, he opted not to speak.

When he finally addressed reporters after another exceptional game, and another road win over Indiana, he was succinct.

"I don't want to make a circus of it," Jokic said. "My whole family was shocked. . . . I love his whole family."

In the immediate aftermath of the tragedy, his play had honored his mentor's legacy better than anything he could've said.

When they first met at Mega in Belgrade, Dejan was tasked with cultivating all of Nikola's gifts. As an eighteen-year-old, Nikola had no concept of professional conduct. It was Dejan's job to mold him and teach him.

"Deki was a guy who gave me freedom," Jokic said. "He showed me the way how you're supposed to do things: act, train, work out, having positive energy, having positive attitude."

It was Dejan's positive attitude that was the most pervasive. His smile was ever-present; his laugh was equally as infectious. It boomed throughout rooms and across basketball courts. Those forces coincided with an impressionable Nikola, nurturing a joy that never left. That lesson was perhaps more profound than the freedom he afforded Nikola on the court.

Once both arrived in the NBA, their relationship shifted. The player-coach dynamic blossomed into a friendship. When the Warriors visited Denver, Nikola hosted Dejan. When the Nuggets traveled to San Francisco, Dejan opened his doors.

By the end of the 2023–24 regular season, with the Nuggets as the No. 2 seed and the Warriors, uncharacteristically, out of the postseason, Nikola still hadn't spoken about his relationship with Dejan at length. As Jokic fixated on dispatching the Lakers from the postseason for a second consecutive season, there was never an opportune time.

But his insights finally came amid Denver's prolonged second-round series against Minnesota, coincidentally during his third MVP press conference. As Jokic spoke, he wore a black shirt with the word "Brate"—brother—on it, and the letters "DM" on the shoulder. Jokic would have you believe that it was mere coincidence he was wearing that shirt, but Jokic's overarching decision to honor his late friend's memory was anything but chance.

The Nuggets' Game Seven ouster eleven days later was demoralizing and ushered in a wave of complicated questions pertaining to Jokic's title window. It was informative, however, that even in the throes of the playoffs, Nikola never lost perspective on what really defined him: the relationships.

"It was just like a really, really quality friendship, with a lot of telling truth between each other and being honest," Jokic said. "I think Deki was a guy who you always want to have as a friend. Someone who's going to tell you how it is with no lying and no trying to hide anything."

Those were, by far, the most fruitful relationships in Nikola's life. He strived to be like Deki—successful, competitive, and sincere. Even before Dejan passed, Nikola managed to achieve all those things. Whatever his legacy amounts to, perhaps the harmony he reached, in becoming an all-time great while refusing to compromise himself, will amount to his greatest achievement.

"For me, seeing a seventeen-year-old kid that I met becoming a grown-up man. . . . [It's] beautiful emotions," Dejan said. "For me, I'm happy that Nikola became MVP, whatever. But for me, the best thing is that he stayed the same person. I really care more about this than him being MVP and NBA champion."

ACKNOWLEDGMENTS

There are many people both directly and indirectly responsible for this book. Without all of you, it never would've happened.

Thank you to Sean Desmond and Daniel Greenberg for believing in the project and to Brian Windhorst for facilitating it. Thanks to Ben Golopol for your scrupulous editing and Nick Kosmider for the endless brainstorming sessions.

To Calvin Booth, Arturas Karnisovas, Michael Malone, Chris Finch, and Wes Unseld Jr., I can't thank you enough for your candor and time. To Tim and Negah Connelly (and Papa John's and Pacifico), thank you for everything.

To Mason Plumlee, Gary Harris, Felipe Eichenberger, and Nebojsa Vagic, your insights were invaluable. Thanks, also, to Marty Pocius, Sparky Gonzales, and the Nuggets PR team, all of whom helped immeasurably.

To Sam Amick and Jeff Zillgitt, I don't know where to start, and I'll leave it at that. To Matt Schubert and AAron Ontiveroz, and all my former colleagues at the *Denver Post*, thank you. To Professor Baughman, your encouragement meant the world. To Burton Chawla, thank you for matching my energy.

To Isidor and Milos, Rafal and Nenad, thank you for trusting me. To Ogi and Milica Stojakovic, thank you for your hospitality and friendship.

Without Marko Ljubomirovic, this book wouldn't exist. He drove me all over Serbia, translated, found subjects, and FaceTimed at all hours of the day. I can't thank you enough.

To Annie and Natalie, thank you for your patience and love. You guys made the book possible. To Mom and Dad, thanks for your ceaseless support.

And thank you, Nikola, for letting me share your story. Hvala, Brate.

INDEX

MVP (2024), 342
MVP Finals (2023), 315327, 338
Novi Sad team, coach Anicic, and
  development of his skills, 28–38
Nuggets and (*see* Denver Nuggets)
Nuggets Championship (2023) and,
  327–29
Nuggets contracts, 97, 170–72, 180,
  278–79, 322
Nuggets demand for conditioning, 79–85
Nuggets discovery of, 63–65
Nuggets draft pick (2014), 74–78
Nuggets offseason work, 149–52, 154
Nuggets playmaker and leader (2018–
  19), 185–203
Nuggets rising star (2016–17), 127–41
Nuggets rookie year (2015–16),
  104–16, 137
Nuggets–Spurs series, playoffs (2019),
  194–99
Nuggets stash year (2014–15), 86–88
Nuggets thermostat (2019–20), 212–
  16, 220–21
Nuggets training camp, 100–103
Olympics (2016) and, 118–22
pandemic and (2020), 222–25
popularity with teammates, 37–38, 44,
  46, 268–70, 297–300, 330–31, 334–35
relationship with his brothers, 25–29,
  36, 37, 39, 46–49, 64, 105, 106, 141,
  176, 295, 315, 336
Rudic as Sombor coach and mentor,
  6–9, 12–20, 24, 26
scouting of, 63–65, 68–73
Serbian FIBA team (2013), 50
Serbian players (Balkan boys) and, 223,
  224, 232–33
Serbian youth basketball, 2–3, 5–9,
  12–16, 17–23, 24–26
sinking off-balance shots, 315
style of play and, 3, 7, 19, 22–23,
  35–36, 51–52, 55–57, 71–72, 77, 87,
  110, 125, 144, 146–47, 238, 244–45,
  255, 264, 297, 303–4, 307, 317
Summer League, Las Vegas, 97–99
suspension (2021), 262–63
talent of, 9, 19, 29–33, 45, 50, 51, 55,
  68, 69, 70–71, 75, 126, 144, 154,
  157, 179, 244, 267, 295
temper of, 262

triple-doubles of, 51, 137, 162–63, 185,
  200, 201, 244, 263, 284, 293, 308,
  312, 315
turning points in his career, 25, 52–53,
  74–78, 86, 278–79, 322
unselfishness as a player, 15, 19, 44,
  87, 102, 119, 130, 131, 133, 135–36,
  154, 166, 177, 178, 210–11, 284,
  285–86, 321, 326, 327
videogames and, 58, 105, 120, 180–82,
  196, 222–23, 266
Vojvodina regional championship
  (2012), 24–25, 334–35
Jokic, Strahinja (brother), 2, 10, 64, 105,
  171, 295, 336
  Jokic's career and, 26–29, 36, 37, 39,
    40, 46–49, 170–71, 259, 278, 315,
    328–29, 332, 336–37
  Jokic's future, prediction about, 53
  Jokic's MVP (2022) and surprise party,
    273–76
  as Jokic's support system, 47–48, 79–81,
    90, 91, 97, 106, 140, 150, 154, 176, 186
  Lamborghini of, 252
  at Nike Hoop Summit, 72
  in Santa Barbara with Jokic, 79–82
  Twitter account, 262–63
Jones, Tyus, 70
Jordan, DeAndre, 119, 120, 280–82, 285,
  297–99, 315, 327–28, 330
Jordan, Michael, 111, 118, 200, 218, 266
Jovancevic, Aleksandar, 29–30, 31, 38
Juc, Rafal, 60–65, 69, 70, 72, 74–76, 80,
  90, 91–92

Kanter, Enes, 199, 255
Karl, George, 66
Karnisovas, Arturas, 62, 64–65, 69–71,
  73, 76, 77, 79, 80, 86, 91, 92, 94, 99,
  117, 118, 148, 152, 202, 212, 288
  Barcelona Olympics (1992) and,
    117–18, 122
  Jokic's first contract, 97
  Jokic's second contract, 170–71
Katic, Rasko, 57, 58
Kerr, Steve, 341
KK So Kos, 18–19
  Cadet championship (2012), 25
  Jokic and coach's mockery, 21
  Jokic playing in (2010–11), 18–25

ABOUT THE AUTHOR

MIKE SINGER was the Nuggets beat writer for the *Denver Post* for five seasons, culminating in coverage of the franchise's first championship. In 2021, he was named Colorado's Sportswriter of the Year. Before the *Post*, he was the national NBA editor at *USA TODAY*. A Cleveland native and proud Wisconsin Badger, Singer's family has been in Denver since 2018.